Achievements and Future Directions of the Long-Term Care Insurance System in Japan

Toward Social "Kaigo" Security in the Global Longevity Society

Hiroshi Sumii
Yuki Sawada

UNIVERSITY EDUCATION PRESS

Achievements and Future Directions of the Long-Term Care Insurance System in Japan:
Toward Social "Kaigo" Security in the Global Longevity Society
by Hiroshi Sumii and Yuki Sawada

Copyright © 2014 by Hiroshi Sumii and Yuki Sawada

All rights reserved.

No part of this book protected by this copyright notice may be reproduced or transmitted in any form or by any means, electronic or mechanical, including photocopying, recording, or by any information storage and retrieval system, without the written permission from the copyright holder.

Cover Design: Miho Hara

Published by:
UNIVERSITY EDUCATION PRESS Co., Ltd.
855−4 Nishiichi,
Minami-ku, Okayama, 700−0953
Japan
http://www.kyoiku.co.jp/

First published 2014

Printed in Japan by MORIMOTO PRINT CO., Ltd

ISBN978−4−86429−254−2

PREFACE

Individuals who are in the twilight years of their lives now receive long-term care (called "Kaigo" in Japan). They have the right to be treated with respect and dignity and to live a fulfilled life even if they need long-term care services. However, until recently, social welfare programs for the elderly have been provided with only limited support services.

The Long-Term Care Insurance (LTCI) Law was approved by the National Assessable on December 9, 1997, and was implemented on April 1, 2000, in Japan after a long process. It provides new types of long-term care services in the health, medical, and social welfare fields. Although LTCI aims to provide elderly Japanese individuals who require long-term care with services such that they can live independently and with dignity, the way to achieve this goal is still unclear; the system still requires adjustments. Official and responsible parties provide different types of long-term care services under the health insurance system, which was designed to serve the needs of the insured and their families. In the Kaigo insurance era, we have to consider the delivery of the ideal model of health and social welfare services that ensures a life with dignity for the elderly.

While social welfare is gradually diminishing, many of the insured and their families are caught between two different systems: health insurance and LTCI. In a society with a rapidly aging population, healthcare professionals in Japan have to offer long-term care services while worrying about the quality of care. In addition, they receive little support in providing better care.

We not only care for the life and living of the insured, but also believe that long-term care should be provided such that individuals in need of care can live with dignity, which would most likely help them to have good quality of life in their later years. Each person should thus be provided with sufficient Kaigo security. The efforts supporting this system could result in a better society in the 21st century and we would like to introduce the strategies in this book to anyone in the world who needs long-term care security. With this publication, we hope that the importance of the Kaigo insurance would be acknowledged and the dream of Kaigo security in Japan realized.

The features and structure of this book are as follows.

Chapter 1 discusses the historical background and policy process of the development of LTCI. Chapter 2 first provides an overview of the system and then describes it in more detail. Chapters 3, 4, and 5 discuss a wide range of various types of LTCI-covered care services while chapters 6 and 7 illustrate the application process for LTCI benefits. Chapters 8 and 9 focus on financing and the costs of the system, and chapter 10 addresses care management and the role of care managers. Chapter 11 focuses on various types of heath and non-health care professionals involved in the system and their work settings and chapter 12 goes over the lessons leant from other countries in developing the LTCI system. Finally, chapter 13 provides information on how the system was revised. In the Appendix, we provide the LTCI eligibility assessment forms, physician's report, and fee criterion for LTCI care services as of April 2000 and 2012.

Unless indicated otherwise, all information contained herein is as of April 2000. This is because we believe that everything has a beginning and that the first steps are the most difficult and therefore the most valuable. Thus, it is important to understand how the system began and developed until it is fully mature.

ACKNOWLEDGEMENTS

This book would not have been published without the support of many individuals who contributed to our understanding of the system presented in this book. We would like to thank Chiemi Tokuyama, Fuminori Mimura, Kana Kageyama, Kazue Tokutomi, Kazumi Araki, Keiko Miyake, Keiko Mori, Keizo Kamo, Masami Hidaka, Masato Kodera, Mayumi Katsura, Midori Kusakabe, Mie Oba, Mika Kunisada, Mitsuharu Taniguchi, Miyuki Ono, Naoto Tokuhara, Naoya Senba, Rumiko Takeda, Sachiko Kasahara, Shinsuke Kitahama, Shinya Hashimoto, Sugako Murakami, Takao Inazu, Tomio Imada, Toru Kameyama, Tsuneichi Kanekura, Yoshiro Fujiwara, and Yuji Maeda.

We would also like to express our special thanks to Mamoru Sato, President of University Education Press, who supported us throughout the publishing process. Ai Yasuda and the staff at University Education Press must also be recognized for their invaluable assistance and support.

This book was published with financial assistance from Grants-in-Aid for the Publication of Scientific Research Results and Scientific Literature, provided by the Japan Society for the Promotion of Science.

Hiroshi Sumii
Yuki Sawada

ABOUT THE AUTHORS

Hiroshi Sumii is a professor of Human Welfare at Prefectural University, Hiroshima, Japan. He received his Doctor of Medicine degree from Tottori University and Ph.D. in Medicine from Okayama University, Japan. He has served as a member to Science Council of Japan conferences and a board member of Japanese Society of Human Sciences of Health-Social Services, Japan Academy of Home Care, and Japan Kaigo Research. An author of over 75 scholarly publications in the field of health and social welfare, Dr. Sumii's research interests include the LTCI system and time studies of nursing activities in hospitals and nursing homes.

Yuki Sawada is a visiting research fellow at the Center for Well-Being and Society and teaches social welfare for the elderly at Nihon Fukushi University, Nagoya, Japan. She received her Master of Science in Gerontology from the University of Southern California and Ph.D. in Social Welfare from Nihon Fukushi University. Dr. Sawada's previous positions include serving as the Social Services Department Manager at Keiro Intermediate Care Facility, Los Angeles, California, and a researcher of Center of Excellence Project of Nihon Fukushi University. She is author of The Management System for Improving Quality of Care in U.S. Nursing Homes (University Education Press, 2012) and a contributor to many journals on the topic of quality of care and staffing issues in nursing homes in both the United States and Japan. All the various tasks involved in publishing this book such as translation, rewriting, and editing were done by her.

TABLE OF CONTENTS

Preface .... *i*
About the Authors .... *iv*
List of Figures and Tables .... *xv*

Chapter 1: Introduction to and Background of Long-Term Care Insurance in Japan: Creating and Maintaining "Kaigo" Security *3*
   Yuki Sawada and Hiroshi Sumii
   Long-Term Care Programs for the Elderly: The Forty-Years Prior to the Enactment of the Long-Term Care Insurance Law   *4*
      Welfare Law for the Elderly   *4*
      A Health Service System for the Elderly   *4*
      Gold Plan   *6*
   Steps toward the Establishment of the Long-Term Care Insurance System   *7*
      Seeking the Right to Choose   *8*
      Involving Public and Private Sectors in Long-Term Care   *9*
      Establishment of the Long-Term Care Insurance Law   *9*
   Purpose and Philosophy of the Long-Term Care Insurance System   *11*
      Transfer of Caregiver Responsibility from Family to Public Authorities   *11*
      Integration of the Medical Care and Social Welfare Services via Long-Term Care Insurance   *13*
      Sharing the Cost of Long-Term Care Insurance with All Citizens   *13*
      Enhancement of Free Choice and Competition between Care Providers   *13*
   Summary   *14*
   References   *15*

Chapter 2: An Overview of Long-Term Care Insurance · · · · · · · · · · · · · · · 17
Yuki Sawada

The Structure of Long-Term Care Insurance   19

    The Contents and Types of Long-Term Care Insurance-Funded Care Services   19
    Insurers (Municipal Governments)   21
    The Insured (Beneficiaries of Long-Term Care Insurance)   21
    Qualifications of Long-Term Care Insurance Benefits   23
    Certification of "Care-Required" and "Assistance-Required"   23
    Financing and Costs of Long-Term Care Insurance   25
    Care Management and Care Plans   26
    Types of Professionals in the Long-Term Care Insurance System   27

Summary   27

References   27

Chapter 3: Home- and Community-Based Care Services · · · · · · · · · · · · · · · 29
Yuki Sawada

Types of Home- and Community-Based Care Services   30

    Home Care (Home Help)   31
    Home Bathing Services   32
    Home Health Care (Visiting Nurse Services)   33
    Home Visit Rehabilitation   33
    Medical Management   34
    Adult Day Care Services   35
    Day Care Rehabilitation (Day Care)   36
    Short-Stay Program for Personal Care   36
    Short-Stay Program for Medical Care   37
    Group Homes for People with Dementia   37
    Care Services for Private Care Facility Residents   38
    Loan of Assistive Devices and Home Modifications   38

Other Related Home- and Community-Based Care Services   39

    Preventive Care Benefits   39
    Special Benefits Provided by Municipalities   39

To What Extent Can Individuals Receive Long-Term Care Services?   40

Summary   40

References   40

Chapter 4: Assistive Devices and Home Modifications ···············42
Yuki Sawada

Assistive Devices   42

Assistive Devices Available for Loan   43
    Wheelchairs   43
    Wheelchair Accessories and Attachments   45
    Hospital Beds   45
    Bed Accessories and Attachments   46
    Pressure Ulcer Prevention and Treatment Devices   47
    Positioning and Adaptive Cushions   47
    Handrails, Grab Bars, and Safety Rails   47
    Wheelchair/Threshold Ramps and Platforms   47
    Walkers   48
    Walking Canes and Crutches   49
    Code Alert Systems   49
    Transfer Lifts   50

Fee Schedule for Loan of Assistive Devices   51

How to Rent Assistive Devices   51

Assistive Devices Available for Purchase   51
    Bedside Commodes   52
    Automatic Urine Collection Devices   53
    Bathroom Aids   53
    Portable Bathtubs   54
    Sling Lifts   54

Long-Term Care Insurance and Welfare of Physically Disabled Persons Programs   55

Home Modifications   55
    Installation of Handrails   56
    Elimination of Thresholds   56
    Floor Modification   57
    Replacement of Existing Doors and Doorknobs   57
    Replacement of Squat Toilets with Western Toilets   57

How to Apply for Reimbursement   58

Points to Note   58

Living Environment Improvements for Promoting Home- and Community-Based Care   59

Suggestions for Home Modifications   60

Summary   60
References   61

Chapter 5: Institutional Long-Term Care Services ···············62
Yuki Sawada

Welfare Facilities for the Elderly   64
    Services and Activities in Welfare Facilities for the Elderly   64

Health Facilities for the Elderly   66
    Services and Activities in Health Facilities for the Elderly   67

Designated Long-Term Care Hospitals   67
    Designated Long-Term Care Beds   69
    Designated Long-Term Medical Care Beds for the Elderly   69
    Designated Long-Term Care Beds for Elderly with Dementia   70

Long-Term Care Insurance-Uncovered Institutional Care Facilities   70
    Almshouses for the Elderly   70
    Low-Cost Elder Homes   70
    Care Houses   71

Medical Insurance-Covered Institutional Care Services   71
    Hospital with Designated Long-Term Care Beds   71
    Medical Insurance-Designated Recovery-Phase Rehabilitation Units   73

Advantages and Disadvantages of Newly Certified Care Facilities   74

Tips for Choosing a Long-Term Care Facility   75

Tips for Receiving High-Quality Care   77

Having a Grievance and Complaint about Institutional Care   77

Summary   81

References   81

TABLE OF CONTENTS ix

Chapter 6: Application Process for Long-Term Care Insurance Benefits 83

Yuki Sawada

The First Part of the Application Process   85

    To Whom and Who Can Apply   85
    How to Handle Residents Who Were Institutionalized Prior to the Enactment of Long-Term Care Insurance   88

Importance of the Application   88

Change of Address for Long-Term Care Insurance Benefits   89

Reapplication of Certification   90

Fees and Costs Involved in Applying for Certification   91

How to Appeal   92

Summary   93

References   93

Chapter 7: Qualification Assessment for Long-Term Care Insurance Benefits 95

Yuki Sawada and Hiroshi Sumii

Three Types of Assessment Methods   96

    Intake Interview   96
    Objective Assessment   97
    Additional Comments by Assessors   103

Issues in Assessing the Status of Applicants   103

Initial Classification by Computer   104

    Calculation of Sum per Category   104
    Calculation of Total Amount of Care Using the "Tree Diagram"   105
    Classification of Care Levels   107

Physician's Report   107

Long-Term Care Certification Committee Review   108

Features of and Issues Pertaining to the Certification System   109

    Issues with Evaluating Only the Physical and Mental Statuses of Beneficiaries   109
    Care Levels Determine the Budget Ceiling   110
    Issues Raised by the One-Minute Time Study   110
    Issues Raised by the Use of Evaluation Items   112

Issues Raised by Applying Only Statistical Processes   *112*
Difficulty in Classifying Levels of Care   *112*

Tips for Not Obtaining a Lower Level of Care than is Needed   *113*

Summary   *114*

References   *114*

Chapter 8: Sources of Financing for Long-Term Care Insurance
.... *116*

Yuki Sawada

Financial Sources of Long-Term Care Insurance   *117*

Insured Persons: The Age of 40 as the Cutoff Point   *118*

Long-Term Care Insurance Premiums   *118*

    Premiums of 1st Category Insured Persons   *118*
        Levy Methods for 1st Category Insured Persons   *119*
        Determining Methods of Premiums for 1st Category Insured Persons   *120*

    Premiums of 2nd Category Insured Persons   *123*
        Levy Methods for 2nd Category Insured Persons   *124*
        Determining Methods of Premiums for Salaried 2nd Category Insured Persons   *125*
        Levy and Determining Methods of Premiums for Self-Employed 2nd Category Insured Persons   *125*

Failure to Pay Premiums Penalties   *125*

    For 1st Category Insured Persons   *126*
    For 2nd Category Insured Persons   *126*

Policy of Premium Reduction and Exemption   *126*

Summary   *127*

References   *128*

Chapter 9: Costs of Long-Term Care Insurance-Covered Services
.... *129*

Yuki Sawada

Long-Term Care Insurance Service Costs   *129*

Fee Structure of Long-Term Care Insurance Services   *131*

TABLE OF CONTENTS *xi*

Fixed Unit Price Method   *132*
Time Period Method   *133*
Care Level Method   *135*
Combination of Time Period and Care Level Method   *138*

Co-Payments and Out-of-Pocket Expenditures   *139*

Co-Payments   *140*
Out-of-Pocket Expenditures   *140*

Benefit Supply Management   *141*

Summary   *141*

References   *146*

Chapter 10: Care Management and Care Managers   *147*

Yuki Sawada

The Conventional Client Allocation System and the Long-Term Care Insurance System   *148*

Care Plans   *148*

Home-Care Care Plans   *150*
In-Facility Care Plans   *150*

Care Planning Process   *150*

Assessment   *150*
Care Providers Discuss and Develop Care Plans   *152*
Implementation of Care Plans   *152*
Follow-up: Monitoring and Reassessment   *152*

Care Managers   *152*

Process of Becoming a Care Manager   *153*
The Role of the Care Manager   *155*
Other Functions   *155*
Providing a Team Approach   *155*
Documentation   *156*

Care Manager's Basic Goals   *157*

Independent Living   *157*
Normalization and Dignity   *157*
Life-Span Development   *158*

Practice of Care Management   *158*

Summary   *161*

References   *162*

Chapter 11: Types of Professionals in the Long-Term Care Insurance System and Their Work Settings 163
Yuki Sawada

Significance of an Interdisciplinary Team Approach   164
Which Professionals Work in Long-Term Care Settings?   165
- Care Managers   165
- Healthcare Professionals   166
  - Physicians and Dentists   166
  - Pharmacists   166
- Nursing Care Professionals   167
  - Nurses   167
  - Certified Care Workers   168
  - Home Care Aides   170
- Rehabilitation Professionals   170
  - Physical Therapists   170
  - Occupational Therapists   171
  - Speech Therapists   171
- Social Services Professionals   172
  - Certified Social Workers   172
  - Long-Term Care Counselors   173
  - Commissioned Welfare Volunteers   173

Who Else Works in Long-Term Care Settings?   174
- Volunteers   174
- Informal Caregivers   175

New Workplace Opportunities Created by Long-Term Care Insurance   175
- Private Enterprises   175
- Japan Agricultural Co-operative and Consumer Co-operative   176
  - Agricultural Co-operative   176
  - Consumer Co-operative   176
- Non-Profit Organizations   176

Summary   177
References   177

Chapter 12: Lessons from European Countries, Australia and the United States 178
Yuki Sawada and Hiroshi Sumii

Denmark   180

Australia   *182*
The United States of America   *183*
The United Kingdom   *186*
Germany   *187*
Summary   *189*
References   *190*

Chapter 13: Revisions to the Long-Term Care Insurance System
.... *192*

Yuki Sawada
Background   *193*
Introduction of the Preventative Care Services Package   *194*
Introduction of New Classification Criteria   *195*
Levy of Cost of Room and Board   *197*
Establishment of Community-Focused Services: Small-Scale Multi-Purpose Care Centers   *198*
Establishment of Comprehensive Community Support Centers   *198*
Introduction of the Public Reporting System of Care Providers' Care Quality   *199*
Other Revisions   *200*
Current Status of the Long-term Care Insurance System   *202*
Summary   *204*
References   *204*

Appendix

- A. Assessment Form: Background Information *208*
- B. Assessment Form: General Assessment *210*
- C. Assessment Form: Additional Comments *218*
- D. Physician's Report *220*
- E. Regional Unit Pricing per Unit as of April 2012 .... *225*
- F. List of Municipalities for Each Region *226*
- G. Fee Criterion for Long-Term Care Insurance Care Services *228*

Index *239*

LIST OF FIGURES AND TABLES

LIST OF FIGURES

Figure 1-1	Historical Events, Aging, and Total Fertility Rates	5
Figure 1-2	Overview of Expected Structure of Health and Long-Term Care Systems as of 1997	10
Figure 1-3	Overview of Long-Term Care Insurance in Japan as of April 2000	12
Figure 2-1	Outline of the Long-Term Care Insurance System	18
Figure 2-2	Application Process Flow Chart for Long-Term Care Insurance Benefits and Certification	24
Figure 4-1	Manual Wheelchair	43
Figure 4-2	Hospital Bed and its Accessories and Attachments	46
Figure 4-3	Portable Wheelchair Ramp	48
Figure 4-4	Platform Forearm Crutch and Reciprocal Walker	49
Figure 4-5	Transfer Lift with Sling	50
Figure 4-6	Bedside Commode and Raised Toilet Seat	52
Figure 4-7	Automatic Urine Collection Devices	53
Figure 4-8	Bathroom Aids	54
Figure 4-9	Example of Home Modification 1	56
Figure 4-10	Example of Home Modification 2	58
Figure 5-1	Sample of a Care Plan in a Health Facility for the Elderly	68
Figure 5-2	Care and Discharge Planning Process Flow Chart	78
Figure 5-3	Sample of an In-Facility Care Plan in a Welfare Facility for the Elderly 1	79
Figure 5-4	Sample of an In-Facility Care Plan in a Welfare Facility for the Elderly 2	80
Figure 6-1	Flow Chart of the Application Process and Care Planning for Long-Term Care Insurance Benefits	84
Figure 6-2	Application Form	86
Figure 6-3	Sample of the Long-Term Care Insurance Card (Front & Back)	87
Figure 6-4	Overview of the Appeal Process and the Responsible Parties	92
Figure 7-1	Visual Assessment Symbol	102

Figure 7-2	Tree Diagram for Dietary Intake	105
Figure 7-3	Calculation of the Base Amount of Time	106
Figure 8-1	Financing of Long-Term Care Insurance	117
Figure 8-2	Premium Levy Methods for 1st Category Insured Persons	120
Figure 8-3	Premium Levy Methods for 2nd Category Insured Persons	124
Figure 9-1	Sample of a Service Receipt	142–143
Figure 9-2	Sample of a Service Provider's Report	144–145
Figure 10-1	Difference between the Conventional Client Allocation System and Long-Term Care Insurance in Providing Care Services	149
Figure 10-2	Flow Chart of the Care Planning Process	151
Figure 10-3	Care Managers' Qualification Criteria and Requirements	154
Figure 10-4	Sample of a Weekly Schedule and Care Plan	160
Figure 11-1	Health and Non-Health Professionals Involved in Long-Term Care Insurance	164
Figure 11-2	Role of Care Managers in Coordination	165
Figure 11-3	Steps to Becoming a Certified Care Worker	169
Figure 12-1	Private Room of a Home for the Aged in Denmark	180
Figure 12-2	Medical and Long-Term Care System in Denmark	181
Figure 12-3	Long-Term Care System in Australia	183
Figure 12-4	Rehabilitation Room at a Nursing Home in the United States	184
Figure 12-5	Long-Term Care Insurance System in Germany	187
Figure 12-6	Private Room of a Care Home in Germany	189
Figure 13-1	Number of Recipients: 2000-2005	193
Figure 13-2	Total Expenditure: 2000-2005	194
Figure 13-3	New Classification of Care Levels	196
Figure 13-4	Cost of Living at Home and in Institutional Settings per Month	197
Figure 13-5	Contribution Rates for Long-Term Care Insurance: 2000 and 2006	200
Figure 13-6	Number of Recipients: 2006-2010	203
Figure 13-7	Total Expenditure: 2006-2011	203

LIST OF TABLES

Table 2-1	Long-Term Care Insurance-Funded Care Services	20
Table 2-2	Persons Insured by Long-Term Care Insurance	22
Table 2-3	Budget Ceiling for Home- and Community-Based Care Services	26
Table 3-1	Types of Home- and Community-Based Care Services	30
Table 4-1	Available Loan Items and Fee Schedule for Rentals	44
Table 4-2	Available Items and Fee Schedule for Purchase	52
Table 5-1	Overview of Long-Term Care Insurance-Certified Care Facilities	63
Table 5-2	Services Available in Welfare Facilities for the Elderly	65
Table 5-3	Sample of Annual Events in Welfare Facilities for the Elderly	65
Table 5-4	Services Available in Health Facilities for the Elderly	67
Table 5-5	Average Cost of Nursing Care per Month by Types of Long-Term Care Facilities	69
Table 6-1	Where to Apply and Who Can Apply	88
Table 7-1	Contents of the 85-Item Scale	98–99
Table 7-2	Classification of the Assessment Method	99
Table 7-3	The Basic Amount of Time by Care Level	107
Table 8-1	Calculation Formulas for Premium Rates	119
Table 8-2	Payment Process of Premiums	121
Table 8-3	Premiums of 1st Category Insured Persons and Aging Rates by Prefecture	122
Table 9-1	Regional Unit Pricing per Unit as of April 2000	130
Table 9-2	Calculation Formula for Determining Fixed Cost of Home Visit Rehabilitation Services	131
Table 9-3	Fee Structures of Long-Term Care Insurance Services	132
Table 9-4	Unit Price of Home Bathing Services (1250 units)	133
Table 9-5	Home Care: Providing Nursing Care for Changing Diapers and Bed Sheets for 30-60 min (402 units)	134
Table 9-6	Unit Price, Extra Charge, and Discount for Home Health Care Services for Less than 60 min (830 units)	135
Table 9-7	Unit Prices for Group Homes by Care Level	136
Table 9-8	Unit Prices for Care Services for Private Care Facility Residents by Care Level	136
Table 9-9	Unit Prices for Welfare Facilities by Care Level	137

Table 9-10 Unit Prices for Day Care Rehabilitation ·· *138*
Table 9-11 Extra Charges for Day Care Rehabilitation ································· *139*
Table 11-1 Significance of an Interdisciplinary Team Approach ···················· *164*
Table 12-1 Trends in European Countries, Australia and the United States, and Japan ·· *179*
Table 13-1 Budget Ceiling for Home- and Community-Based Services: 2000 and 2006 ··· *196*
Table 13-2 Calculation Formulas for Premium Rates as of 2006 ···················· *201*

Achievements and Future Directions of the Long-Term Care Insurance System in Japan: Toward Social "Kaigo" Security in the Global Longevity Society

1

Introduction to and Background of Long-Term Care Insurance in Japan: Creating and Maintaining "Kaigo" Security

Providing long-term care to frail elderly is an issue relevant to not only families but also society as a whole. In April 2000, long-term care insurance (LTCI), a mandatory social insurance, was implemented in Japan, in which a new concept of "Kaigo" (literally, "long-term care") and policies in the field of healthcare, medical care, and social welfare, were introduced after a legislation drafted by the LTCI Law. The LTCI system, which was created in reference to the LTCI system in Germany, has led to the construction of a new long-term care system for the elderly, providing a wide range of long-term care services to people requiring them in order to reduce the burden on family caregivers. Until then, people requiring long-term care were mainly cared for by their families, especially by daughters-in-law, which tended to isolate them from society. Further, many elderly people requiring long-term care were not appropriately cared for and often ended up being abandoned by their families, and they are sometimes abused by their children because of the children's frustration.

This introductory chapter discusses the historical background of LTCI (Figure 1-1), the process involved in the development of the LTCI system, and the changes made by this new care system.

LONG-TERM CARE PROGRAMS FOR THE ELDERLY: THE FORTY-YEARS PRIOR TO THE ENACTMENT OF THE LONG-TERM CARE INSURANCE LAW

Welfare Law for the Elderly

Until the implementation of the LTCI Law in April 2000, the Welfare Law for the Elderly, which was established in 1966, was used as a basic law/regulation for elderly care. This law mandated the provision of long-term care services to the elderly through a system called "*sochi*" (literally "patient-allocation system").

Under the sochi system, regardless of one's needs and desire, the municipal governments alone determined the contents of long-term care services, such as which institutional care facility or home- and community-based care service should be provided, and decided who is eligible for benefits. In this allocation system, almost all expenses were covered by the recipients themselves and/or the persons responsible for the recipients' welfare. The amount of out-of-pocket expenses was calculated based on recipients' incomes and the income tax of responsible persons.

A Health Service System for the Elderly

In the first half of the 1980s, Japan's national health-care expenditure broke through the 20-trillion-yen mark, and by 1999, it had exceeded 30 trillion yen. This was because of the increase in the number of elderly people who were admitted to hospitals ever since the institutional care services provided by long-term care facilities under the Welfare Law for the Elderly were placed under budgetary restraints and hospitals started

1 Introduction to and Background of Long-Term Care Insurance in Japan   5

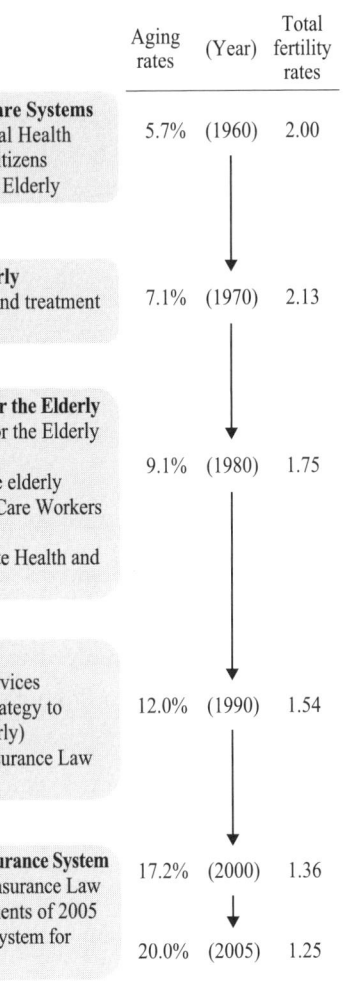

Figure 1-1   Historical Events, Aging, and Total Fertility Rates

to provide more beds to elderly people. Because all citizens in Japan are covered by medical insurance and free to choose their hospitals and doctors regardless of income level, the elderly preferred to be placed in hospitals when they become frail instead of in long-term care facilities, which usually have long waiting lists.

In order to reduce these high expenses, the Health and Medical Care Services Law for the Elderly was enacted in 1982 to cover all medical care services, including hospital admissions, for the elderly, and in 1986, the first long-term health care facilities were established to provide accommodation for them.

Gold Plan

In 1989, the Gold Plan was developed and implemented to expand the number of long-term care facilities, home- and community-based services, and professionals involved in long-term care. This plan, also called the "Ten-Year-Strategy to Promote Health and Welfare for the Elderly," aimed to reach its target numbers of care facilities, home- and community-based services, and manpower over a 10-year period, by 1999.

Nevertheless, before reaching the target numbers, it became evident that the target number was too low because of the rapid increase in the number of elderly people requiring long-term care. Hence, in 1994, the national government decided to revise the original plan by significantly increasing the numerical targets in the "New Gold Plan."

This plan generated public interest regarding caring for the elderly as a major public issue and became a cornerstone for the development of a new public long-term care system for the elderly.

STEPS TOWARD THE ESTABLISHMENT OF THE LONG-TERM CARE INSURANCE SYSTEM

Aiming to establish a new elderly care system, the Ministry of Health and Welfare (MHW)[1] Study Group, which was tasked to plan elderly support systems, mentioned the need for a public insurance program for elderly care in December 1994. The study group pointed out that the conventional social welfare systems were not consistent with the current condition of aging in Japan and that the necessity of establishing a new elderly care system was discussed from only the perspectives of issues in the field of healthcare, medical care, and social welfare services. Therefore, the MHW Study Group proposed the development of a new long-term care system such as LTCI.

The MHW Study Group also attributed the limitations of the conventional social welfare system to the shortage of public financial resources and revealed that it has become more difficult for municipal governments to manage the client allocation system by using the general tax revenue. The group further pointed out that although the conventional system became operational under high economic growth, the system would not be fully effective in an economic recession.

There were also issues that needed to be addressed in the field of medical services and the social security system. The issues with medical services were that individuals in need of long-term care were hospitalized not for medical care but for long-term care or social admission, which reduced the number of beds available for people who actually needed medical care. Moreover, health care insurance was consumed by socially admitted elderly because there was no proper insurance system for their long-term care needs. The healthcare cost associated with long-term hospitalization had also risen significantly, decreasing the funds available for medical insurance. Although the medical budget was doing well in the 1970s, an era that had a surplus of medical doctors, it gradually fell into difficult times in the 1980s, and the restrictions imposed, especially on the national medical expenditure, became tighter. The study group thus decided that Japan could learn from Germany, which had, at the time, a public LTCI system that provided long-term care. With the introduction of LTCI, the national medical expenditure was expected to be reduced by resolving the issue of long-term hospitalization in hospitals, thereby reducing the number of patients hospitalized for non-medical purposes.

At the same time, there were issues with the social security system. Elderly people were receiving pension as guaranteed income, covered by medical insurance, and were receiving extra money as a personal needs allowance if they were admitted to welfare facilities. In other words, the pension payment was not properly utilized for daily living in old age, and discrepancies in the conventional social security system became apparent. The MHW Study Group finally concluded that an elderly care system framed by LTCI would successfully solve the problems in the social security system.

Seeking the Right to Choose

In the conventional systems, the types of care services and providers that one utilized were determined not by individuals in need of care, but governmental offices through the client/patient allocation system or medical insurance. It was apparent that this system was operating against the trends of modern times and that there was a need to create a system that enabled patients to choose the care service and service provider that they want. For this, Japan looked toward Australia, which, at that time, had already had a system of determining the eligibility of beneficiaries, who were then able to choose from the services available at their care level. However, this requires a large number of long-term care facilities to choose from and financial resources to build more facilities. Nevertheless, the budget was extremely limited at that time and it was considered inappropriate to increase or use taxes for medical insurance and health care service systems for the elderly. The MHW Study Group, therefore, proposed that the LTCI system should be created in a way that is different from existing social welfare programs.

Involving Public and Private Sectors in Long-Term Care

In this matter, Japan learned from the United Kingdom, where local governments conduct care management, which includes assessing the needs and creating care plans for the elderly and coordinating care services, while care services are provided by private organizations that have contracts with the local governments. This decreased the burden on the state in long-term care.

Establishment of the Long-Term Care Insurance Law

After a long interval of 33 years after the National Universal Health Insurance was established in 1961, the Council on Social Security, in response to the proposal of the MHW Study Group, proposed to begin planning the new public LTCI system on July 4, 1995. The most important point in their recommendation was that the new LTCI system obliges elderly individuals to share the costs of providing LTCI services via insurance premiums and replace the conventional client allocation system by the LTCI system (Figure 1-2).

Most of the discussion was carried out among parties interested in long-term care. On April 22, 1996, the Council on Health and Welfare for the Elderly submitted their report called "Foundation of LTCI for the Elderly" to the Minister of Health and Welfare. Since consumption tax was scheduled to be increased from 3% to 5% in April 1997, the report was written with the assumption that LTCI should be financed by extra general tax revenues collected from the increased portion (2% of 5%) of consumption tax and proposed that a social insurance model be adopted in the creation of the

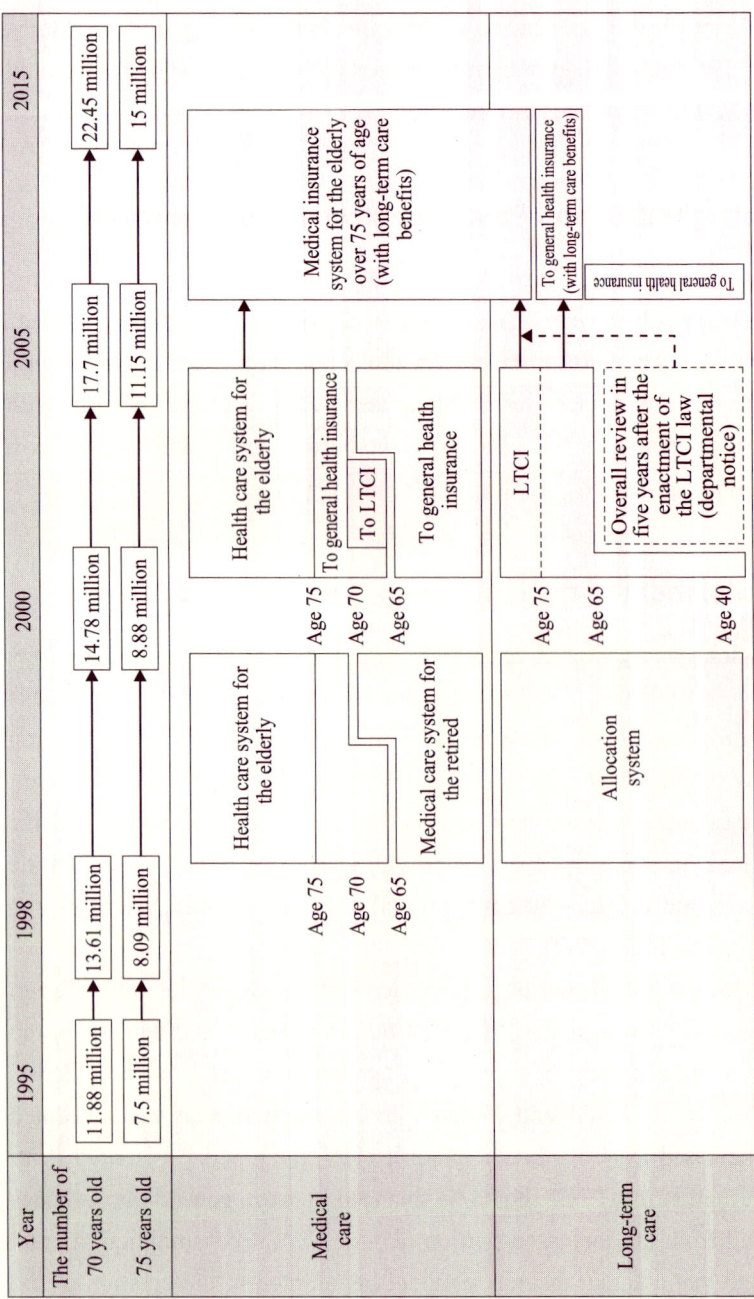

Figure 1-2 Overview of Expected Structure of Health and Long-Term Care Systems as of 1997

Source: Sumii, H., et al. (2008). Introduction to Long-Term Care Insurance in Japan-To Support "Kaigo" Security.

LTCI system.

Moreover, a non-profit group called "Ten Thousand Citizens' Committee to Realize a Public Elder-Care System" launched a campaign to establish a public long-term care system in September 1996, which expanded the network of care providers throughout the country and expressed their ideas of what constitutes a successful long-term care system.

Three bills related to LTCI ("LTCI Bill," "Enactment of the LTCI Law Bill," and "Medical Services Law Reform Bill") were submitted to the National Assembly in November 1996. During the discussion on the bills, a counter bill on "Long-Term Care Security for the Elderly by Tax" was submitted by the opposition party, and municipal governments requested a careful deliberation. However, on December 9, 1997, three bills related to LTCI were passed in the National Assembly despite the absence of opposition parties.

PURPOSE AND PHILOSOPHY OF THE LONG-TERM CARE INSURANCE SYSTEM

In April 2000, the LTCI system was implemented with the following aims: to (1) help family caregivers by providing care services and transferring caregiving responsibility from them to the governments; (2) integrate medical care and social welfare services; (3) share the cost of LTCI with all citizens; and (4) ensure free choice for consumers and competition between care providers. Figure 1-3 shows an overview of LTCI as of April 2000.

Transfer of Caregiver Responsibility from Family to Public Authorities

Until the enactment of the LTCI system, families, mostly women, were caring for their bedridden and frail family members in the community. Since caregiving for a loved one places a lot of burden on caregivers, the

	1st category insured persons	2nd category insured persons
Beneficiaries	· Persons aged 65 and above.	· Persons aged between 40 and 64 with medical insurance.
Insurance premium	· Determined by each municipality government according to income level. · Deduction from pension payments as a general rule.	· Determined by each medical insurance agency using a mathematical formula and the national average premium amounts.
Eligibility criteria	· Persons in need of long-term care because of being bedridden or having dementia (certified as care-required). · Persons in need of assistance with ADLs^2 and/or IADLs^3 such as cooking and dressing (certified as assistance-required).	· Persons in need of long-term care or assistance because of having one or more of the 15 specified diseases[4] associated with aging.

Apply for LTCI benefits ⇅ Notice of approval and issue of insurance card   Provide services ⇅ Pay co-payments

Municipalities (insurers)		Service providers
· Operate and manage the LTCI system. · Issue the insurance cards. · Conduct certification assessments. · Secure and maintain long-term care services.	Reimbursement for services ⇒	· Designated organizations (e.g., social welfare and medical corporations, private sectors, nonprofit organizations). · Provide home-and community-based care, institutional care, and preventive services.

Figure 1-3   Overview of Long-Term Care Insurance in Japan as of April 2000

LTCI system aimed to relieve some of it by providing in-kind benefits. Providing a cash allowance for family care was discussed during the process of planning for LTCI, but many women's groups and feminists argued that providing money does not help to relieve the burden of caregivers since the money would most likely go to the household budget, leaving little at the caregiver's disposal. Accordingly, care services such as home care and adult day care services, with no cash allowance for family caregivers, were provided to transfer caregivers' burden and responsibility from the family to public authorities.

Integration of the Medical Care and Social Welfare Services via Long-Term Care Insurance

Another purpose of the LTCI system was to integrate medical care and social welfare services as defined by the LTCI Law. Until LTCI was enacted, medical care was paid for by medical insurance, and social welfare services were covered by general revenues. However, with the establishment of LTCI, funds for existing medical care were unified with those for existing social welfare services. This integration allowed not only the provision of care services from a single financial source but also the creation of comprehensive long-term care plans with medical care and social welfare services.

Sharing the Cost of Long-Term Care Insurance with All Citizens

The philosophy of the LTCI system was to have older people themselves share the cost of LTCI. The LTCI Law states that, based on the idea of joint solidarity between citizens, "the LTCI Law will provide a long-term care system" (Article 1) and that "citizens are required to equally share the cost of the system" (Article 4). Thus, Japanese citizens are now responsible for their insurance premiums as well as co-payments.

However, the purpose and philosophy of the LTCI Law were not fully discussed before establishing the system, and the law was formulated mainly to secure financial resources for LTCI; beneficiaries who were the targets of long-term care services were not consulted during the process.

Enhancement of Free Choice and Competition between Care Providers

By changing the system of sochi (allocation system) into that of a contract, the new LTCI system enabled frail elderly to utilize various care services and to choose their care provider. It also provided an opportunity for private for-profit organizations to enter the social welfare industry for the elderly, which was previously run by only the public sectors and social welfare corporations. This loosened the responsibilities of the public sectors and brought the principle of competition and market fundamentalism into the field of long-term care.

Until then, the public sectors and social welfare corporations had been providing health and social services in accordance with national regulations and standards of care. When they were cited for the violation of regulations/standards, these corporations were required to immediately implement any suggestions given by the respective government authorities after administrative inspections. However, it is questionable whether private, for-profit organizations will follow suit. It is possible that long-term care services are now being provided by providers who may be more concerned about receiving reimbursements from the LTCI system instead of improving and maintaining the quality of care. Therefore, the quality of care is uncertain because of the reforms in the basic social welfare structure. As such, it would be evaluated in accordance with the amount of reimbursements, i.e., "more money, better service."

SUMMARY

It took almost 40 years, from the time of implementation of the National Universal Health Insurance and pension coverage for all citizens until 2000, to establish the LTCI system as a new branch of social insurance that provides long-term care services for older people in Japan. Importantly, when the LTCI Law was enacted, medical care and social welfare services were integrated into a social insurance program, and a system to shift the burden of caregiving from family caregivers to the government was created; individuals were required to contribute to long-term care, were offered free choice, and competition was generated between care providers.

Notes

1) MHW of Japan was reorganized into the Ministry of Health, Labour and Welfare (MHLW) through the Central Government Reform in 2001.
2) Activities of daily living: The basic activities of everyday life that individuals perform such as eating, toileting, bathing, dressing, and transfers to and from the bed and/or wheelchair.
3) Instrumental activities of daily living: A series of life functions necessary for independent living in a community setting such as preparing meals, taking medications, shopping for groceries, using the telephone, and managing money.
4) Specified diseases associated with old age: (1) amyotrophic lateral sclerosis (ALS); (2) Ossification of posterior longitudinal ligament (OPLL); (3) osteoporosis with fractures; (4) multiple system atrophy (formerly known as Shy-Drager Syndrome); (5) spinocerebellar syndrome; (6) spinal canal stenosis; (7) presenile dementia; (8) progeria; (9) diabetic neuropathy, diabetic nephropathy, and diabetic retinopathy; (10) cerebrovascular disease; (11) Parkinson's disease; (12) arteriosclerosis obliterans; (13) chronic rheumatoid arthritis; (14) chronic obstructive pulmonary disease (COPD); (15) osteoarthritis with significant deformation in the hip or knee joint on both sides. The number of specified diseases was increased to 16 in April 2006 after including terminal cancer.

References

Campbell, J. C. & Ikegami, N. (2000). Long-Term Care Insurance Comes to Japan. Health Affairs, 19(3), 26-39.

Ihara, K. (2012). Japan's Long-Term Care Insurance Programs. http://www.kaigo.gr.jp/JLCIhp.htm (accessed June 8, 2013).

Japan Kaigo Support Association (2000). SOS Signals for Qualification of Long-Term Care Benefits [*Yokaigo Nintei SOS*]. Tokyo: Index Press.

Japanese Society of Medical Social Work (2001). Comprehensive Guidebook to Medical Welfare in the Era of Long-term Care Insurance [*Kaigo Hoken Jidai no Iryo Fukushi Sogo Gaide*]. Tokyo: Igaku-Shoin Ltd.

Kaigo Gijyutsu Zensho Henshu Iinkai (1999). Easy-to-Understand Long-Term Care [*Wakariyasui Kaigo*]. Kyoto: Minerva-Shobo.

Ministry of Health and Welfare (1996). Establishment of the Long-Term Care Insurance System for the Elderly [*Koreisha Kaigo Hoken Seido no Sosetsu ni tsuite*]. Tokyo: Gyosei Corporation. http://www.kaigo.gr.jp/JLCIhp.htm (accessed September 5 2012).

Sumii, H. (1998). Theory and Practice of Care Model [*Kaigo Model no Riron to Jissen*].

Okayama: University Education Press.

Sumii, H. (2002). The Start of Long-Term Care Insurance [*Kaigo Hoken no Start*]. In Institute of Japan Care Work (Ed.), Introduction to Long-Term Care Insurance [*Kaigo Hoken Nyumonsho*] (pp.1-22). Tokyo: Index Press.

Sumii, H., et al. (2008). Introduction to Long-Term Care Insurance in Japan–To Support "Kaigo" Security. International Journal of Welfare for the Aged, 19, 17-39.

2

An Overview of Long-Term Care Insurance

Recently, the population of Japan has been aging sharply along with a notable decrease in birthrate. This rapid aging leads to a huge increase in costs for social security programs such as long-term care, pension, and health care. At the same time, the burden on the younger working population, who are mainly responsible for paying insurance premiums, increases due to the aging population and declining birthrate.

Prior to the arrival of the LTCI system, there were several types of social security programs in Japan, such as the social insurance program, public assistance program, public health program, social welfare program, and war veterans' coverage. These programs provided a set of health care benefits to all eligible persons who paid insurance premiums in case of emergencies and any life-threatening events such as injuries, disease/ disability, and accidents. Unemployment insurance benefits provided regular payments in cases of unemployment. There were also workers' compensation insurance benefits for accidents at the work place or during working hours and several other types of pension plans for the stability and continuation of life after retirement. These social security programs

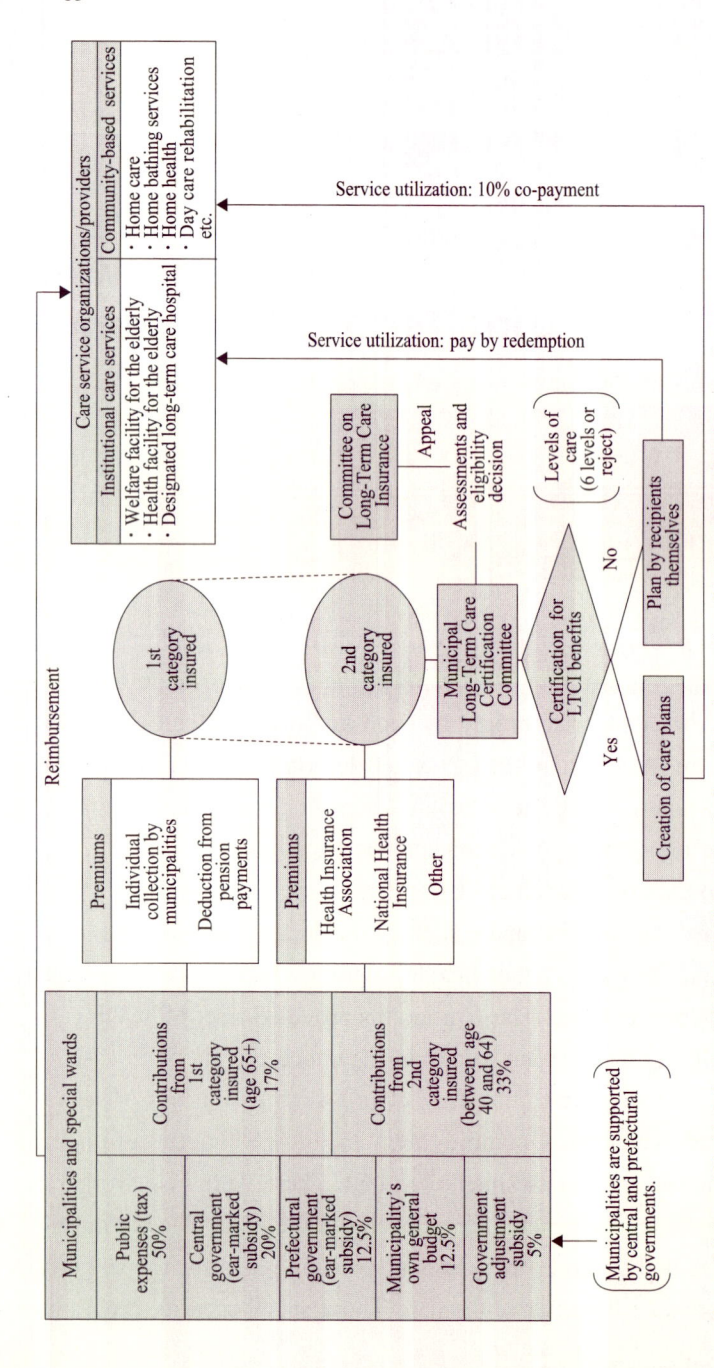

Figure 2-1 Outline of the Long-Term Care Insurance System

Source: Ministry of Health, Labour and Welfare (2009) Preparing for Smooth Implementation of the Long-Term Care Insurance System.
Note: "Assistance-required" beneficiaries can utilize only community-based care, whereas "care-required" beneficiaries can receive both community-based care services and institutional care. In 2000, for half a year, financial resources related to insurance premiums were supported by the central government. As for supporting family caregivers, a cash benefit funded by municipalities with a subsidy from the central government is provided for elderly members whose level of care required is level 4 or 5 for 1 year without using any public care services funded by LTCI.

allowed people to prepare for unpredictable events beforehand and played an important role in decreasing damages in such events by allowing people to pay cash out of their insurance coverage and obtain medical care services and hospitalization.

However, no unified social security program existed that delivered the full range of long-term care services. Therefore, the LTCI program, a new social insurance program of the social security system, was developed to provide a combination of health/medical and social welfare services to beneficiaries in the event that they become unable to take care of themselves. This chapter provides an overview of the LTCI program (Figure 2-1).

THE STRUCTURE OF LONG-TERM CARE INSURANCE

The LTCI program is a public mandatory social insurance program operated by municipalities under the central government legislation in Japan. The following section briefly explains the structure of LTCI such as the contents and types of LTCI-funded care services, insurers and insured persons, certification of care-required and assistance-required, financing and costs of LTCI, care management and care plans, and various types of professionals in the LTCI system.

The Contents and Types of Long-Term Care Insurance-Funded Care Services

There are 3 types of care services: (1) long-term care services for persons classified as "care-required," (2) disease/disability prevention services for persons classified as "assistance-required," and (3) special services funded by each municipality. Among the care services available to care-required and assistance-required persons, there are 15 types of long-term care services that LTCI will cover under home- and community-based care services and 3 types under institutional long-term care services (Table 2-1). Home- and community-based care services include not only home care, home health, adult day care, and home rehabilitation services (see Chapter 3) but also loans on assistive devices, such as wheelchairs and hospital beds, and home modifications (see Chapter 4). Institutional care services are provided by 3 different types of care facilities: (1) welfare facilities for the elderly; (2) health facilities for the elderly; and (3) hospitals with designated long-term care beds (see Chapter 5). The special services that each municipality covers in its financial and social resource include transportation services, drying of futon (bedding), and home-delivered meals.

Once a person is officially certified as care-required, 1 or more of 15 types of home-and community-based care and 3 types of institutional long-term care services are provided. If a person is classified as "assistance-required," then he/she would be allowed to use only home-and community-

Table 2-1 Long-Term Care Insurance-Funded Care Services

	Long-term care insurance-funded care services
Home- and community-based care	1. Home care (home-help visits for caregiving and/or housekeeping) 2. Home bathing services 3. Home health care (e.g., visiting nurse services) 4. Home visit rehabilitation 5. Medical management (home visits for medical advice and supervision of care plans by health care professionals) 6. Adult day care services 7. Day care rehabilitation 8. Short-stay program for personal care (respite care) 9. Short-stay program for medical care 10. Group home for people with dementia 11. Care services for private care facility residents 12. Loan of assistive devices (e.g., wheelchairs and specialty beds) 13. Reimbursement for purchasing assistive devices 14. Reimbursement for home modifications 15. Care management
Institutional long-term care	1. Welfare facility for the elderly (a type of nursing home) 2. Health facility for the elderly (a type of skilled nursing facility) 3. Designated long-term care hospital

based care services that are provided as disease/disability preventative services and not institutional long-term care and in-facility care for dementia.

Insurers (Municipal Governments)

Insurers of LTCI are municipalities and 23 special wards in Tokyo (referred to as "municipalities" in this book) that are responsible for the operation and maintenance of the LTCI system. These insurers play a central role in supervising and controlling the overall flow of the process, such as collecting insurance premiums, receiving applications for LTCI benefits, determining the type of care that should be provided, and checking whether those benefits are appropriately offered. Municipalities are the insurers of the National Health Insurance (NHI) for those who are self-employed.

For the LTCI system, municipalities are not required to manage the entire system on their own. Both the national and prefectural governments are supposed to provide financial support, supervision, and assistance to operate and manage the LTCI system.

The Insured (Beneficiaries of Long-Term Care Insurance)

Insured persons are all individuals aged 40 and over who pay insurance premiums on LTCI. They are categorized as "1st category insured" and "2nd category insured" persons. Both categories of insured persons are required to be residents of the prescribed municipality.

As shown in Table 2-2, 1st category insured persons are those aged 65 and above, and 2nd category insured persons are members of the medical insurance program aged between 40 and 65. First category insured persons can apply for LTCI benefits when some assistance is required with activities of daily living (ADLs; e.g., bathing, toileting, dressing,

Table 2-2 Persons Insured by Long-Term Care Insurance

	1st category insured	2nd category insured
Eligibility	Persons aged 65 and above.	Medical insurance members aged between 40 and 65.
Beneficiaries	Individuals requiring assistance or long-term care.	Individuals who require assistance due to a particular illness such as cerebro-vascular disease.
Premiums (contributions)	Collected by municipalities.	Insurers collect contributions as medical insurance premiums, then pay as a package.
Levy and levy methods	· Fixed amounts of premiums based on income level. · For those who receive more than a certain amount of pension, the premium will be deducted from pension payments. · Otherwise, fees are collected by regular methods.	· Health insurance organization: Standard care insurance premiums. · National Health Insurance: Premiums are paid on a pro-rata basis.

and transfers to and from the bed and/or wheelchair) and instrumental activities of daily living (IADLs; e.g., preparing meals and homemaking) due to a decline in physical and mental conditions caused by aging and/or due to being bedridden or having symptoms of dementia (Figure 1-3).

Second category insured persons can utilize LTCI benefits only when their physical and mental abilities decline due to having one or more of the 15 specified diseases associated with old age (e.g., Parkinson's disease, cerebrovascular disease, and dementia) specified by the MHLW. In other words, LTCI services cannot be delivered to those with a temporary sickness that is not a result of aging and those who are physically disabled due to an injury or a birth defect. The reason for limiting eligibility is that the present LTCI system was created mainly for the elderly and to address the anticipated shortage of care for the elderly; caring for disabled people requires in-depth consideration and optimal policy reform, which the LTCI system is not designed to meet. Physically disabled persons who do not qualify for LTCI care services (e.g., personal home care, day care, short-term stay) are covered by the municipal's own social welfare services programs, as per the Law for the Welfare of Physically Disabled Persons, even if they are aged over 40.

Qualifications of Long-Term Care Insurance Benefits

Under LTCI, only those who are certified as "care-required" and "assistance-required" are eligible for LTCI-covered care services. The care-required level is defined strictly according to the level of the person's physical and mental disability that requires continuous care over a 6-month period, whereas the assistance-required level is determined depending on the possible level of long-term care that one would require in the future. Considering the above facts, it can be said that LTCI is not for all insured people; rather, it is for those who really experience difficulties in daily life.

Certification of "Care-Required" and "Assistance-Required"

In order to be eligible for and receive LTCI-funded care services, individuals have to obtain certification for LTCI benefits after undergoing an onsite evaluation of physical and mental conditions conducted by each municipality. To receive the certification, people need to submit an application form to their local municipal government (see Chapter 6).

Figure 2-2 outlines the basic process of applying for and receiving long-term care services. Once the application is submitted, the onsite assessment of physical and mental status using an 85-item assessment scale (as of April 2000) is conducted by the municipal government. The results of the assessment are then analyzed by a computer program developed by the national government that classifies applicants into one of 6 care levels (or rejects) as an initial classification. Once this step is completed, a group of experts called the "Long-Term Care Certification Committee" will review the results of the initial classification, as well as reports submitted by the applicants' primary attending physician, and

Application
When individuals feel the need for long-term care/assistance, they or their family members need to submit an application form to a clerk at the office of their municipality.

⬇

Assessment of functional and cognitive status
Care managers (such as care specialists designated by municipalities) visit the homes or the nursing facilities where the applicants reside and check the applicants' health condition by using the national standardized assessment form.

⬇

Review of application, assessment results, and physician's report
Based on the result of the onsite assessment and a report from the applicant's doctor, the Long-Term Care Certification Committee, consisting of specialists in medicine, health, and social welfare, then decides if long-term care is required and classifies the applicants into 1 of 6 levels of care categories.

⬇

Eligibility decision
Eligibility is decided according to the assessment and is conveyed to the applicants within 30 days of application.

Figure 2-2   Application Process Flow Chart for Long-Term Care Insurance Benefits and Certification

will finally classify each applicant's level of care. "Assistance-required," which is intended for disease/disability services, is the lowest level; the other levels are called "care-required" (see Chapter 7).

It usually takes up to 30 days to inform the applicant of the eligibility decision. If an applicant is physically and mentally independent, he/she will be informed of being ineligible for LTCI benefits by the municipalities.

Beneficiaries' care levels have to be re-evaluated every 6 months. However, by considering the physical and mental conditions of the beneficiaries, the certificate may be renewed for an additional 3 months or up to 1 year, if the Long-Term Care Certification Committee approves the need for additional care.

Financing and Costs of Long-Term Care Insurance

All insured individuals are required to pay premiums (see Chapter 8). The MHLW made it clear that, once they are entitled to the care services funded by LTCI, recipients must pay 10% of an explicitly defined monetary amount as co-payment and share the cost of meals provided in the institutions (see Chapter 9). Nevertheless, LTCI beneficiaries are not required to pay for the creation of care plans by care managers.

The budget ceiling of the explicitly defined monetary amount of LTCI services is determined according to the care level required. For example, if a beneficiary requires community-based care at home, then the budget ceiling ranges between JPY 61,500 and JPY 358,300 per month (Table 2-3).

For recipients who are required to pay fees exceeding JPY 37,200 per month, the balance would be refunded. However, individual expenses from purchasing devices such as wheelchairs or home modifications would not be refunded if the cost exceeds the budget ceiling. Therefore, some policies to reduce the burden of personal expenses are necessary, especially for low-income people.

Table 2-3 Budget Ceiling for Home-and Community-Based Care Services

Level of care	Budget ceiling per month (JPY)
Assistance-required	61,500
Care-required level 1	165,800
Care-required level 2	194,800
Care-required level 3	267,500
Care-required level 4	306,000
Care-required level 5	358,300

Note: As of April 2000

Care Management and Care Plans

Originally adopted from that of nursing homes in the United States, the LTCI system introduced a concept of "care management" in Japan and required the development of a care plan (by either beneficiaries themselves or care managers) in order to receive LTCI benefits. The care plan is a care scheme that accommodates a variety of care services to meet the needs of beneficiaries, and is a part of care management, which is defined by the Council on Health and Welfare for the Elderly as a series of activities supporting elderly persons in need of care to have constant and appropriate care services that meet their needs.

There are two types of care plans: (1) home-care care plan and (2) in-facility care plan (see Chapter 10). While the home-care care plan is formulated within the budget ceiling of each care level, the in-facility care plan is created to indicate what actions will be carried out by facility staff. Since elderly individuals and their families lack information as to what type of care services and providers are available and how social resources and human resources vary by region, it would be better to have a care manager develop care plans for beneficiaries.

Types of Professionals in the Long-Term Care Insurance System

There are various types of health care professional such as physicians, nurses, nurse's aides (called "care workers" in Japan) and rehabilitation personnel, as well as non-health care professionals such as commissioned welfare volunteers involved in the LTCI system (see Chapter 11). Care managers are responsible for developing care plans for LTCI beneficiaries according to their needs and desires. They use an interdisciplinary team approach to provide appropriate care to beneficiaries.

SUMMARY

Before going into details about the LTCI system, this chapter provided an overview of it to describe the roles of the insurers and insured, financial sources to assure the operation of the system, eligibility criteria and related assessment procedures, and care management for the coordination of various types of home- and community-based and institutional care. It also briefly introduced the health and non-health professionals involved in the LTCI system (e.g., care managers). The LTCI system includes a wide range of care services, from home care efforts to adult day care, loans on assistive devices, residential repairs, and institutional care services. These services will be discussed in detail in the following chapters.

References

Asahi, K. (1999). Points of Long-Term Care Insurance [*Kaigo Hoken no Point*]. Tokyo: Kiri-Syobo.

Campbell, J. C. & Ikegami, N. (2000). Long-Term Care Insurance Comes to Japan. Health Affairs, 19(3), 26-39.

Fujiwara, Y. (2002). What is Long-Term Care Insurance? [*Kaigo Hoken towa Nanika*]. In Institute of Japan Care Work (Ed.), Introduction to Long-Term Care Insurance [*Kaigo*

Hoken Nyumonsho] (pp.23-32). Tokyo: Index Press.

Fukushi Jichitai Unit (2000). Quick Understanding of Long-Term Care Insurance Law [*Kaigo Hokenho Hayawakari*]. Tokyo: Houken Corp..

Ihara, K. (2012). Japan's Long-Term Care Insurance Programs. http://www.kaigo.gr.jp/JLCIhp.htm (accessed June 8, 2013).

Japanese Society of Medical Social Work (2001). Comprehensive Guidebook to Medical Welfare in the Era of Long-Term Care Insurance [*Kaigo Hoken Jidai no Iryo Fukushi Sogo Gaide*]. Tokyo: Igaku-Shoin Ltd.

Ministry of Health, Labour and Welfare (2009). Preparing for Smooth Implementation of the Long-Term Care Insurance System. http://www.mhlw.go.jp/english/wp/wp-hw/ (accessed September 1 2012).

Murasawa, I. (2000). Twelve Chapters for Understanding Long-Term Care Insurance [*Kaigo Hoken ga Wakaru 12sho*]. Tokyo: Diamond, Inc..

Sumii, H. (1998). Theory and Practice of Care Model [*Kaigo Model no Riron to Jissen*]. Okayama: University Education Press.

3

Home- and Community-Based Care Services

The LTCI system delivers a wide range of home- and community-based care services to assist frail elderly to attain or maintain the maximum level of functioning and to live at home independently. Home- and community-based care services are beneficial and convenient to many elderly people because the services are provided at their homes.

As a rule, beneficiaries who are certified as "assistance-required" are entitled to only home- and community-based care services while those certified as "care-required" can receive institutional long-term care. In other words, home care services and in-facility services cannot be used at the same time.

This chapter first reviews the types of home- and community-based care services that are funded by LTCI (except care management, which is discussed in Chapter 10), and then discusses care services funded by social welfare programs. The last section will address how much home- and community-based care service is available for each care level.

TYPES OF HOME- AND COMMUNITY-BASED CARE SERVICES

The purpose of home- and community-based care is to facilitate the independence of beneficiaries and their families, help them to live with dignity, and provide a connection between the beneficiaries/their families and social resources in the community. For these purposes, LTCI provides 15 types of home- and community-based care services, including care services provided at a person's home (e.g., home care and home health care), outpatient care services (e.g., adult day care and day care rehabilitation), leasing assistive devices, and home modifications (Table 3-1).

When one is classified as "assistance-required," he/she is entitled to

Table 3-1 Types of Home- and Community-Based Care Services

	Home-and community-based care services
"Care-required" levels	1. Home care
	2. Home bathing services
	3. Home health care
	4. Home visit rehabilitation
	5. Medical management
	6. Adult day care services
	7. Day care rehabilitation
	8. Short-stay program for personal care
	9. Short-stay program for medical care
	10. Group home for people with dementia
	11. Care services for private care facility residents
	12. Loan of assistive devices
	13. Reimbursements for purchasing assistive devices
	14. Reimbursements for home modifications
	15. Care management
"Assistance-required" (provided as preventive care)	All benefits mentioned above, except group home for people with dementia.
Municipal original benefits	Benefits implemented by the ordinance of the municipality.

receive any type of home-and community-based care up to the budget ceiling of their care level except "group homes for people with dementia." A person who is certified as "care-required" has a free choice between community-based care and institutional long-term care.

Home Care (Home Help)

Home care aides (called home-helpers or care workers in Japan) would visit the homes of those aged 65 and above and are in need of assistance for physical care and some activities of daily living such as cooking, cleaning, and shopping. This service helps these elderly persons live independently and reduces the burden on caregivers.

Home care, also called home-help, services could be physical-care-focused, homemaking-focused, or a combination of both services, with different fee schedules for each type of service. Similarly, there are different types of home visits, such as stay-for-a-while, routine-visit-care, and night-shift-visit care services.

The physical-care-focused stay-for-a-while care service provides assistance with bathing, eating and toileting, dressing, sponge baths, hair washing, and transportation to doctor's appointments. A home care aide usually stays for a couple of hours until he/she finishes providing all the required care services.

The homemaking-focused stay-for-a-while care service provides services such as cooking, washing clothes, vacuuming, and grocery shopping. The length of visit is approximately 1-2 hours.

Routine-visit-care provides sponge baths and assistance with position change, fluid intake, and toileting. A home care aide usually comes for a short period of time (usually 30 min) to provide care.

The night-shift-visit care is provided by 2 nursing staff members and they usually assist with position change to prevent beneficiaries from developing bedsores while sleeping.

A mixed version of the physical-care-focused and housework-assistance-focused visiting care services was established because it is difficult to separate physical care and assistance in a household, and because it is provided according to recipient's needs. For instance, if the recipient is able to take a bath and do some housework independently, but requires assistance with washing hair, then the mixed version is provided.

It is important to note that, when one utilizes the home- and community-based care funded by LTCI, it is not advisable to demand beyond the scope of service of the home care aides and to disregard the home care aide's advice. However, there may be some home care aides with limited nursing experience and skills. Thus, it is important to choose a reliable person and agency that are able to provide appropriate care.

Home Bathing Services

Bathing does not only keep the body clean—it also refreshes one. Individuals who wish to take a bath at home with the help of a home care aide can choose the home bathing service and those who want to take a bath at a nursing facility with the nursing staff's help can choose the day service.

It is important to note that although assistance with bathing is hard work for caregivers, it is also mentally and physically difficult for the elderly recipients. Moreover, because recipients may sometimes need to undergo preliminary medical check-ups before taking a bath, it is important to consult with the attending physician regularly. Therefore, it is important to choose an agency/facility whose bathing schedule is flexible and to confirm whether bathing services can be used without causing any problems to the elderly.

Home Health Care (Visiting Nurse Services)

Home health care provides medical and nursing care, which are not provided by home care services, to individuals with stabilized health conditions and aims to help elderly people in need of long-term care to recuperate and live independently in the community.

Expert nursing staff members, such as nurses and health professionals, visit the homes of the elderly persons from a home visit nursing care station, hospital, and/or health clinic, and provide the necessary recuperation therapies according to physicians' orders.

Home health care is often provided, particularly for the treatment of bedsores and wounds and managing tube feeding, intravenous fluids, respiratory function, urethral catheterization, and colostomy. It also provides domiciliary oxygen therapy, enemas for constipation and fecal impaction, assistance with eating, toileting and bathing, sponge baths, and physical and occupational therapies. It is delivered only when a beneficiary's physician authorizes and writes an order for the above services.

Because beneficiaries can choose their service providers, they should check the number of available staff members that the provider has and their qualifications, in addition to the information related to its affiliated care providers in case the level of care changes.

Home Visit Rehabilitation

Home visit rehabilitation is planned under the physician's medical management. A physical and/or an occupational therapist visits the home of the recipient, who undergoes physical and occupational therapies and other necessary rehabilitative activities. Home visit rehabilitation aims to maintain the recovery of physical functioning to promote independent living in elderly persons who are in the recovery phase and to provide information related to their rehabilitation to their family members. It also aims to improve the performing of ADLs and quality of life (QOL) in beneficiaries so that they can live with dignity.

This service can be provided by only designated hospitals, health clinics, and health service facilities. It is thus recommended to check the provider and the availability of doctors and other health care professionals specializing in rehabilitation when applying for this service.

Although travel expenses for this service are covered by LTCI, recipients are required to pay if the service is provided outside the service area.

Medical Management

This service provides doctor, dentist, pharmacist, and nationally registered dietitian visits to the recipients' homes to examine their health status, provide medical advice, and supervise their care plans. It is mainly for LTCI beneficiaries who reside at home.

Physicians observe the condition of the recipients while they are eating, sleeping, toileting, showing problem behaviors, and engaging in ADLs. Physicians then provide medical advice to both the recipients and their families after an interview. Physicians can also provide advice on hospitalization and institutionalization. It is recommended to seek advice on whether hospitalization and/or institutionalization is necessary for a recipient from a family doctor who understands the daily mental and physical condition of the recipient. When meeting with the physician, it is important to report the recipient's actual condition accurately and honestly, and it is recommended that family members, especially those who live with the recipients, communicate frankly with the doctor regarding any concerns or changes that they have about the recipient.

Medical management consists of doctors' home visits, visiting dental services, and home-based medication management programs. Doctors' home visits are generally provided to those with chronic diseases, dementia, and physical disabilities. Visiting dental services are usually provided for elderly persons who have oral, gum, and/or denture problems. Home-based medication management programs provided through visits by pharmacists or other medication experts are conducted to analyze the medications that the recipients take to determine if the medications (dosage, frequency) are prescribed appropriately and if they are causing any negative side effects, and to resolve any therapeutic duplication.

Adult Day Care Services

Adult day care services are provided to individuals aged 65 and above by long-term care facilities such as health facilities for the elderly, which provide transportation for the recipients. This service is also called the "day service" or "day trip for nursing care" because it can be used on a daily basis.

This service provides meals, functional restoration training, and assistance with bathing and toileting. It is intended for those with physical weaknesses, those who are bedridden, and those who have dementia, although some facilities target only elderly persons with dementia.

Adult day care has its advantages—elderly people can socialize and communicate with others, preventing them from feeling isolated. Some day care centers also provide recreational activities. However, the costs for transportation and meals are paid out of the beneficiaries' own pockets. In addition, they would have to pay for facility stock items such as absorbent incontinence pads, if applicable, because such expenses are not covered by LTCI. The availability and frequency of the service also varies between facilities, so it is important to check and confirm such details before utilization.

Day Care Rehabilitation (Day Care)

Day care rehabilitation service, formally known as "day care," provides rehabilitative care, meals, and bathing services at health or medical care facilities for elderly people. This service aims to restore and maintain recipients' mental and physical conditions and to support their independent living.

Day care rehabilitation service is widely utilized by people with functional disorders, who recuperate at home, are infirmed, bedridden, and/or have dementia. It targets persons with lower levels of LTCI certification.

Under the physician's order and supervision, physical and occupational therapies and functional training are provided by rehabilitation professionals such as physical therapists and occupational therapists.

Similar to home visit rehabilitation, the fees for transportation to and from home visit rehabilitation and meals, and similar to adult day care, facility stock items such as absorbent incontinence pads, are also paid for by the recipients, not LTCI.

Short-Stay Program for Personal Care

This program provides personal care such as assistance with bathing, toileting, and eating to elderly people aged 65 and above who are staying temporarily at a care facility for the elderly. The main targets of this program are elderly people who are bedridden and those with dementia.

This service is useful for when family members responsible for caring for these elderly recipients become unavailable for a short period of time and for reducing the burden of care on family caregivers. However, this service should be used within the budget ceiling of the care level, and, as before, LTCI does not cover the meals and absorbent incontinence pads provided during the short-stay.

Short-Stay Program for Medical Care

If a doctor orders it, an individual aged 65 and above can stay at a medical facility temporarily to receive medical care, rehabilitation, and assistance with ADLs when his/her caregiver is unavailable to provide care. This service is usually provided at health facilities for the elderly, designated long-term care hospitals, and hospitals with designated long-term care beds.

The targets of this program are elderly people whose health condition is stable but are bedridden and require some medical attention. Although this service is useful for reducing caregivers' mental and physical burden, similar to other services, it does not cover meals and items needed for daily living.

The biggest difference between short-stay programs for medical care and for personal care is that medical care short-stay focuses on providing not only personal care but also medical care, including rehabilitation and nursing care.

Group Homes for People with Dementia

This service provides assistance with ADLs and rehabilitation in group homes or small-scale units in long-term care facilities to those who qualify for LTCI benefits and have a diagnosis of dementia. The main purpose of this service is to offer care in order to slow the progression of symptoms of dementia so that the resident would be able to live as independently as possible. The eligibility criteria for admission into group homes include (1) aged 65 and above with a middle stage of dementia, including those with pre-senile dementia aged below 65 years; (2) are difficult to be taken care of at home due to some environmental factors; (3) are physically independent; and (4) have no difficulties living together with others. Beneficiaries classified as assistance-required are not eligible for this service.

Care Services for Private Care Facility Residents

LTCI provides assistance with ADLs, rehabilitation, and nursing care services to those living in facilities such as private elder homes and care houses. This service targets elderly individuals who require long-term care but do not qualify for institutional long-term care or who desire to meet their various needs on their own. Similar to some aforementioned services, daily expenses such as diapers and meals incurred from this service are not covered by LTCI.

Loan of Assistive Devices and Home Modifications

LTCI covers fees for renting assistive devices such as wheelchairs and hospital beds that are designated by the Minister of Health, Labour and Welfare (Minister of HLW) (see Chapter 4). However, not all devices could be loaned; some LTCI-approved devices, called "specialty assistive devices" (e.g., bedside commodes and specialty bathtubs), are unsuitable for loan but are available through purchase. Purchasers of such devices must first pay the full amount and obtain a reimbursement of 50% of the cost, or up to JPY 100,000, per year.

In order to help recipients to live at home, LTCI also covers fees for home modifications. When recipients of these services modify their homes, they first have to pay the full amount and then obtain a reimbursement of 90% or up to JPY 200,000 per person from LTCI. In principle, home modifications are limited to only one time per house, except in cases of moving to another place and/or when the care level increases by 3 levels (e.g., assistance-required level 1 to care-required level 4). If there are more than two beneficiaries in the same family/house, and each person requires different types of modifications at different times, then both modifications are covered by LTCI.

OTHER RELATED HOME- AND COMMUNITY-BASED CARE SERVICES

Preventive Care Benefits

To be eligible for LTCI benefits, one is required to receive certification for long-term care. Therefore, the services funded by LTCI are unavailable for those not certified as care-required or assistance-required. However, these people may have a need for care services even if they are uncertified, which may lead to them requiring long-term care in the future. Therefore, with the introduction of LTCI, municipal governments have become responsible for providing their own preventive care programs for those who are ineligible for LTCI benefits. For example, some municipalities offer daily living equipment, home modification programs, and functional training programs to prevent elderly individuals from being housebound. The national government also provides subsidies to municipalities that deliver their own social welfare programs that promote preventive care programs for those ineligible for LTCI.

Special Benefits Provided by Municipalities

In the LTCI system, services such as "additional services" and "on-the-side services" are provided by each municipality, which are funded by LTCI insurance premiums collected from 1st category insured persons aged 65 and above, in addition to the benefits provided by LTCI. An "additional service" entails adding a certain amount of money to the budget ceiling to increase the frequency and number of the service(s) provided, such as home visit care. "On-the-side" service refers to services such as meals-on-wheels or haircut services that are not covered by LTCI. Because both addition and on-the-side services are provided by each municipality, the contents and types of services vary between municipalities.

TO WHAT EXTENT CAN INDIVIDUALS RECEIVE LONG-TERM CARE SERVICES?

The care services that could be provided at beneficiaries' homes are limited by the budget ceiling, which ranges from JPY 61,500 to JPY 358,300 (Table 2-3) and determined according to the beneficiaries' care levels. Therefore, before choosing the contents and types of services, it is important for beneficiaries to check the amount of the budget ceiling, which is written on the insurance card. In general, recipients have to pay 10% of the full costs of care services.

SUMMARY

Home- and community-based care services include a wide variety of services ranging from home care, home health aide services, and adult day care that temporarily relieves family caregivers of their responsibility in the home or in the community to LTCI beneficiaries. These services are provided widely so that the home- and community-based care recipients could delay or avoid institutionalization as much as possible. Despite the wide range of home- and community-based care services available, beneficiaries' family members still have to provide some forms of care. Lastly, when considering the type of service to receive, beneficiaries should check the budget ceiling.

References

Asahi, K. (1999). Points of Long-Term Care Insurance [*Kaigo Hoken no Point*]. Tokyo: Kiri-Syobo.

Hiramatsu, K. (1998). Strategies of Long-Term Care Insurance and Medical Care Services [*Kaigo Hoken to Iryo Shisetsu Service no Senryaku*]. Tokyo: Ishiyaku Publishers, Inc..

Ministry of Health and Welfare (2000). Basic Textbook for Care Managers [*Kaigo Shienin Kihon Text*]. Tokyo: Chojyu Shakai Kaihatsu Center.

Tokuhara, N. & Ono, M. (2002). What are Community-Based Care Services of Long-Term Care Insurance? [*Kaigo Hoken no Kyotaku Service towa*]. In Institute of Japan Care Work (Ed.), Introduction to Long-Term Care Insurance [*Kaigo Hoken Nyumonsho*] (pp.83-96). Tokyo: Index Press.

Watanabe, S. (1997). Knowledge of Long-Term Care Insurance [*Kaigo Hoken no Chishiki*]. Tokyo: Nikkei Publishing Inc..

Yamasaki, Y., et al. (1999). Management of the Long-Term Care System [*Kaigo Hoken System no Management*]. Tokyo: Igaku-Shoin Ltd..

4

Assistive Devices and Home Modifications

The LTCI system covers the rental and purchase fees for a number of assistive devices and home modifications. Because of this coverage, people requiring long-term care can rent expensive assistive devices such as hospital beds and wheelchairs at a low cost, and choose one that is suitable for their level of function. It is recommended for beneficiaries to take advantage of these services to attain or maintain safe and comfortable living environments for themselves.

This chapter explores the types of assistive devices and looks at the types of home modifications that are covered by LTCI.

ASSISTIVE DEVICES

An assistive device is a tool, product, or type of equipment that helps elderly and/or disabled people perform particular tasks and activities and alleviate difficulties that they have in their daily living.

LTCI provides both assistive devices and reimbursements for purchasing assistive devices to its beneficiaries who reside in their own homes. Although the MHLW designates certain devices to be covered by LTCI, almost all assistive devices available in the market can be rented. Nevertheless, some individuals do not wish to rent these devices, and some are averse to using a bedside commode that others might have used before. These people can purchase such devices and obtain reimbursements of up to JPY 100,000 from LTCI per year.

ASSISTIVE DEVICES AVAILABLE FOR LOAN

LTCI-approved assistive devices that are available for loan include wheelchairs and wheelchair accessories/attachments, hospital beds and bed accessories/attachments, pressure ulcer prevention and treatment devices, positioning and adaptive cushions, handrails, wheelchair/threshold ramps, walkers, canes and crutches, code alert systems, and transfer lifts (Table 4-1).

Wheelchairs

A wheelchair is a chair mounted on 4 wheels. It is usually used by ill or disabled persons and designed to be a replacement for walking. Types of wheelchairs include manual wheelchairs, attendant-propelled wheelchairs, and powered chairs.

Manual wheelchairs (Figure 4-1) enable individuals to move by themselves. Users can steer by turning the steering wheels or foot pedals.

Attendant-propelled wheelchairs require attendants to push from behind. Some such wheelchairs have adjustable back support that is suitable for people who have difficulty remaining in one position for an extended period of time.

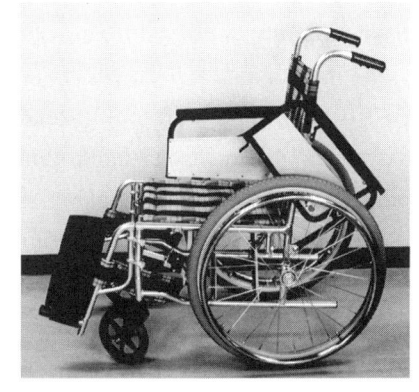

Figure 4-1 Manual Wheelchair

Table 4-1   Available Loan Items and Fee Schedule for Rentals

Loan items	Standard rental fee schedules per month (JPY)
Wheelchairs	6,000 - 10,000
Powered wheelchairs	20,000
Wheelchair accessories and attachments	from 500
Specialty/hospital beds	10,000 - 22,000
Bed accessories and attachments: · mattresses · over-the-bed tables · side rails	 2,000 500 300 - 1,500
Pressure ulcer prevention & treatment devices	5,000 - 6,000
Positioning & adaptive cushions (devices for changing positions)	2,000
Handrails, grab bars, and safety rails	2,000 - 4,000
Wheelchair ramps	4,000 - 8,000
Walkers	2,000 - 3,000
Walking canes and crutches	1,000
Code alert systems	8,000
Transfer lifts	13,000 - 20,000

Note: As of April 2000

Powered chairs are equipped with electric motors and are suitable for those who cannot propel manual wheelchairs by themselves and/or have difficulty in propelling for extended periods of time.

It is important for users to choose their wheelchairs carefully because ill-fitting wheelchairs could lead users to have painful contractures, skin breakdown, lower-back pain, and/or pressure sores. Thus, when considering using a wheelchair, it is recommended that potential users consult physical and/or occupational therapists to choose the most suitable wheelchairs.

Wheelchair Accessories and Attachments

Wheelchair accessories and attachments include a wide range of devices such as wheelchair seats, back cushions, desks, and trays that help to provide proper positioning and assist reading and eating while seated. They are covered by LTCI when rented together with a wheelchair.

Wheelchair seat and back cushions and pads are used for comfort and to relieve pressure, prevent pressure ulcers, and promote better blood circulation. With these accessories, users can sit comfortably and in the proper position for a long period of time even if they have difficulty maintaining a seating position.

Wheelchair desks and trays, usually attached to the wheelchair armrest, allow the user to eat, write, read, and do other tasks while in the wheelchair.

Wheelchair brakes are used for slowing or stopping a wheelchair through the absorption or transfer of the energy of momentum. Users can move or stop safely with this device. There are two types of brakes: (1) lever brakes, which enable the user to adjust the braking force, and (2) toggle brakes, which require less force to stop the wheelchair.

Although some electric accessories are available for wheelchairs, certain types of wheelchairs do not allow multiple electric accessories; thus, one needs to be careful when installing them.

Hospital Beds

Hospital beds, also called specialty beds or electric beds, are beds specially designed for individuals in need of some form of health care that requires some parts of the bed, such as the head or foot, to be angled (Figure 4-2). Rental and purchase of hospital beds are covered by LTCI; beneficiaries are reimbursed up to 100,000 JPY.

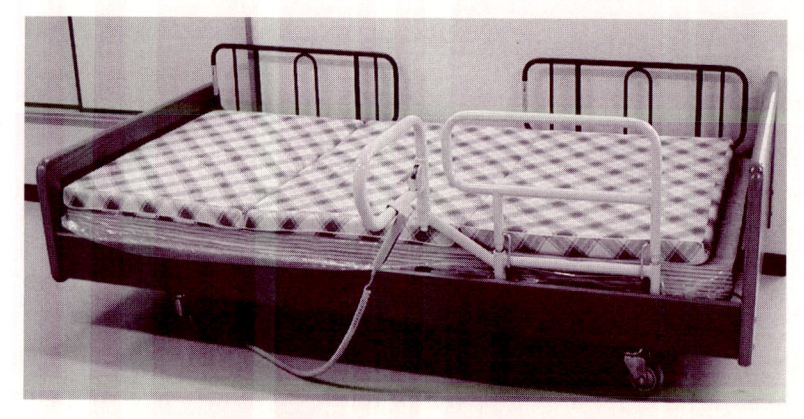

Figure 4-2   Hospital Bed and its Accessories and Attachments

Bed Accessories and Attachments

Rentals of some bed accessories and attachments such as regular mattresses, bedside rails, handrails, and pressure relief mattresses for pressure ulcer prevention are covered by LTCI only when hospital beds are rented at the same time. When choosing a mattress, users and their families should choose one that is highly hygroscopic, breathable, and elastic, and that does not compromise the features of a hospital bed (especially those pertaining to the raising of certain parts of the bed).

A bedside rail provides assistance for getting in and out of bed and transfer to and from a wheelchair. It is usually attached to the bed frame and used to help prevent an individual, or even bedding, from falling on the ground. There is a type of bedside rail that opens outward (as shown in Figure 4-2) that is especially useful for transferring to and from a wheelchair when compared to that of regular bedside rails. Other types of bedside rails, such as plug-in bedside rails, folding bedside rails, and full-length bed rails, are also available. An over-the-bed table can also be rented, with the cost covered by LTCI.

Pressure Ulcer Prevention and Treatment Devices

There are pressure relief mattresses, which provide relief and alleviate pressure while maintaining proper body support and firmness, that prevent and treat pressure ulcers and promote blood circulation. These mattresses could be filled with foam, gel, water, or air with an electric air mattress pump.

A pressure relief mattress is very soft such that a user's body sinks down into the mattress. This may make rolling over and getting up difficult for the user. Accordingly, another type of mattress that is thin and less soft might be more suitable for those who can roll over by themselves.

Positioning and Adaptive Cushions

Positioning and adaptive cushions may be used to change the orientation of one's posture while changing diapers and clothes and taking a bed bath. An air pod or cushion is placed under one's body, which helps to change the position of one's body.

Handrails, Grab Bars, and Safety Rails

A handrail is a narrow rail attached to a wall or side of a stairway to prevent falling while providing stability and support for elderly persons when moving around or transferring to a wheelchair. If handrails cannot be mounted on the wall, parallel bars and floor-to-ceiling grab bars can be installed. These could also be installed in the shower, bathtub, and toilet.

Wheelchair/Threshold Ramps and Platforms

A portable wheelchair/threshold ramp or platform provides a gradual incline to cross thresholds or small stairs and can eliminate possible tripping hazards (Figure 4-3). The length of a ramp needs to be 6 to 8 times longer than the length of a step to allow wheelchair users to easily push themselves to the top.

There are folding wheelchair/threshold ramps with 2 side rails and ramps that can be folded into half or 3 parts. There are also indoor ramps or platforms that can be used inside a house or room without being mounted to the floor. Non-slip pads or treads are usually attached to ramps and platforms.

Figure 4-3   Portable Wheelchair Ramp

Walkers

A walker is a 3-sided walking tool consisting of left and right frames joined by a middle pipe that allows the user to stand and walk in the center of the frame. This structure allows users to ambulate safely.

There are several of types of walkers, namely, standard walkers, four-wheel walkers, four-wheel walkers with armrest, front-wheel walkers, reciprocal walkers (Figure 4-4; right), stair-climbing walkers, and one-handed hemi walkers. Users should choose their walkers according to their body function and the environment in which they will use it.

Walking Canes and Crutches

A walking cane is a weight-bearing tool used to assist in walking and prevent accidental falling. It is particularly helpful if no handrail is installed. There are several of types of walking canes and crutches, such as standard canes, quad canes (the two most popular types of canes), axillary crutches, Canadian crutches, and non-axillary crutches known as forearm crutches, elbow crutches, Lofstrand crutches, and platform forearm crutches (Figure 4-4; left); users should choose canes or crutches according to their needs. For example, axillary crutches are used by people who can support a large percentage of their weight, while people with decreased muscle mass in their arms and hands should use stronger canes such as Lofstrand crutches.

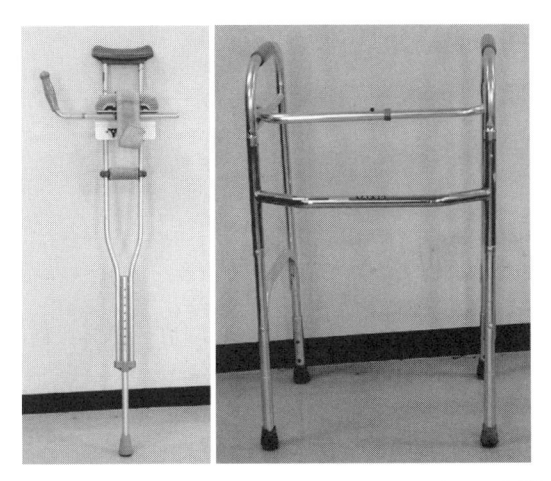

Figure 4-4 Platform Forearm Crutch and Reciprocal Walker

Code Alert Systems

A code alert system is a device worn on the wrists of people with dementia that monitors their activities. The system informs caregivers of possible wandering, prevents elderly persons from getting lost, and ensures a quick response for people with dementia who require assistance.

Transfer Lifts

A transfer lift is an assistive device used to transfer individuals whose mobility is limited between a bed and a chair or other places (Figure 4-5). Although LTCI covers lift rentals, beneficiaries need to purchase a sling lift. There are portable lifts, ceiling lifts, and wall-mounted lifts.

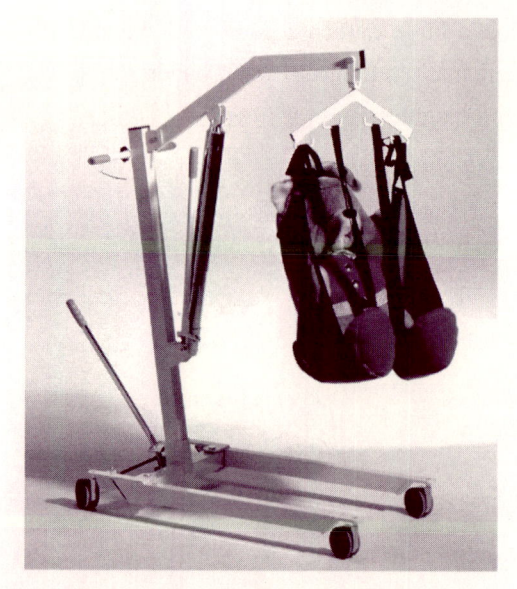

Figure 4-5   Transfer Lift with Sling

FEE SCHEDULE FOR LOAN OF ASSISTIVE DEVICES

Assistive devices that are covered by LTCI include wheelchairs, wheelchair accessories and attachments, hospital beds, bed accessories and attachments, handrails, slopes, walkers, canes, transfer lifts (except power lifts), code alert systems, and devices that prevent and treat pressure ulcers or assist in position change.

Beneficiaries have to pay only 10% of the total rental cost if the total cost is within the budget ceiling. The standard fee schedule for renting assistive devices is shown in Table 4-1.

HOW TO RENT ASSISTIVE DEVICES

A care plan has to be developed with the help of a care manager, reflecting the needs of a beneficiary, before any assistive device could be rented. Care managers then choose the most suitable devices for beneficiaries by considering their care and functional levels, lifestyle, economic status, and families' preferences.

ASSISTIVE DEVICES AVAILABLE FOR PURCHASE

Some specialty assistive devices can be purchased through the LTCI system. These include bedside commodes, automatic urine collection devices, and assistive devices for bathing, portable bathtubs, and sling lifts (Table 4-2).

When purchasing such devices, beneficiaries must first pay the full amount and then submit the required documents (e.g., application form, insurance card indicating their care level, bank account information, receipts of payment, and brochures of the purchased devices) for reimbursement from LTCI. The names of purchased assistive devices should be indicated on the receipts and brochures so that the municipalities are able to confirm if these devices are LTCI-approved. Beneficiaries are reimbursed 90% of the

Table 4-2 Available Items and Fee Schedule for Purchase

Items	Standard fee schedules (JPY)
Bedside commodes	20,000-60,000
Automatic urine collection device	1,700-25,000
Bathroom aids	10,000-30,000
Portable bathtubs	65,000-100,000
Sling lifts	30,000-40,000

Note: As of April 2000

cost up to JPY 100,000 per year.

The following section outlines the types of assistive devices available for purchase.

Bedside Commodes

A bedside commode is a chair-like movable and portable toilet with a container below the toilet that can be placed and used in the living room (Figure 4-6: right). When using the bedside commode, privacy is protected by spraying deodorant and setting up privacy screens/curtains.

There are plastic and wooden commodes and raised toilet seats. Users should always use commodes that are stable and that allow users

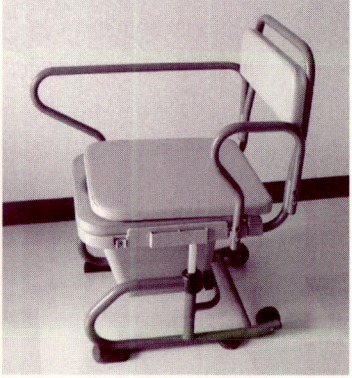

Figure 4-6 Bedside Commode and Raised Toilet Seat

to touch the ground with their feet. The raised toilet seat, a vinyl-covered padded toilet seat, can be placed on top of the regular toilet bowl to add height (Figure 4-6: left).

Automatic Urine Collection Devices

An automatic urine collection device is a specialized medical device that enables the collection of urine while someone is lying in the bed; thus, it can be used by those who have limited mobility (Figure 4-7). As it is able to store urine in a container, users do not have to dispose of urine frequently and need not be afraid of an odor. However, since some noise is created during urine collection, users may hesitate to use it at night or in a quiet setting.

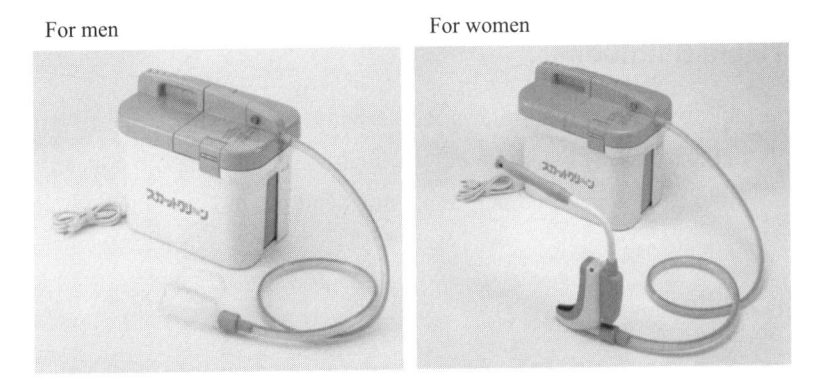

For men   For women

Figure 4-7 Automatic Urine Collection Devices

Bathroom Aids

Bathroom aids such as tub grab bars, shower chairs, bath chairs, tub and shower benches, and draining boards are used in bathrooms to provide support for getting in and out of the tub and comfort when taking a shower/ bath for extended periods of time (Figure 4-8). Users should choose these

54

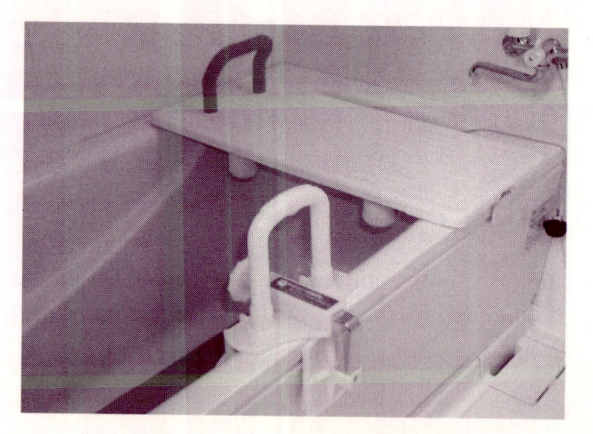

Figure 4-8   Bathroom Aids

aids according to the type of their bathtubs and their ways of bathing.

Portable Bathtubs

A portable bathtub is a simple movable bathtub that allows one to bathe easily in the room. Only simple bathtubs without plumbing are covered by LTCI, although there are inflatable bathtubs and folding portable bathtubs.

Sling Lifts

A sling lift is a tool used to transfer patients in the home or in other settings. Users should choose one that fits their bodies and that is strong enough to hold their weight while being soft enough for comfort.

LONG-TERM CARE INSURANCE AND WELFARE OF PHYSICALLY DISABLED PERSONS PROGRAMS

In addition to LTCI, there is the Welfare of Physically Disabled Persons (WPDR) program, a social services program established by the Welfare of Physically Disabled Persons Law (the WPDR Law), which allows disabled persons to rent and purchase assistive devices.

When dual eligibles, that is, those eligible for both LTCI and WPDR (i.e., elderly disabled persons), rent or purchase assistive devices, the fees are primarily covered by LTCI, with the WPDR supplementing payments made by LTCI.

The WPDR can be used to cover devices that are not covered by LTCI. For example, a ready-made wheelchair (covered by LTCI) may be ill-fitting and, as mentioned earlier, may lead to painful contractures, skin breakdown, lower-back pain, and/or pressure sores. In such cases, dual eligibles could use the WPDR to cover made-to-order devices.

HOME MODIFICATIONS

Home modification is an important process of making safety changes to a home/apartment so that it is safer for elderly people. Home modification funds are available through LTCI and distributed through municipal governments. LTCI reimburses the following 5 types of modifications: (1) installation of handrails, (2) elimination of thresholds by building wheelchair/threshold ramps, (3) floor modification, (4) replacement of existing doors with sliding doors and doorknobs, and (5) replacement of squat toilets with Western toilets. Since reimbursing the engineering fees for construction is the main purpose of this benefit, home modifications that do not require construction will be replaced with LTCI-approved rental assistive devices.

Installation of Handrails

Fees for the installation of handrails along internal and external walls and sides of stairways, main entrances, balconies, restrooms, and bathrooms are covered by LTCI (Figure 4-9).

Beneficiaries can install round or flat-bottom handrails horizontally, vertically, or in an L-shaped manner according to their needs and heights. For beneficiaries whose houses are made of wood, soil and base reinforcement may be required before installing the handrails, with the fees for reinforcement covered by LTCI.

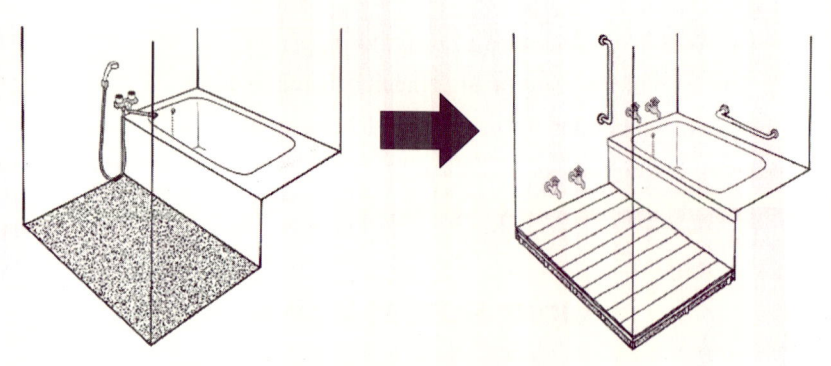

Figure 4-9　Example of Home Modification 1

Elimination of Thresholds

There are many thresholds and tripping hazards in Japanese houses and eliminating these hazards will enable the elderly to move safely and easily. With financial support from LTCI, beneficiaries can eliminate thresholds and tripping hazards throughout their houses by, for instance, lowering the height of the entrance, building a ramp, and/or elevating the height of the bathroom floor.

However, LTCI does not cover the installation of large mechanical devices such as stair, mobility, and wheelchair lifts to eliminate thresholds.

If a beneficiary needs to install one of these, he/she needs to apply for home modification programs funded by his/her local municipality.

Floor Modification

The tatami, the most popular type of mat used as flooring material in Japanese houses, is not suitable for wheelchair use. Therefore, LTCI allows beneficiaries to replace their tatami mats with flooring materials such as linoleum, rubber, and vinyl. However, LTCI does not cover the attachment of non-slip materials to floors. If beneficiaries need to attach only non-slip materials, then they have to purchase these out of their own pockets.

Replacement of Existing Doors and Doorknobs

Since some doors, especially hinged doors, can be a hassle for wheelchair or walker users, LTCI will cover the replacement of hinged, bi-folded, and accordion doors with sliding doors. If an existing sliding door is too heavy to be opened and closed properly by users, the cost of replacing it with a lighter door (but not an automatic door) will be covered by LTCI. For individuals who have difficulty grasping or turning knobs, LTCI will cover the replacement of knobs with lever handles.

Replacement of Squat Toilets with Western Toilets

The cost of replacing squat toilets with Western ones that have heated bidet toilet seats is covered by LTCI (Figure 4-10). However, the cost for installing plumbing before replacing a non-flush toilet with a flush toilet is not reimbursed by LTCI.

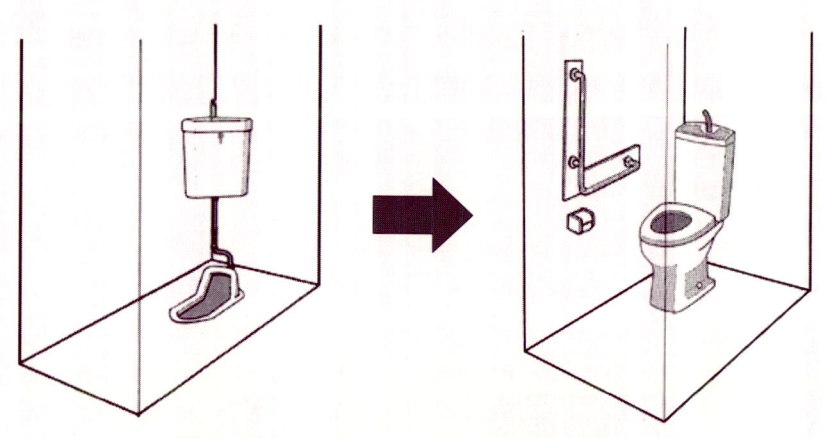

Figure 4-10 Example of Home Modification 2

HOW TO APPLY FOR REIMBURSEMENT

For home modifications, recipients have to first pay the full amount to the contractors and then submit an application form along with a receipt of the modifications to the local municipality. When the application is approved, LTCI will reimburse up to JPY 200,000 per person in a lifetime. However, if individuals who have modified their homes with help from LTCI move to another location or if their care level increases by 3 levels, then they are entitled to receive another home modification benefit (up to JPY 200,000) funded by LTCI.

POINTS TO NOTE

There are some points to note concerning home modifications. First, this financial allowance for home modifications is applicable to only the homes in which LTCI beneficiaries reside. If a beneficiary resides in a rental apartment/home and the owner approves of the modification of the property, then the residents can modify it with reimbursement from LTCI. However, if the residents of rental apartments/homes are required to restore the apartment to its original condition for whatever reason, the cost of restoration will not be covered by LTCI. Therefore, beneficiaries should discuss this with the owners before modifying the apartment.

Second, beneficiaries can apply for reimbursements only after the completion of modifications. In addition, if they become unable to reside in the modified home for some reason, they will have to pay the full modification cost themselves.

LIVING ENVIRONMENT IMPROVEMENTS FOR PROMOTING HOME- AND COMMUNITY-BASED CARE

As discussed above, LTCI reimbursements for home modifications are limited to beneficiaries because LTCI home modification benefits are not designed to increase the property value of people's homes. The costs of modifying homes, which should be done according to municipal regulations, are substantial. When individuals have difficulty living independently at home, they should consult with the relevant professionals such as their care managers, physical and occupational therapists, and architects. Recently, a new certification called "housing environment coordinators for the elderly and disabled people" has been established by The Tokyo Chamber of Commerce and Industry, which provides appropriate home modification consultation for the elderly and disabled.

At the same time, professionals who provide consultation for LTCI beneficiaries on home modifications are reimbursed up to JPY 2,000.

It has become increasingly important to improve the living environments of elderly persons according to their physical function and families' ability to provide care. In order to prevent dissatisfaction after home modification, it is highly recommended that beneficiaries visit showhouses and showroom displays, try to use materials and equipment designed especially for impaired individuals and their families, and find a reliable contractor. Beneficiaries could also obtain examples of home modification and information from hospitals, health care facilities, and their care managers.

SUGGESTIONS FOR HOME MODIFICATIONS

Since the utilization of assistive devices and home modification benefits could improve beneficiaries' care level and ease the burden on other family members, it is important to choose assistive devices and home modification plans in accordance with the level of the beneficiaries' physical function and their lifestyles.

Care managers, as well as architects, interior designers, and contractors approached, must possess skills and knowledge in home modifications for impaired individuals. However, since there is no specialized certification for that purpose, and some, especially contractors, may not have enough skills and knowledge to create an appropriate modification plan and/or modify differently from the plan requested by the clients, clients are advised to occasionally check on them during the modifications.

Lastly, it is better to consult with these professionals regarding the costs before starting any modifications to ensure that the budget ceiling is not exceeded.

SUMMARY

There is a wide range of assistive devices and home modifications available for LTCI beneficiaries. Similar to home- and community-based care services, appropriate use of these devices and modifications may delay and/or prevent institutionalization. However, purchasing assistive devices and home modifications may be very expensive depending on recipients' needs. Therefore, before making a decision on whether to purchase such devices or begin modifications, one should consult with healthcare professionals.

References

Hidaka, M., Katsura, M., & Kameyama, T. (2002). What are Assistive Devices and Home Modifications of Long-Term Care Insurance? [*Kaigo Hoken niyoru Fukushi Yogu to Jyutaku Kaishu towa*]. In Institute of Japan Care Work (Ed.), Introduction to Long-Term Care Insurance [*Kaigo Hoken Nyumonsho*] (pp.117-136). Tokyo: Index Press.

Kandel, J. & Adamec, C. (2009). The Encyclopedia of Elder Care. New York: Facts on File.

Kuroda, D. (2000). Issues of the Supply System of Assistive Devices [*Fukushi Yogu Kyokyu System no Kadai*]. Sogo Rehabilitation, 28(1), 75-82

Mura, T., et al. (1999). The Supply System of Assistive Devices [*Fukushi Yogu no Kyokyu System*]. Sogo Rehabilitation, 27(9), 831-835.

NHK Fukushi Bangumi Shuzai Han (2000). Silver Care: Home Modifications and Assistive Devices [*Silver Kaigo: Sumai no Kufu to Fukushi Yogu*]. Tokyo: Junposha, 2000.

Ota, T. & Takemoto, Z. (2000). A Guide for Extensive Use of Long-Term Care Insurance [*Kaigo Hoken 100% Katsuyo Guide*]. Tokyo: Chuokeizai-Sha, Inc..

Sumii, H., et al. (2001). Well-Understanding of Rehabilitation and Long-Term Care Techniques [*Mite Yoku Wakaru Rehabilitation Kaigo Gijyutsu*]. Tokyo: Hitotsubashi-Shuppan, 2001.

Tokyo Chamber of Commerce and Industry (2001). Textbook for 2nd-Class Certification for Housing Environment Coordinators [*Fukushi Jyukankyo Coordinator Kentei 2 kyu Text*]. Tokyo: Tokyo Chamber of Commerce and Industry.

5

Institutional Long-Term Care Services

The institutional long-term care services funded by LTCI are provided by 3 types of long-term care facilities: (1) LTCI-certified welfare facilities for the elderly, (2) LTCI-certified health facilities for the elderly, and (3) LTCI-designated long-term care hospitals that are managed by public sectors such as prefectures and municipalities as well as private sectors, both for profit and non-profit (Table 5-1).

Elderly individuals who have been classified into care-required levels can be admitted to those LTCI-certified long-term care facilities. Beneficiaries and their families can choose the types of institutions and providers to use and sign a contract by themselves. They need to consider the type and characteristic of each facility in order to receive high-quality care. Usually, there is a long waiting list for admission. Considering this circumstance, it would be helpful to plan ahead and reserve a bed/room in advance.

The following section outlines the most common types of institutional care services covered by as well as some of the institutions not covered by LTCI.

Table 5-1 Overview of Long-Term Care Insurance-Certified Care Facilities

	Founders/responsible organizations	Staffing	Size of resident's room	Basic principles/mission
Welfare facilities for the elderly	· Prefectures · Municipalities · Social welfare corporations	Care managers and other staff assigned by the MHLW ordinance.	More than 10.65 m^2	To provide bathing care, excretion care, assistance with meals, functional training, health management, and other long-term care, in order to enable the elderly to live as independently as possible, with the aim of returning the elderly to their own homes.
Health facilities for the elderly	· Municipalities · Medical corporations · Social welfare corporations · Other	Medical doctors, nurses, care managers, and other staff assigned by the MHLW ordinance.	More than 8 m^2	To provide nursing care and functional training under medical doctor's supervision and based on in-facility care plan, in order to enable the elderly to live as independently as possible with the aim of returning them to their homes.
Designated long-term care hospitals	· National government · Municipalities · Medical corporations · Public benefit corporations · School corporations	Care managers and other staff assigned by the MHLW ordinance.	More than 6.4 m^2*	To provide nursing care and functional training under medical doctor's supervision and based on in-facility care plans, in order to enable the elderly to live as independently as possible.

* The size of a patient's room in a general hospital is at least 4.3 m^2.

WELFARE FACILITIES FOR THE ELDERLY

A welfare facility for the elderly, established by the Welfare Law for the Elderly of 1963, is designated by the LTCI Law as a long-term care facility for LTCI beneficiaries. Elderly individuals who are bedridden or who are suffering from dementia and unable to take care of themselves can be admitted to such facilities. These facilities accept elderly persons who have no relatives, have only aged caregivers, or have trouble making a living due to low income.

Due to the Ten-Year-Strategy to Promote Health and Welfare for the Elderly (also known as Gold Plan 21), some municipalities have achieved their targeted number of facilities available for their residents, as indicated by the Health and Welfare Plan for the Elderly. However, some facilities still have a long waiting list for admission.

The co-payment for welfare facilities is the lowest among other types of LTCI long-term care facilities, and it can be reduced further for low-income elderly.

The welfare facilities are required to employ a care manager to create in-facility care plans and provide long-term care to support their residents in living a life with dignity and as close to how they had lived at home as possible.

Services and Activities in Welfare Facilities for the Elderly

Welfare facility residents are provided with various types of care services: assistance with getting up, meals, toileting, changing clothes and bathing, personal hygiene, position change, and medication (Table 5-2). Many welfare facilities provide buffet-style meals to their residents and rearrange their dining rooms to create a relaxed atmosphere. There are also specialty bathtubs for bedridden elderly.

Table 5-2   Services Available in Welfare Facilities for the Elderly

· Assistance with ADLs (e.g., bathing, toileting, eating)
· Nursing care
· Functional training
· Health management

Beneficiaries and their families should check with the facilities about their bath schedules, availability of assistance with bathing, and policy of privacy protection when they are looking for a suitable long-term care facility, because some facilities may not be able to accommodate their requests owing to the work schedules of their nursing staff.

If they are in relatively good shape, residents can join rehabilitative activities, such as walking and physical exercises, provided by the facilities. Many facilities have their own annual events to entertain their residents and have them experience seasonal changes. Table 5-3 shows an example of annual events. Nursing staff members also try to entertain their residents as much as possible. In addition, because it is a good chance

Table 5-3   Sample of Annual Events in Welfare Facilities for the Elderly

	Events
January	New Year party, new year's visit to a shrine, playing Karuta (Japanese card games)
February	Setsubun (the day before the beginning of spring) festival, video viewing
March	Momo-no-Sekku (Doll Festival/Girl's day) party, video viewing
April	Cherry-blossom viewing, outing
May	Boys' Festival, shopping
June	Memorial ceremony for Deity of Mercy, outing
July	Tanabata (the Star Festival), Karaoke party
August	Bon Festival, summer festival
September	Full moon party, Keiro-Kai (Respect-for-Elderly Day)
October	Autumn festival, sports festival
November	Karaoke festival, shopping
December	Christmas Day, year-end party, mochi pounding

for residents to communicate with their families and other residents, staff members encourage family members and residents to attend as many events as possible.

Community-focused nursing facilities are increasingly important. Nursing home residents may be able to go shopping or to an entertainment center in a wheelchair. In this aspect, the relationship between the facilities and their local communities is critical.

HEALTH FACILITIES FOR THE ELDERLY

A health facility for the elderly is a new type of facility introduced by partial amendments to the Health and Medical Care Services Law for the Elderly in 1986, and was first established in 1988 as an intermediate care facility that bridges medical centers and welfare facilities. It is designed for individuals whose conditions have stabilized and are not expected to change substantially and who do not require hospitalization but require some medical attention and rehabilitation before they are able to return home.

Long-term care services in health facilities for the elderly are provided by a care team consisting of doctors, nurses, care managers, physical and occupational therapists, and nurse's aides. Care teams have four principles: (1) promoting independent living, (2) providing home rehabilitation, (3) inducing in residents the feeling of being at home, and (4) establishing ties with the community and homes. The goal of a care team is to assist facility residents to return to their own homes as quickly as possible. However, the reality is that there are fewer residents who can return home and more residents waiting to be transferred to a welfare facility for the elderly.

In the past, the longer the elderly stays in the health facility, the lower the fee for nursing care. This payment system could have contributed to residents' increased length of stay. There is thus a need to consider useful strategies that assist the elderly in returning to their own homes.

Services and Activities in Health Facilities for the Elderly

Nursing care, medical supervision, functional training, other medical care, and care for ADLs are provided at health facilities for the elderly according to beneficiaries' care plans (Table 5-4). These facilities provide care with more emphasis on rehabilitation compared to other types of facilities. The aim of their care is to maximize residents' abilities in order to improve their mind and body function for returning home. The elderly can receive both group and individual rehabilitation provided by rehabilitation professionals such as physical and occupational therapists. Figure 5-1 shows a sample care plan created for a health facility resident.

Table 5-4   Services Available in Health Facilities for the Elderly

· Assistance with ADLs
· Nursing care
· Medical supervision
· Medical care
· Functional training by rehabilitation professionals

DESIGNATED LONG-TERM CARE HOSPITALS

Designated long-term care hospitals provide both medical and long-term care. They are mostly for elderly who have a substantial need for medical attention and long-term care. Chronic patients who require long-term care or who cannot receive sufficient care at home may be admitted to this facility. Compared to the other two types of facilities, this better resembles a hospital, with in-house medical doctors, nurses, nurse's aides, and other professionals such as pharmacists, nutritionists, and radiologic technologists.

As shown in Table 5-5, the average fee for care provided at a designated long-term care hospital is JPY 442,000 per month, which is the highest among LTCI-certified long-term care facilities. However, although residents have to pay more, the higher quality medical and nursing sys-

Resident's name: _____

Time	Approach plan	Responsible staff	Activity of daily living performed by patient
4:00	Monitoring for sleep pattern	Nurses Nurse's aides	
6:00	Encourage toileting	Nurses Nurse's aides	Toileting Getting up, washing face, brushing teeth, dressing
8:00	Assistance with eating, washing dentures Check vital signs	Nurses Nurse's aides Nurses	Eating breakfast, washing dentures, toileting
10:00	Activity		Participation in activity
12:00	Assistance with eating, washing dentures Encourage toileting	Nurses Nurse's aides	Eating lunch, washing dentures, toileting Watching TV
14:00	Assistance with bathing, changing clothes		Fluid intake, bathing
16:00	Encourage toileting		Toileting
18:00	Assistance with eating, washing dentures Encourage toileting	Nurses Nurse's aides	Eating dinner, washing dentures, toileting
20:00	Encourage toileting	Nurses Nurse's aides	Toileting
22:00	Monitoring for sleep pattern		Going to bed, sleeping
24:00	Encourage toileting	Nurses Nurse's aides	Toileting
2:00	Encourage toileting		Toileting
4:00			
As needed/emergency services			
Other services			Haircut, medical consultation, dermatologist's consultation, nail clipping

Figure 5-1   Sample of a Care Plan in a Health Facility for the Elderly

Table 5-5 Average Cost of Nursing Care per Month by Types of Long-Term Care Facilities

	Average level of care-required	Fees for nursing care (JPY)	Fees for meals (JPY)	Total (JPY)
Welfare facilities for the elderly	3.23	272,000	58,000	331,000
Health facilities for the elderly	2.85	296,000	58,000	354,000
Designated long-term care hospitals	3.64	378,000	64,000	442,000

tems make up for the higher cost.

Designated long-term care hospitals provide larger floor space than that of regular hospital beds (Table 5-1) and have three types of beds: (1) designated long-term care beds; (2) designated long-term medical care beds for the elderly; and (3) designated long-term care beds for elderly with dementia.

Designated Long-Term Care Beds

Many hospitals offer some beds for long-term care, which have a higher ratio of nurse's aides to patients. Patients who require a long convalescence owing to chronic conditions are admitted to long-term care beds. The size of such patients' rooms and corridors is larger than that of those in general hospitals, which is necessary because many long-term care patients use wheelchairs as their sole method of locomotion.

Designated Long-Term Medical Care Beds for the Elderly

Some hospitals offer long-term medical care beds that are used to provide both long-term care and medical care to patients who have stabilized chronic diseases but still require medical attention, nursing care, and rehabilitation.

Designated Long-Term Care Beds for Elderly with Dementia

Some hospitals also provide long-term care beds that are used in mental treatments and long-term care to elderly patients who have symptoms of dementia and problem behaviors and who require long-term hospitalization. Psychiatric care is provided by in-house psychiatrists and psychiatric social workers.

LONG-TERM CARE INSURANCE-UNCOVERED INSTITUTIONAL CARE FACILITIES

Some residential care services are not covered by LTCI, namely, almshouses for the elderly, low-cost elder homes, and care houses.

Almshouses for the Elderly

Almshouses for the elderly provide residences mainly for low-income people. Although municipalities decide who are eligible to live there, those eligible are usually elderly aged 65 or over who are able to take care of themselves but are unable to live at home due to some family matters. Nurse's aides, counselors, nutritionists, and cooks provide support for daily living. Residents are usually charged according to their ability to pay.

Low-Cost Elder Homes

Elderly individuals who wish to live at low-cost elder homes must sign contracts for admission directly with the facilities and pay for it themselves. There are 2 types of homes: A and B. Type A is for residents who wish to have their meals provided by the home and Type B is for those who are capable of preparing their own meals. Elderly aged 60 or over can live in either type of homes. If an elderly couple who are both aged over 60 wish to share a room, they have the right to do so upon consent from the home. Individuals who have difficulty living at home for family reasons or housing situations can live in this kind of homes.

Care Houses

Care houses (literally "care homes") resemble condominiums in which residents can lead a more carefree life. Elderly persons aged 60 or over who are able to take care of themselves are eligible to live there. Residents can receive consultations from nurses and nurse's aides and meal services. They can also use the care services provided by LTCI if needed.

MEDICAL INSURANCE-COVERED INSTITUTIONAL CARE SERVICES

Medical insurance also covers some institutional care services, namely, hospitals with designated long-term care beds, LTCI-designated long-term care beds, and medical insurance-designated recovery-phase rehabilitation units.

Hospital with Designated Long-Term Care Beds

Hospitals for the elderly have been criticized for overdosing and overtreating patients, poor staffing and surroundings, social admission, and so forth. These criticisms have motivated hospitals to refine their services, systems, and attitudes.

After the MHLW institutionalized the Inpatient Management Fee for Exceptionally Approved Elderly Care Hospitals in 1990, hospitals with designated long-term care beds were established by the 2nd amendment of the Medical Care Act in 1992. After transitioning from fee-for-service to flat-rate payments, hospitals have responded to many problems (e.g., female caregivers providing round-the-clock care to bedridden elderly patients, poor surroundings for care, and over-prescription) and hospitals with designated long-term care beds have also changed their attitudes toward long-term care by increasing their staffing ratio to provide more individualized care for their patients. As a result of the LTCI Law implemented in April 2000, hospitals with designated long-term care beds were divided into 2 types: (1) beds that LTCI covers (LTCI-designated long-term care beds) and (2) beds that medical insurance covers (medical insurance-designated long-term health care beds). However, to reduce the social admission of elderly people to hospitals, the MHLW is currently working to convert medical insurance-designated long-term health care beds into LTCI-designated long-term care beds.

These two groups of beds differ in some respects. First, the conditions of patients are different, as described below.

Long-Term Care Insurance-Designated Long-Term Care Beds:
To be eligible for LTCI-designated long-term care beds, patients must meet the following conditions:

1) Be certified as care-required level 1 to 5; and
2) Be 65 years or older or
3) Be 40-64 years old with one or more of the 15 specified diseases (except those patients with complications of diabetes, chronic respiratory diseases, terminal cancer, neural-incurable diseases, and dialysis).

Medical Insurance-Designated Long-Term Health Care Beds:
Patients admitted to medical insurance-designated long-term health care beds are those who require:

1) Intensive care due to having complications of diabetes, chronic respiratory diseases, terminal cancer, neural-incurable diseases, and

dialysis; and
2) Acute phase rehabilitation.

Patients who are below age 40 and those aged between 40 and 64 with one or more of the 15 specified diseases cannot be admitted to medical insurance-designated long-term health care beds.

Second, hospitals with LTCI-designated long-term care beds are required to hire care managers, whereas hospitals with medical insurance-designated long-term health care beds are not required to do so.

Medical Insurance-Designated Recovery-Phase Rehabilitation Units

Generally, there are 3 phases of rehabilitation: (1) acute phase within 2 weeks of disease onset, (2) recovery phase within 6 months after the acute phase, and (3) chronic phase. Medical insurance-designated recovery-phase rehabilitation units aim to provide rehabilitation during the recovery phase and help patients restore their physical capacities such that they can live and remain at home for as long as possible.

As medical insurance-designated rehabilitation units were established after a revision of fee schedules to medical reimbursement in 2000, an increasing number of medical facilities have converted their medical insurance-designated long-term health care beds into this type of rehabilitation unit. In order to provide enough rehabilitation programs during the recovery phase, these medical facilities have higher staffing ratios and stricter eligibility and length of stay rules than regular rehabilitation units.

Eighty percent of the rehabilitation unit must be occupied by patients who demonstrate the necessity of recovery phase rehabilitation. Therefore, these units target patients who:

1) Had cerebrovascular diseases or damage to the spinal cord within the last 3 months;

2) Had fracture of the femur, lower leg, pelvis, etc., within the last 3 months;
3) Had disuse syndrome due to being bedridden after surgery or pneumonia treatment within the 3 last months; or
4) Are in a state similar to the above 3 conditions.

The number of recovery phase rehabilitation units is expected to increase from now on and play a central role between acute care hospitals and the home.

ADVANTAGES AND DISADVANTAGES OF NEWLY CERTIFIED CARE FACILITIES

Conventional long-term care facilities had been using a group-based approach and assembly-line system in which long-term care was offered to residents in a sequential manner. However, newly certified LTCI-institutional care facilities are expected to promote care for residents in an environment that retains and improves residents' dignity and that recognizes their individuality. For example, conventional long-term care facilities were not required to provide a private room for each resident; however, lately, the MHLW has been encouraging facilities to offer private rooms or small unit-based care.

If care facilities adopt small unit-based care, then their residents will be divided into small groups of about 10. Dining rooms, restrooms, and bathrooms are installed and nursing staff is assigned to each unit (area). Residents in a unit receive care from the same nursing staff every single day, 7 days a week. This approach is rather different from the conventional group-based approach; therefore, the staff members involved need to change their perspective and attitudes toward providing care and have the aim of enhancing residents' dignity.

Although this change of perspective and attitude may provide a new way forward in providing quality care, it can have a negative effect on residents, who might have to pay more out of their own pockets. Indeed, the MHLW has called for contributions from these residents for renovations made to care facilities and for the increased labor force due to converting from a group-based approach to a unit-based care approach. This is in addition to co-payments, fees for meals, and facility stock items. Consequently, low-income earners may receive only group-based care while high-income earners receive individualized care based on their needs.

If individualized care were necessary for maintaining a life with dignity, then it should be provided to all individuals who require long-term care. Therefore, a system that provides individualized care equally to all residents is needed.

TIPS FOR CHOOSING A LONG-TERM CARE FACILITY

Choosing a care facility for a family member is one of the most difficult decisions people have to make in their lives. As mentioned earlier, there are 3 types of facilities to choose from in Japan: (1) welfare facilities, (2) health facilities, and (3) hospitals with designated long-term care beds. Welfare facilities for the elderly attempt to provide a home-like environment, health care facilities for the elderly are transitional facilities that provide mainly rehabilitation, and hospitals with designated long-term care beds provide both medical support and long-term care.

There are several questions people can ask when looking for a long-term care facility:

Basic information
- Where is the facility?
- Who owns the facility?
- What is their mission?

Quality of care
- How is its quality and quantity of care?
- Does the facility have regular resident care conferences?
- Does the facility invite residents to attend resident care conferences?
- Does the facility have enough staff?
- How does the staff assist with ADLs?
- Do its care managers listen to residents' preferences and include them in the care plan?
- What kind of restraints does the facility have for residents with dementia (e.g., restraining band, locked unit)?
- What policies and procedures does the facility have for preventing pressure ulcer?

Quality of life
- Does the facility allow time to bathe?
- Does the facility treat residents in a respectful manner?
- Does the facility have grievance and complaint procedures?
- Does the facility protect resident's privacy?
- How are the meals?

Staffing
- How is the quality of staff (personality, skills, and knowledge)?
- How does the staff handle phone calls and visitors?
- Does the staff have active and positive attitudes?

Emergencies
- Is the facility affiliated with a hospital?
- Does the facility have an arrangement with a hospital for emergencies?

Availability
- Does the facility offer rehabilitation?
- Does the facility have visiting hours?
- Does the facility have volunteers?
- What kind of recreational activities does the facility have?

- Does the facility provide transportation?
- Does the facility have private rooms?
- Does the facility have unit-based care?

It is highly recommended to visit the facility before making a final decision.

TIPS FOR RECEIVING HIGH-QUALITY CARE

Once elderly persons are admitted to a LTCI-certified facility, each facility must make in-facility care plans for each resident that include goals and outcomes of care, specific nursing actions to help the resident achieve the outcomes and goals, and a possible discharge plan. An overview of the care and discharge planning process is shown in Figure 5-2.

Because an individual care plan is important for both the receiving and providing of satisfactory care services, residents and their families need to confirm and verify the contents of care plans. In order to receive high-quality care, residents as well as care providers should participate in the planning of care. A sample of a care plan used in welfare care facilities for the elderly is shown in Figures 5-3 and 5-4.

HAVING A GRIEVANCE AND COMPLAINT ABOUT INSTITUTIONAL CARE

A decade ago, people tolerated the low quality of care provided by long-term care facilities because they assumed that the facility and its staff members knew best. However, care recipients in both facilities and homes are now bolder in expressing their complaints about the quality of care. They can file their complaints to the municipal department in charge of LTCI and/or complain to their care managers. Some facilities have also set up a grievances and complaints system for their residents to ensure that their

Facility-visit prior to admission
This is very important when choosing a facility. The applicant should ask various questions.
It is essential for the applicant to feel that the facility is suitable for him/her.
The applicant should meet with residents and staff members.

⬇

Qualification assessment conference
Not only the applicant and his/her family but also staff such as care managers, social workers, nurses, and nurse's aides participate in the resident care conference.
Mutual understanding and sharing of the same goals are essential for resident care.

⬇

Admission
Changes in the surrounding affect the elderly mentally and physically.
Residents should notify the staff when having problems.

⬇

Creation of in-facility care plans
Care managers must explain the points of their in-facility care plans.
The residents and their families could express their wishes, if any.

⬇

Providing care based on the care plan
It is important for residents to make an effort to participate in various rehabilitative activities.
Residents and their families should check if care is provided based on the care plans.

⬇

Reassessment and revision of care plans
Nursing staff will administer reassessment. Residents and their families should express their wishes, if any. Good communication is essential.

⬇

Discharge planning
Facility staff will visit the place where the resident will be discharged to and provide information on assistive devices and care techniques.

⬇

Discharge to his/her home
Facility staff will follow-up on discharged residents regularly.

Figure 5-2 Care and Discharge Planning Process Flow Chart

5 Institutional Long-Term Care Services   79

In-Facility Care Plan (1)

(First)/Referral/Continued   (Certified)/Pending

Resident's name: _____ Birth date: _____ Address: _____

Name of staff creating care plan: _____

Name and address of facility: _____

Date of planning (modifying a plan): _____   Date of first planning: _____

Date of certification: _____   Duration of certification: _____

Level of care-required: Level 1 / (Level 2) / Level 3 / Level 4 / Level 5   Other: _____

Resident's and family's preference on care	Resident has severe memory loss and incontinence, and his wife has difficulty in ambulation. Under these circumstances, the resident's family think that they cannot take care of both of them at home and requested to have a facility take care of the resident.
Opinions of the Long-Term Care Certification Committee	
Comprehensive care plan	We provide care for incontinence in order to prevent him from feeling ashamed and to keep him clean. We will attempt to control his bowel movements.

Figure 5-3   Sample of an In-Facility Care Plan in a Welfare Facility for the Elderly 1

In-Facility Care Plan (2)

Needs/concerns/ problems	RESIDENT GOALS			APPROACH PLAN			
	Long-term goal	Duration	Short-term goal	Duration	Action	Responsible person	Frequency	Duration
Constipation Needs support for cleaning up after BM	Will have regular bowel movements	3 months	Finding the rhythm of his bowel movements	1 month	Check for BM Wife to supply Yakult Providing hot tea at teatime Record his BM	Nurses Nurse's aides	After each meal At night At breakfast At 3 pm	2/3/2001-3/15/2001
Unable to locate bathroom at night Incontinence at night	Will be able to locate bathroom at night	6 months	Encourage toileting Directing resident to bathroom	1 month	Encourage toileting Record time and frequency of toileting	Nurses Nurse's aides	At 9 pm 12 am 3 am 6 am	2/3/2001-3/15/2001

Figure 5-4 Sample of an In-Facility Care Plan in a Welfare Facility for the Elderly 2

voices will be heard.

SUMMARY

Institutional care services funded by LTCI include LTCI-certified welfare facilities for the elderly, LTCI-certified health facilities for the elderly, and LTCI-designated long-term care hospitals. These facilities are managed by prefectures, municipalities, and the private sector, such as social welfare corporations and medical corporations. Assistance with ADLs and IADLs, rehabilitative and recreational activities, and care management are available. Some facilities also provide private rooms and unit-based care to their residents.

LTCI does not cover some of the care services provided by institutional care facilities and residential care homes. These include almshouses for the elderly, low-cost elder homes, care houses, some of hospital with designated long-term care beds, and medical insurance-designated recovery-phase rehabilitation units.

Before a final decision can be made on whether one should be admitted to long-term care facilities, a thorough consideration should be given to the quality of care and life, availability of nursing staff, activities and emergency care, and personal preferences of the beneficiaries and family, so that beneficiaries are able to receive quality care.

References

Asahi, K. (2000). Guide of Long-Term Care Insurance for Recipients and Ombudsmen [*Riyosha to Ombudsmen no tameno Kaigo Hoken Gaide*]. Tokyo: Kiri-Syobo, 2000.

Ishikawa, M. (2000). Care and Rehabilitation for the elderly [*Koreisha Care to Rehabilitation*]. Tokyo: Kosei-Kagaku-Kenkyuujo.

Institute of Japan Care Work (2001). Techniques for Rehabilitative Care [Rehabilitation Gijyutsu]. Tokyo: Hitotsubashi-Shuppan, 2001.

Japanese Society of Medical Social Work (2001). Comprehensive Guidebook to Medical Welfare in the Era of Long-Term Care Insurance [*Kaigo Hoken Jidai no Iryo Fukushi*

Sogo Gaide]. Tokyo: Igaku-Shoin Ltd.

Kondo, K. & Ooi, M. (2000). Rehabilitation for Stroke [*Nosocchu Rehabilitation*]. Tokyo: Ishiyaku Publishers, Inc..

Miyake, K., Kusakabe, M., & Takeda, R. (2002). What are Institutional Long-Term Care Services of Long-Term Care Insurance? [*Kaigo Hoken no Shisetsu Kaigo Service towa*]. In Institute of Japan Care Work (Ed.), Introduction to Long-Term Care Insurance [*Kaigo Hoken Nyumonsho*] (pp.97-116). Tokyo: Index Press.

6

Application Process for Long-Term Care Insurance Benefits

LTCI care services are provided to only individuals who are 1st and 2nd category insured and who are certified as either "care-required" or "assistance-required" after the application process and certification from the municipalities.

The application process includes the following three steps: (1) complete the application form, (2) submit all required documents to the municipal government office, and (3) go through an onsite qualification assessment and interview with assessors from the municipal governments. These processes can be complicated and frustrating for the recipients, who are older adults.

This chapter and the next aim to explain the application process for LTCI. In this chapter, the first part of the application process — completion and submission of application form — is presented. Information about the process of reapplication and appeals, and fees involved in the application process are also discussed. Figure 6-1 shows an overview of the application process.

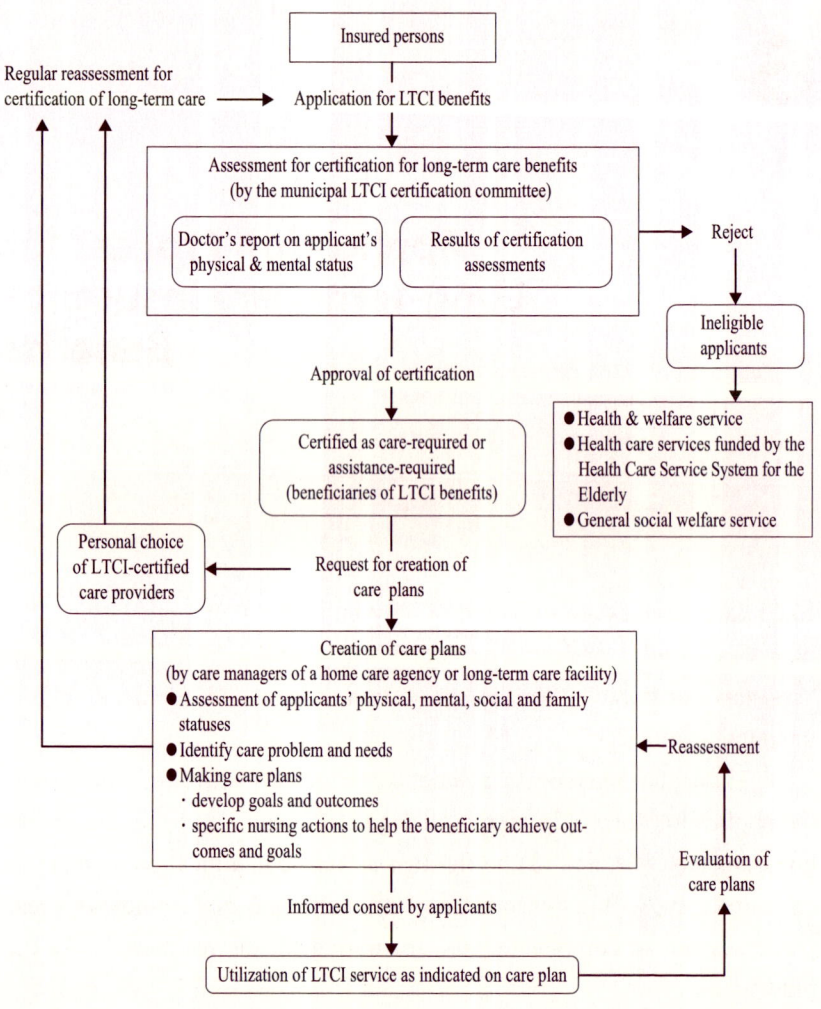

Figure 6-1 Flow Chart of the Application Process and Care Planning for Long-Term Care Insurance Benefits

THE FIRST PART OF THE APPLICATION PROCESS

To Whom and Who Can Apply

When 1st category insured persons wish to begin receiving long-term care, they have to complete an application form (Figure 6-2) and submit it to their local municipal office (LTCI section) with their LTCI card (Figure 6-3). Second category insured persons, who have not received their LTCI card, also have to visit their local municipal office and provide their physical and mental statuses and family situation in written form.

The completed application can be submitted by the applicant himself/herself, the applicant's family member who has been authorized to represent the applicant in accordance with civil law, or public consultants on social and labor insurance. LTCI-certified home care agencies and LTCI-certified facilities can also apply for long-term care on behalf of the applicant. If one chooses to have a care agency or facility apply for benefits, then he/she needs to submit the completed application to its staff. Table 6-1 summarizes where and who can apply for LTCI benefits.

Although the insured person and his/her family can apply directly to the municipal office, it might be advisable to have an agency apply for it because filling in the application could be difficult for some applicants. If some care services are already being provided, then it is possible for an applicant to request that his/her care provider or care manager process it. Agencies rarely charge applicants for assisting in filing an application.

Because it is required for applicants to apply at the local municipalities where they are registered as residents, they need to notify the municipal government of any changes in address and reapply at the new municipal office within 14 days of moving.

86

ID number

Name, address, and phone number of the facility in which the applicant currently resides (if applicable).

If currently hospitalized, indicate the name of the hospital.

If currently receiving home- and community-based care, leave this blank.

If an agent is applying on behalf of the applicant, indicate the name, address, and phone number of the agency. An agency seal is required.

Information of attending physician

Application date; important for retroactive recording.

介護保険〔要介護認定・要支援認定〕申請書
〇〇市長
次のとおり申請します。

被保険者番号		申請年月日	平成 年 月 日
		生年月日	明・大・昭 年 月 日
被保険者	氏 名	性 別	
	住 所		
			電話番号
	介護保険施設入所・入所している場合（短期入所を除く）	入院・入所施設名所在地	
		入院・入所施設名所在地	

提出代行者	名称	該当に〇（居宅介護支援事業者・介護老人福祉施設・介護老人保健施設・介護療養型医療施設・地域包括支援センター）
	住所	〒 印

主治医	主治医の氏名		医療機関名	
	所在地	〒		電話番号

2号被保険者（40歳から64歳の医療保険加入者）のみ記入			
医療保険者名		医療保険被保険者証記号番号	
特定疾病名			

介護サービス計画を作成するために必要があるときは、要介護認定・要支援認定にかかる調査内容、介護認定審査委員による判定結果・意見、及び主治医意見書を居宅介護支援事業者、居宅サービス事業者又は介護保険施設の関係者に提示することに同意します。

	本人氏名	印

Section for 2nd category insured persons; name of the applicant and diagnosis (one or more of the 15 specified diseases).

Applicant's signature and seal

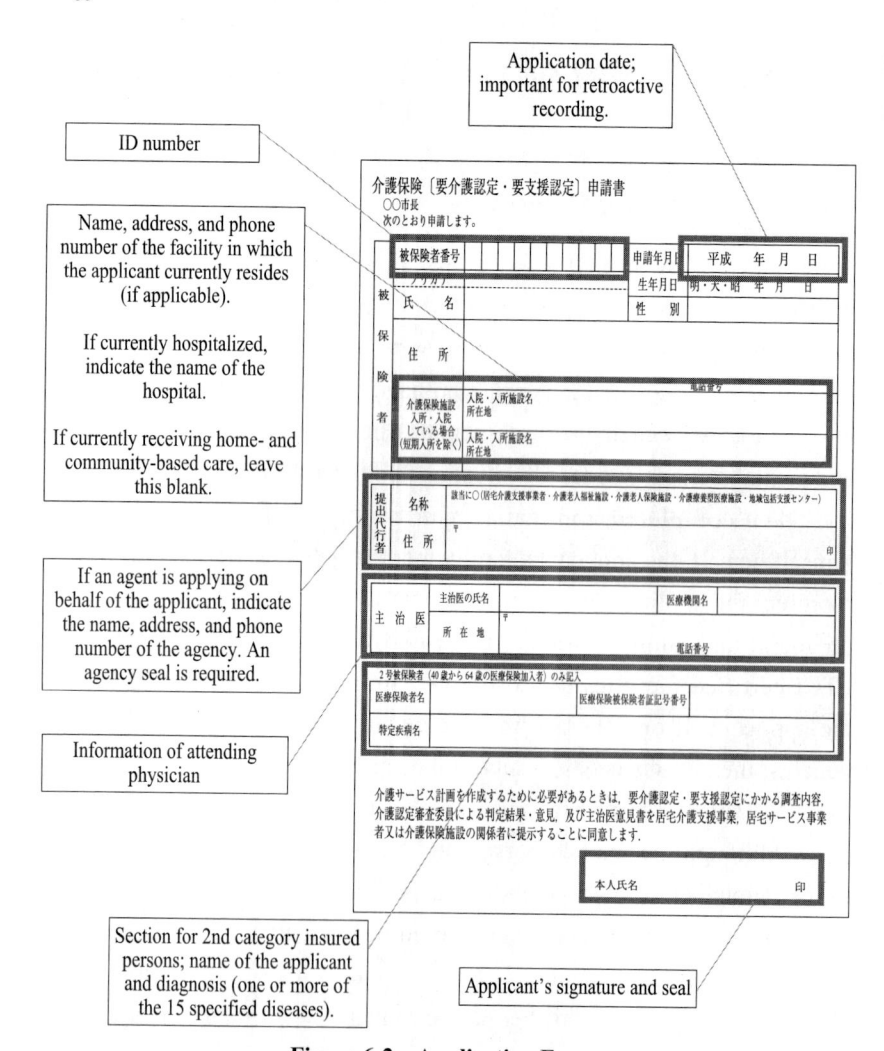

Figure 6-2 Application Form

6 Application Process for Long-Term Care Insurance Benefits *87*

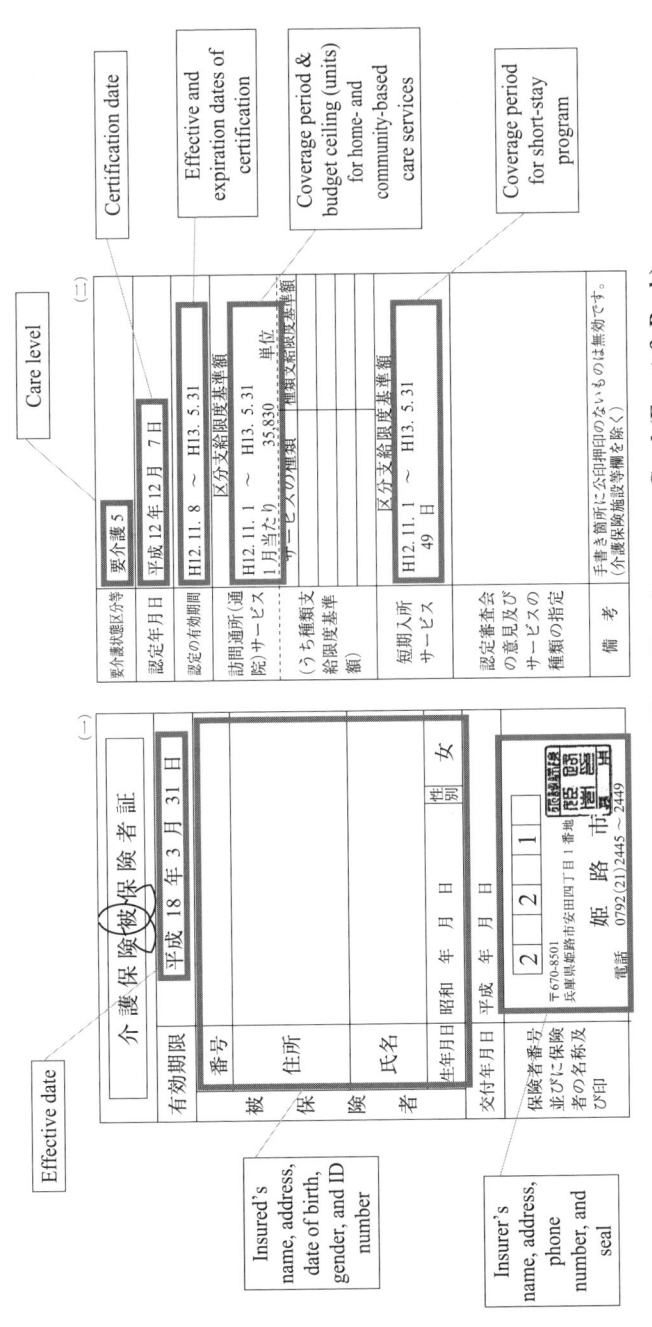

Figure 6-3 Sample of the Long-Term Care Insurance Card (Front & Back)

Table 6-1   Where to Apply and Who Can Apply

Where to apply:
1) LTCI section at the municipal office
2) LTCI-certified care providers, if applicable

Who can apply:
1) Insured persons
2) Family of the insured (authorized representative)
3) LTCI-certified home care agencies and long-term care facilities (applicant's care providers)
4) Public consultant on social and labor insurance (the agent of the Law for Public Consultants on Social and Labor Insurance)

How to Handle Residents Who Were Institutionalized Prior to the Enactment of Long-Term Care Insurance

If a person had been already admitted to a welfare facility for the elderly prior to the enactment of LTCI (April 1, 2000), then he/she is allowed to remain in the facility for another 5 years, until 2005, even if he/she is not eligible for LTCI benefits. After April 1, 2005, institutional care cannot be provided if the resident does not meet the eligibility criteria and the resident may have to be discharged. For residents who do not qualify for LTCI institutional care but who were admitted prior to the enactment of LTCI, the municipality responsible for placing them in long-term care facilities under the patient-allocation system has to bear the cost of and continue to provide institutional long-term care under their own social welfare programs.

IMPORTANCE OF THE APPLICATION

LTCI benefits are retroactive to the application date. Hence, the application day is important because beneficiaries can receive long-term care as soon as they become frail. All processes from application to the notification of the results fall within 30 days. If care services are provided during these 30 days, they will still be reimbursed by LTCI. In other words, the services are available at any time from when an application is filed, even if official certification has not been obtained. However, since the budget ceiling cannot be determined until the care level is established, careful attention is needed in the above case because applicants need to pay their full "future" fees and they would have to pay the balance if the charges exceed the yet-to-be-determined budget ceiling. Consequently, the use of LTCI services might be limited in such cases, and applying for it in advance, even if one has no use for it, is a way to prevent the above situation.

Individuals who do not wish to have LTCI services but social services programs such as preventive services and independent living support services funded by each municipality may require the LTCI qualification assessment to indicate them as "NOT ELIGIBLE" for LTCI benefits.

However, not applying for the certification might be an advantage in some cases. For example, if one wishes to have only home care services, then it might be better to not apply for LTCI since home care services funded by medical insurance is cheaper than that of LTCI.

CHANGE OF ADDRESS FOR LONG-TERM CARE INSURANCE BENEFITS

When a recipient moves within the jurisdiction of a municipality, he/she is required only to notify of the address change to continue receiving any LTCI benefits. If the recipient moves out of the jurisdiction of municipality that approved certification for LTCI benefits, then it is necessary to re-apply for new certification at the new local municipal government office within 14 day of moving with a certification approval notice that was issued by the previous municipal government. However, since an onsite qualification assessment is conducted using a nationally standardized assessment tool and classification criteria, the care services provided will be based on the aforementioned criteria until the expiration date.

When a recipient moves from a municipality where there are insufficient long-term care facilities to another municipality with more sufficient long-term care facilities for admission, a problem arises. That is, the number of LTCI-covered institutional care services that the municipality who accepts the recipient as its new resident must provide and the municipality's burden for financing the institutional care services under its budgets will increase, while the number of institutional care services and the financial burden that the municipality that the recipient had lived in before will decrease. Therefore, financial burden concentrates primarily on the municipality that accepts the recipient. Hence, the "Exceptions for institutionalized insured persons in LTCI-certified facilities (the LTCI Law, Article 13)" was established, and the municipality that the recipient had lived in before the move would fund the LTCI service as the primary insurer for that particular recipient.

REAPPLICATION OF CERTIFICATION

As a general rule, the approved/certified care level is effective for only 6 months. If beneficiaries wish to keep the services after the expiration date, then they have to reapply for the certification. The procedure is similar to that of a first-time application.

Recipients are also required to report any changes in their physical and mental status while receiving care. Reapplication is required especially when physical status declines and the level of care increases during the period of certification. Recipients must therefore be careful about increasing the number and frequency of care services or exceeding the budget ceiling without reapplying, as they would need to pay the balance if they exceeded the budget ceiling, which dates from when they first exceed the budget to the date that they reapply for the LTCI.

Reapplication is not necessary when there is no need to increase the number and frequency of care services. However, when one's physical status improves, it is important to consider whether one should reapply. When the level of care decreases, the budget ceiling decreases accordingly; thus, the care service that was being provided might no longer be available, and even if one decides to keep the care service, the balance after exceeding the decreased budget ceiling must be paid by the recipient.

The advantage of reapplying is that the recipient's co-payment might lower when the level of care needed lowers. That is, when a recipient who had been classified into care-required level 3 receives a certification for care-required level 2 at the time of reapplication, the co-payment for LTCI care services might decrease.

FEES AND COSTS INVOLVED IN APPLYING FOR CERTIFICATION

Unlike the costs for home- and community-based care, institutional long-term care, and creation of care plans covered by LTCI, the cost of obtaining a physician's report, which is a required document for LTCI certification, is covered by the municipalities because it is part of the paperwork needed for certification. Incidentally, the cost of obtaining a physician's report is determined by the ordinance of each municipality. However, to establish a baseline and to standardize across municipalities, the MHLW has determined the base standard amount to be JPY 5,000 for new applicants who live at home and JPY 4,000 for renewals. For institutionalized/hospitalized residents/patients applying for the first time, it is set as JPY 4,000 and as JPY 3,000 for a renewal.

The physicians appointed by the municipalities would create physician's reports for applicants who do not have a primary doctor. The cost of diagnosis and a basic physical examination (including blood pressure, a simple x-ray of the chest, blood tests, and urine test) are covered by the local authorities, similar to the physician's report.

HOW TO APPEAL

If an insured person has a complaint or is dissatisfied with the results of the qualification assessment or premium rates, he/she is entitled to express his/her views and request the local Long-Term Care Certification Committee for a review (Figure 6-4).

If a complainant is dissatisfied with the response to his/her complaint, he/she may appeal in writing to the Committee on LTCI at the prefectural level within 60 days of notice. However, the LTCI care service is assumed to be provided based on the current level of care while his/her complain is under review by the committee, and since the review could take a long time, many complainants usually decide to reapply for the certification instead.

If dissatisfaction remains after receiving the results of an appeal, the complainant could file a lawsuit against the municipal government to

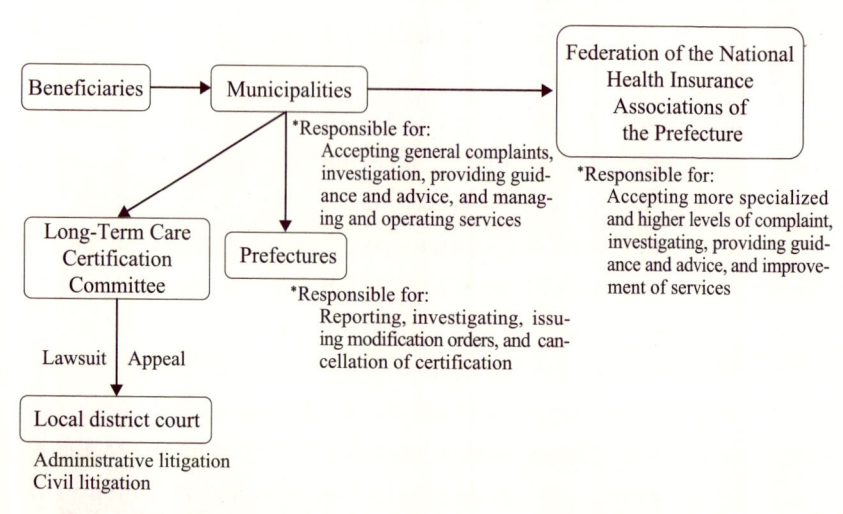

```
Beneficiaries ──▶ Municipalities ─────────────▶ Federation of the National
                                                  Health Insurance
                    *Responsible for:             Associations of
                    Accepting general complaints, the Prefecture
                    investigation, providing guid-
                    ance and advice, and manag-  *Responsible for:
                    ing and operating services    Accepting more specialized
Long-Term Care                                    and higher levels of complaint,
Certification      Prefectures                    investigating, providing guid-
Committee                                         ance and advice, and improve-
                    *Responsible for:             ment of services
                    Reporting, investigating, issu-
Lawsuit | Appeal    ing modification orders, and can-
                    cellation of certification
        ▼
Local district court

Administrative litigation
Civil litigation
```

Figure 6-4 Overview of the Appeal Process and the Responsible Parties

request that the results of the certification be cancelled and/or ask for new certification at the local district court within 3 months of receiving the appeal results.

SUMMARY

This chapter presented the first part of the application process for LTCI benefits. Insured persons who become frail and require long-term care services have to undergo a complex application process and many applicants need all the help they can get. Assistance with application is available from LTCI-certified home care agencies, public consultants on social and labor insurance, and care managers who would usually help at no charge. Applicants are also not required to pay for a physician's report because it will be covered by the municipal government as part of the application process. All applicants have the right to appeal if they are dissatisfied with the LTCI system.

References

Campbell, J. C. & Ikegami, N. (2000). Long-Term Care Insurance Comes to Japan. Health Affairs, 19(3), 26-39.

Hidaka, M. & Kodera, M. (2002). Application and Consultation for Long-Term Care Insurance [*Kaigo Hoken no Shinsei to Sodan niwa*]. In Institute of Japan Care Work (Ed.), Introduction to Long-Term Care Insurance [*Kaigo Hoken Nyumonsho*] (pp.47-58). Tokyo: Index Press.

Kagawa, K. (2001). Process of Application to Utilization [*Shinsei kara Riyo madeno Tejun*]. PT Journal 35, 134.

Kawamura, T. (2000). This is Enough — A Quick Understanding on Long-Term Care Insurance [*Korede Jubun Kaigo Hoken Hayawakari*]. Tokyo: Jistugyo no Nihon Sha.

Ministry of Health and Welfare (1998). Long-Term Care Insurance Q&A [*Kaigo Hoken Seido Q & A*]. Tokyo: Chuohoki Publishing CO., Ltd..

Momose, T. and Wada, K. (1999). Long-Term Care Services and Long-Term Care Insurance [*Kaigo Shien Service to Kaigo Hoken*]. Tokyo: Kenpakusha.

Okuno, E. (2000). Issues related to Long-Term Care Insurance and Policies of Disabled Persons [*Kaigo Hoken Seido to Shogaisha wo meguru Kadai*]. Sogo Rehabilitation, 28, 41-45.

Sato, Y., Mizumaki, N. & Obata, Y. (1997). All Aspects and Practice of Long-Term Care Insurance [*Kaigo Hoken no Zenyo to Jitsumu Taisaku*]. Tokyo: Nihon Horei.

7

Qualification Assessment for Long-Term Care Insurance Benefits

When individuals wish to utilize LTCI care services, as explained in the previous chapter, they have to apply at their municipal office. The purpose of qualification assessment for LTCI benefits is to determine applicants' care levels. After submitting the application form, an onsite assessment will be conducted to classify applicants into one of 6 care levels or reject them. An initial classification decision will be made by analyzing the results of the onsite assessment using a computer program created by the national government. Based on the results of computer analyses, the final classification decision on the care level of each applicant is then determined by the Long-Term Care Certification Committee (mentioned previously). According to the LTCI Law, the decision for eligibility must be conveyed to the applicants within 30 days of application. Once they are deemed eligible, beneficiaries can utilize care services up to the budget ceiling of their level of care (except for some services that may change the budget ceiling). Thus, the certification system plays an important role in the LTCI system.

Since the establishment of the LTCI certification system, there have been complaints that some applicants are classified into a lower care level even though they have dementia/Alzheimer's-related behavioral problems or have a significant decline in physical performance and more issues throughout the process of LTCI certification.

This chapter will address those issues in addition to the last part of the application process, onsite qualification assessment and interview, and classification process.

THREE TYPES OF ASSESSMENT METHODS

When an individual applies for LTCI certification at the municipal office, a municipal staff member who holds a national professional license such as physician, nurse, care manager, or social worker, will conduct an onsite assessment to determine the physical and mental status of the applicant. This onsite assessment is conducted in various settings including the home and care facilities. It usually takes approximately 1 hour and consists of (1) an intake interview that gathers basic information and the needs of the applicant, (2) an objective assessment that consists of 85 items, and (3) a space for descriptive statements of some specific aspects on the assessment form.

Intake Interview

Basic information such as the applicant's name and address, care services the applicant is currently utilizing, current living environment, availability of informal support, and experience of abuse and neglect are gathered during the intake interview.

Even though the intake interview is important for determining the identity of the applicant, the assessment form does not provide enough space for the assessor to record the obtained information. In addition, the Long-Term Care Certification Committee hardly reviews the information obtained during the interview because the MHLW instructs the committees to not use this information as hard evidence for classifying the applicant.

Objective Assessment

The MHLW has developed an 85-item objective assessment instrument for the certification system[1]. Of those 85 items, 73 items contain response scales of 2 to 4 levels and are grouped into 7 categories (Table 7-1). The remaining 12 items concern the medical care/treatments that the applicants are currently receiving. This assessment form consists of items drawn from several other assessment forms and its validity and reliability has not been determined, which might pose an issue to the validity and reliability of the assessment made.

Among the 85 items, 2 items require assessors to observe the applicant performing specific tasks, 13 items require physical checkups, and the rest require interviews with the applicants and/or applicants' families (Table 7-2).

The assessment, which usually takes approximately 1 hour, may not be enough time to be acquainted with the applicants. Therefore, assessors may have difficulty completing the assessment form for first-time applicants and may have to rely heavily on the applicants' and families' responses.

The following section discusses the 7 categories of assessment items and describes issues with assessors and the items used for assessment.

Group 1. Paralysis and Contractures

Diseases, such as Parkinson's disease, which affect the central nervous system and impair motor skills, are included in the paralysis and contractures category. The assessors usually ask the applicants whether they experience paralysis and/or contractures in order to evaluate the levels of their physical ability. However, some assessors frequently

Table 7-1 Contents of the 85-Item Scale

\multicolumn{3}{c}{GROUP 1 (paralysis and contractures)}
Paralysis:	Left-upper extremity	Right-upper extremity
	Left-lower extremity	Right-lower extremity
	Other	
Contractures of joints:	Shoulder	Elbow
	Hip	Knee
	Foot and ankle	Other

\multicolumn{2}{c}{GROUP 2 (basic movements)}
Rolling over	Ambulation
Getting up	Sitting with feet off the ground
Standing	Sitting with feet on the ground
Transfer	

\multicolumn{2}{c}{GROUP 3 (complex movements and tasks)}
Standing up	Getting in/out of the bathtub
Standing on one foot	Bathing (washing body)

\multicolumn{2}{c}{GROUP 4 (special care)}
Bedsores	Swallowing
Cutaneous diseases	Ability to raise hand/arm up to chest level
Urination	Cleaning up after urination
Bowel movements	Cleaning up after bowel movements
Dietary intake	

\multicolumn{2}{c}{GROUP 5 (personal care)}
Oral hygiene	Ability to button and unbutton clothes
Washing of face	Ability to put on and remove garments
Combing hair	Ability to put on and remove a pair of pants
Nail hygiene	Ability to put on and remove a pair of socks
Cleaning own room	Apathy or loss of interest in surroundings
Administration of medication	
Management of money	
Severe memory loss	

\multicolumn{2}{c}{GROUP 6 (communication, hearing, memory, and recall ability)}
Vision	Ability to express self
Hearing	Ability to recall current season
Understanding of daily routine	Ability to recall own name
Short-term memory	Ability to recall birthday
Responds to instructions	Ability to recall current location

GROUP 7 (problem behaviors)	
Paranoia	Restlessness
Making up stories	Ability to locate own home/room
Delusion/ auditory hallucination	Insists on going out alone
Vulnerable emotion	Hoarding
Day-night reversal	Ability to keep watch on a stove
Verbal and physical aggression	Destruction of objects/clothes
Repetitive	Socially inappropriate behavior
Screaming	Pica behavior
Resists care	Troublesome sexual behavior
Wandering	
SPECIAL MEDICAL CARE	
Intravenous fluids	Respirator
Central venous nutrition	Tracheostomy treatment
Dialysis	Pain management
Stoma care	Tubal feeding
Oxygen therapy	Treatment of pressure ulcer
Monitoring (e.g., blood pressure, heart rate, oxygen level)	
Catheter (condom or indwelling)	

Note: As of April 2000

Table 7-2 Classification of the Assessment Method

Assessment methods	Number of items
Ability observation	2
Ability testing	13
Re-testing of ability in a safe manner when assessors are unable to determine applicants' responses on the checklist	10
Comprehensive interpretation of ability observation and testing result by considering the general situation of the applicant	16
Interview with the applicants and their families	23
Comprehensive interpretation of interview results	21
Total	85

fail to ask such questions and these impairments are missed.

Group 2. Basic Movements
The items related to basic movements require interviews with the applicants. If communication with applicants is difficult, then interviews with caregivers are conducted. If appropriate, assessors may have the applicants perform certain tasks in order to test their mobility. If the applicants are able to move between surfaces (e.g., to/from: bed, chair, wheelchair, bath/toilet, or standing position) without assistance or live alone, they are more likely to be determined as "independent."

Group 3. Complex Movements and Tasks
Items related to complex movements and tasks (e.g., standing up, getting in/out of a bathtub) are evaluated in the same way as evaluating basic movements (Group 2). As for bathing/washing the body, the assessors would interview the applicant/family and interpret the applicant's ability by considering the general situation of the applicants.

However, an issue with this group is that, when assessing the applicants for the first time or when assessors are not familiar with the applicants, it is difficult to appropriately evaluate applicants' ability, and the assessment results might vary between assessors.

Group 4. Special Care
This category includes bedsores, cutaneous diseases, the ability to raise the hand/arm up to chest level, swallowing, urination, bowel movements, cleaning after urination, cleaning after bowel movements, and dietary intake. Cutaneous disease includes treatments for athlete's foot and scabies. Bedsores, cutaneous diseases, and the ability to raise the hand and arm up to chest level are assessed

during the interview or observation.

Swallowing, urination, and bowel movements are assessed via interviews with applicants. When communication with the applicant is difficult, the interview and assessment are conducted with family members.

However, this category contains items related to urination and bowel movements that are sensitive and usually accompanied by a sense of shame. Thus, applicants may report in a more "socially accepted" manner, which may lead to inaccurate evaluations by assessors. Therefore, there is a need for the assessors to confirm with the applicants' family regarding these items.

Moreover, some items in this group such as swallowing, urination, bowel movements, and dietary intake are classified as "special care" even though it would be more appropriate to classify them as "basic care" because these are basic activities of daily living and should be considered non-special in nature.

Group 5. Personal Care

This category contains items related to oral hygiene, washing of the face, combing of the hair, and nail hygiene. All items are assessed through interviews and comprehensive interpretation of ability while considering the situation of applicants.

However, assessment of these items may vary between assessors depending on their interpretation of the interview responses, and items of "severe memory loss" and "apathy or loss of interest in surroundings" are categorized as "personal care" even though they seem more appropriate as group 6 or 7 (described below) items.

Group 6. Communication, Hearing, Memory, and Recall Ability
This group includes a wide range of abilities such as vision, hearing, ability to express oneself, response to instructions, and understanding of the daily routine.

Vision is assessed with the symbol shown in Figure 7-1, and hearing is assessed based on ongoing conversation during the assessment. When assessing applicants with dementia or those with communication problems, the results may vary.

Items concerning the ability to express oneself, response to instructions, and orientations are evaluated through interviews. If communication with the applicant is difficult, then assessors will interview the applicant's family for confirmation.

Group 7. Problem Behaviors
Items in this group, which concern behaviors such as paranoia, delusion or auditory hallucinations, verbal and physical aggression, and hoarding and socially inappropriate behaviors, are assessed by the same methods for "severe memory loss" and "apathy or loss of interest in surroundings" in Group 5.

Items in this group may be the most difficult among all other

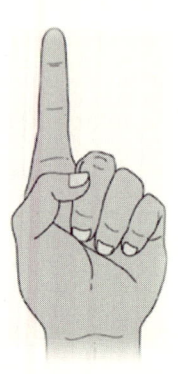

Figure 7-1 Visual Assessment Symbol

items to be accurately assessed, since the applicants are less likely to report having such problem behaviors. Indeed, there was a case in which an applicant was rejected for LTCI benefits even though he had severe dementia, paranoia, and verbally abusive, hoarding, and socially inappropriate sexual behaviors, and scored 15 out of 30 on the Hasegawa Dementia Scale, one of most commonly used assessment tools for screening of dementia in Japan, because the applicant reported not having such behaviors. Thus, the assessors may interview family members in the absence of the applicant to obtain more accurate data.

Additional Comments by Assessors

The assessment form provides space for assessors to record any additional comments. For example, for the ability of rolling over in Group 2, assessors are required to respond on a scale of 1 (*capable*) to 3 (*incapable*) and to indicate in the space provided if the applicants needed "assistance" with rolling over. However, some assessors do not follow the protocol and do not fill in that section.

In addition, some assessors do not indicate if they had problems in assessing specific abilities that may influence the classification of the applicants' care levels.

ISSUES IN ASSESSING THE STATUS OF APPLICANTS

It is difficult to obtain accurate data on applicants' physical and mental status. Some physical and mental impairments or problems can be detected only after care services are provided because (1) physical and mental conditions change every day; (2) cognitive skills, decision-making skills, and activity participation may not decline at the same speed in people with dementia; and (3) there are some cases in which applicants, in the presence of a stranger, are able to perform tasks that they usually are unable to perform.

In addition, during interviews with applicants and/or their families, which is the main assessment method for this category, applicants are unlikely to say "*I can't*" or "*I'm incapable*" when asked if they can perform such tasks and are more likely to overestimate their abilities. In addition, they and their family members may be old and thus may not be able to answer these questions appropriately. Hence, some formal and/or informal support systems such as care managers and friends from the community are required to help provide more accurate answers during the interviews for these types of cases.

INITIAL CLASSIFICATION BY COMPUTER

Once the onsite assessment is completed, the results are analyzed using a computer program developed by the national government to perform an initial classification of the applicants into one of 6 care levels or reject their application. The following section outlines the process of the initial classification.

Calculation of Sum per Category

Seventy-three of the 85 items are categorized into 7 categories: (1) paralysis and contractures; (2) basic movements; (3) complex movements; (4) special care; (5) personal care; (6) communication, hearing, memory, and recall ability; and (7) problem behaviors (Table 7-1), and each item is assigned a certain point. The points from all 7 categories are totaled after calculating the total point for each category.

Calculation of Total Amount of Care Using the "Tree Diagram"

The total amount of care (in minutes) needed for the applicant is calculated by using 9 "tree diagrams," in which a cluster of branches is drawn for each decision to be made and the branches represent the assessment items and the total point of each category.

For example (Figure 7-2), if one requires no assistance or supervision in dietary intake (eating), the analysis will follow a path to the left branch. If one requires limited or extensive assistance, then the path to the right branch of the diagram is followed. These branches further diverge into smaller branches that factor in the sum of points obtained for the middle-level category of personal care. If the sum is less than 6.0, then the path to the left branch is chosen; if the sum is more than 6.1, then the path to the right branch of the diagram is chosen. The last branches will reveal the total minutes of care needed for dietary intake, which is the average length of care (minute/day) acquired from a study called the "One-Minute Time Study."

There are tree diagrams for dietary intake, transfer, urination, bathing,

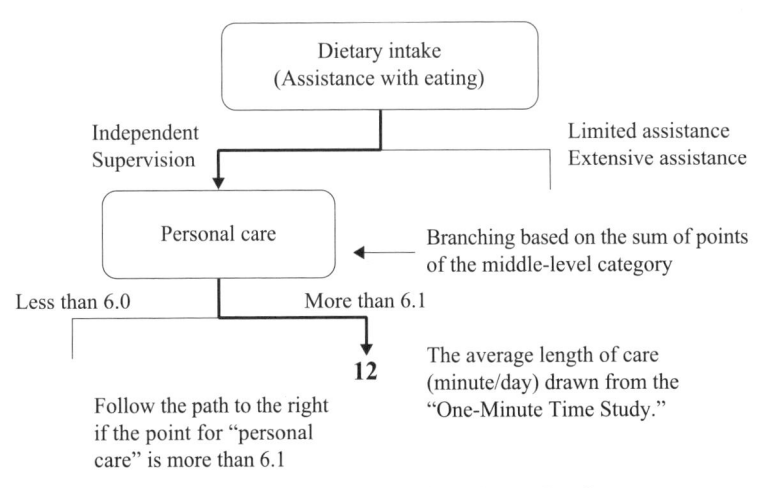

Figure 7-2 Tree Diagram for Dietary Intake

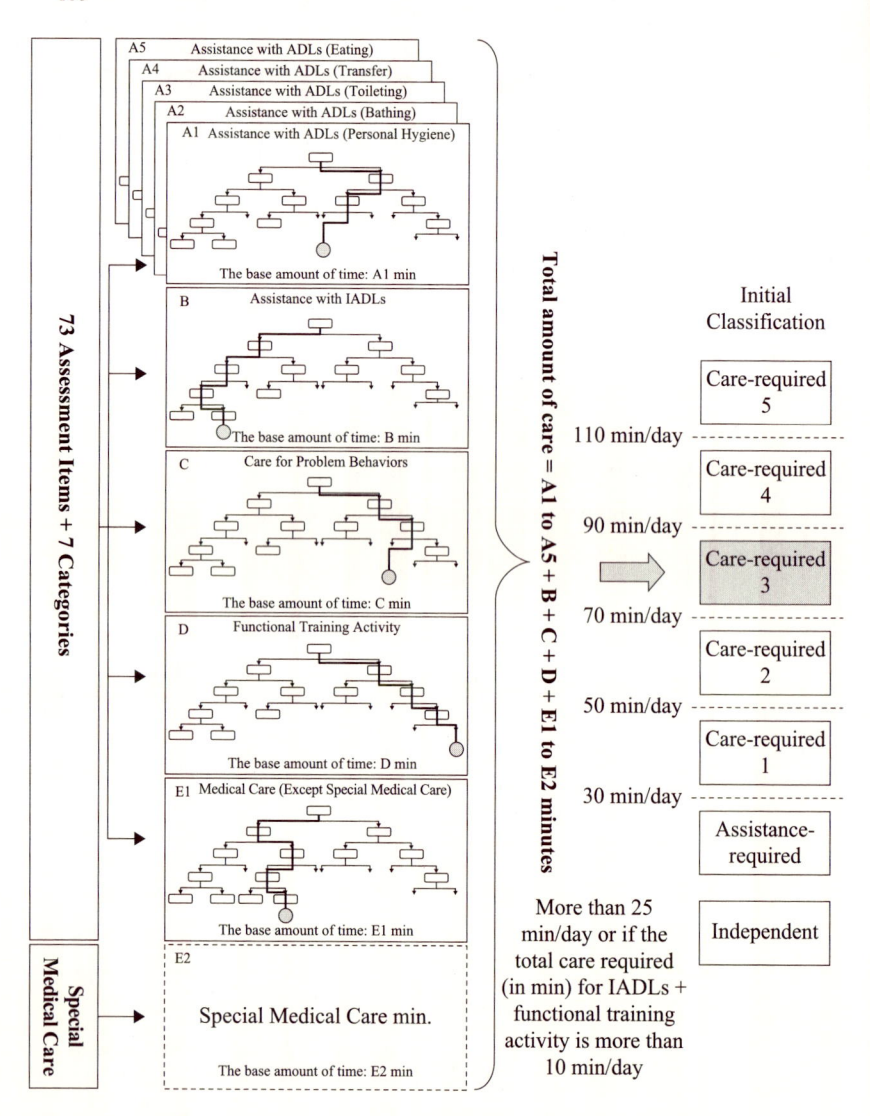

Figure 7-3   Calculation of the Base Amount of Time

Table 7-3　The Basic Amount of Time by Care Level

Level of care	The basic amount of time
Assistance-required	The base amount of time is less than 30 min and; · The base amount of time is more than 25 min or · The total time for the base amounts of time for IADLs and functional training-related activities is more than 10 min.
Care-required level 1	The base amount of time is more than 30 min and less than 49 min.
Care-required level 2	The base amount of time is more than 50 min and less than 69 min.
Care-required level 3	The base amount of time is more than 70 min and less than 89 min.
Care-required level 4	The base amount of time is more than 90 min and less than 109 min.
Care-required level 5	The base amount of time is more than 110 min.

personal hygiene, IADLs, problem behaviors, functional training activity, and medical care. By adding the amount of time obtained from all 9 diagrams and the amount of time spend for special medical care, the base amount of time used for the certification of both care-required and assistance-required levels would be obtained.

Classification of Care Levels

The applicants are then classified into a care level or rejected according to the base amount of time. The care level increases every 20 min of the total amount of time care is required (in min), which can be calculated by adding up all care required min drawn from each of the tree diagrams (Figure 7-3 and Table 7-3). The computer program used for the certification system can be downloaded or purchased at bookstores.

PHYSICIAN'S REPORT

Reports from the applicant's primary doctor include applicants' (1) previous and/or existing injuries and diseases, (2) special medical treatments received within the last 14 days, (3) physical and mental status, (4) need for long-term care, and (5) other information that requires special attention. The doctors should be able to provide information on the applicants' injuries, diseases, and medical treatments, but they may require the applicants' or family's input for reporting the applicants' need for LTCI, because the doctors' primary role is to diagnose and treat sick individuals. Therefore, the quality of primary doctor's reports may vary between doctors.

LONG-TERM CARE CERTIFICATION COMMITTEE REVIEW (FINAL CLASSIFICATION)

A municipal Long-Term Care Certification Committee, usually consisting of 5 members, will review all assessment results, including initial classification, descriptive statements, and the doctor's reports. They review these to determine whether the need for LTCI is due to having one or more of the 15 specified diseases (if the applicant is a 2nd category insured), to confirm the accuracy of the results of the onsite assessment and computer analysis, and to check if other factors need to be considered for LTCI classification.

If they find a discrepancy, then the committee members will re-check the results of the onsite assessment and computer analysis before making a final decision on the care level.

A problem with the final decision made by the committee on care level is that the committee members usually spend only a few minutes on average for each application without meeting the applicant. In addition, because the final decision is made by the municipalities, the decision may vary between municipalities.

FEATURES OF AND ISSUES PERTAINING TO THE CERTIFICATION SYSTEM

As mentioned in the introduction of this chapter, there are more issues pertaining to all processes of the LTCI certification system. The following sections address these issues.

Issues with Evaluating Only the Physical and Mental Statuses of Beneficiaries

First, the 85-item assessment scale focuses on ADLs and rather neglects IADLs (e.g., taking and making phone calls, cooking, doing laundry, and shopping); these activities are important for elderly living at home, and competencies in such activities could delay or avoid institutionalization. Therefore, it is important to assess IADLs as well.

Second, even though they actually require assistance with ADLs and IADLs, elderly people who live alone are likely to be determined as independent by assessors in performing both ADLs and IADLs just because they live at home alone. These elderly people are thus less likely to be eligible for LTCI benefits. Similarly, elderly people who have mental or internal disorders but are able to perform IADLs are likely to be determined as independent even if they require care services and are less likely to be eligible for LTCI benefits.

Third, not considering personal and environmental factors such as living arrangements, availability of caregivers, family's employment and health status, and income levels when municipal committees make decisions on care levels is an issue in Japan. If family and financial situations are not considered during the LTCI certification process, then it would be non-discriminatory (i.e., people who require the benefits will be given them regardless of their social situations). However, because other social welfare systems, such as public assistance, that provide financial assistance to low income recipients in Japan review the applicants' family situation and the income of the beneficiaries and their families, the LTCI system, which does not give priority to people who need it most, is considered by some as not fulfilling its goal as a social welfare system.

Care Levels Determine the Budget Ceiling

The budget ceiling of each care level limits beneficiaries' access to LTCI benefits. The LTCI Law states that the type and number of care services received must be considered in accordance with the insured person's needs and desires to ensure that he/she remains at home for as long as possible. However, the budget ceiling of each level limits the type and number of services that they can utilize and does not correspond with reality. For instance, the budget ceiling of JPY 358,300 for the 4th or 5th level of care is not enough for many beneficiaries, because many of them require more care (Kamo, K. & Sumii, H. 2002). There are also many beneficiaries who require more services due to some personal and environmental factors. Therefore, discrepancies between what the LTCI Law mandates and the actual situation could lead to beneficiaries obtaining less care than they require.

Issues Raised by the One-Minute Time Study

The One-Minute Time Study, which followed nursing staff members in long-term care facilities for 24 consecutive hours and obtained data to develop the LTCI certification and payment system, was conducted by the MHLW to determine the care cost, amount of time that care facility staff spend caring for their residents, and resident characteristics in institutional settings and revealed some problems.

The results of this study indicated that as much as 40% of care facility residents required 0 min (i.e., no need) of bathing care. Because many facilities bathe and shower their residents only twice a week, this may not be captured in the study period, leading to the result of 0 min of bathing and shower. Moreover, even if these facilities provided bathing services during the study period, the incidents would be disregarded if researchers could not identify the residents and if the service was provided to more than 7 residents at the same time. Therefore, the findings of this study may not be accurate.

A similar issue was found for functional training activity; the amount of time nursing staff spent providing such activities was considered as 0 if they were not provided during the study period.

Problem behaviors such as wandering, making disruptive sounds, and engaging in physically and verbally abusive behaviors require nursing attention, especially when it occurs during nighttime. However, the study indicated that only 9.5% of nursing staff provided more than 1 min and 0.9% spent more than 10 min assisting such problem behaviors. This low figure is problematic and further study is warranted. In addition, the data suggest that the care level for individuals with dementia and problem behaviors could be lower if these individuals are able to carry out ADLs and IADLs independently.

The study also revealed that the amount of time that nursing staff spent assisting with eating was significantly low for residents who could not swallow. This is probably due to the reduced amount of time that nursing staff need to spend on spoon-feeding the residents, because many of them have a G-tube inserted through the abdomen that delivers nutrition straight to the stomach.

Unfortunately, although the results from this study are problematic, they were used to develop the certification computer program to perform initial classification, which could greatly influence the benefits that applicants could receive.

Issues Raised by the Use of Evaluation Items

The computer program was written such that the length of time needed for caring for an applicant increases if his/her behavior improves and the number of episodes of problem behavior decreases. This is because it is assumed that the amount of time that nursing staff spent providing recreational activities and functional training activities significantly increases when the number of episodes of problem behavior decreases. This part of the computer program should be changed such that this does not happen.

Issues Raised by Applying Only Statistical Processes

The tree diagrams used for the certification process were created strictly by applying statistical process/methods without critical review from nursing/ medical professionals. In addition, it has been pointed out that statistical inference, a process of drawing conclusion by using a tree diagram, is undeveloped, and could be problematic. Hence, the tree diagram may not be an ideal method of determining the care levels that applicants require.

Difficulty in Classifying Levels of Care

Classifying beneficiaries into one of 6 levels of care using the estimated amount of care in minutes is problematic because the accuracy of the initial classification results drawn from the computer program is low. Indeed, the difference between "independent" and "care-required level 1" is only 6 min. In other words, the classification is not supported by significant differences between levels in the length of care required.

TIPS FOR NOT OBTAINING A LOWER LEVEL OF CARE THAN IS NEEDED

The main reason for applicants being classified into a lower level of care than they need is that the classification system relies heavily on the results of an onsite assessment and physician's report. Thus, it is important to have the assessment results and report accurately reflect whether the beneficiary is in need of long-term care. Below are some tips for not obtaining a lower level of care than is needed:

1) Keep personal health information and medical history current and available; it is important to record and update personal medical conditions, diagnosis, treatment plans, and medications prescribed for that particular medical condition so that applicants can inform their assessors of any undated medical conditions. If an applicant is disabled, it is helpful to have a disability certificate available. It is also important to record any symptoms of diseases such as dementia. If one has problem behaviors, it is necessary to keep track of when, where, how, and what triggered the behavior and to use the worst case as a baseline.

2) Contact primary doctors as often as possible and inform them of any medical conditions.

3) Have a third party available at the time of the onsite assessment, especially if the applicant has difficulty communicating.

4) Inform assessors of any health/medical/mental condition in detail. It is always helpful to be informed of the worst-case scenario.

5) If possible, provide assessors with a copy of any documents that validate the applicant's need for long-term care.

SUMMARY

Both the onsite assessment and computer analysis determine applicants' needs and provide information on whether applicants are frail enough to qualify for LTCI benefits, with the municipal committee deciding on the applicant's care level. The onsite assessment is conducted by municipal staff with a professional license. Questions regarding physical and mental health and functional ability are included in the assessment form to determine applicants' range of capabilities and needs. Computer analysis is conducted to initially classify applicants into one of 6 care levels. The municipal committee then reviews the results to make a final decision on the care level required. Despite the many issues regarding the onsite assessment, computer analysis, and the municipal committee's review, the certification system for LTCI benefits plays a significant role in determining the LTCI services provided.

Note

1) The number of assessment items decreased to 79 in 2003, increased to 82 in 2006, and decreased again to 74 in 2009.

References

Campbell, J. C. & Ikegami, N. (2000). Long-Term Care Insurance Comes to Japan. Health Affairs, 19(3), 26-39.

Doi, T. (2000). Nationwide Inequity: People Who Lose and Gain from Certification of Long-Term Care Insurance [*Zenkoku Ichiritsu Fukohei: Sonsuru Hito Tokusuru Hito ga deru Yokaigo Nintei*]. Tokyo: Hobun Publishing Corporation.

Ishida, K. & Sumii, H. (1999). Unconvinced about Certification on Long-Term Care Benefits: Secrets of Long-Term Care Insurance's Black Box [*Nattoku Dekinai Yokaigo Nintei – Kaigo Hoken Black Box No Himitsu*]. Tokyo: Hobun Publishing Corporation.

Ishida, K., et al. (2000). SOS of Certification of Long-Term Care Benefits: Not to Regret about Long-Term Care Insurance [*Yokaigo Nintei SOS: Kaigo Hoken de Nakanai Tameni*]. Tokyo: Index Press.

Jyosyukaido for Windows (2000). In Ishida, K., et al. (2000) SOS of Certification of Long-Term Care Benefits: Not to Regret about Long-Term Care Insurance [*Yokaigo Nintei SOS: Kaigo Hoken de Nakanai Tameni*]. Tokyo: Index Press.

Kamo, K. & Sumii, H. (2002). What is the Long-Term Care Insurance certification system? [*Yokaigo Nintei towa Nanika*]. In Institute of Japan Care Work (Ed.), Introduction to Long-Term Care Insurance [*Kaigo Hoken Nyumonsho*] (pp.59-82). Tokyo: Index Press.

Ministry of Health and Welfare (1999). Handouts of Prefectural Certification of Long-Term Care Benefits Administrative Division Meeting [*Todofuken to Yokaigo Nintei Tantosha Kaigi Shiryo*]. Ministry of Health and Welfare.

Momochihama Care Management Kenkyukai (1999). Simulation of Certification of Long-Term Care Benefits [*Yokaigo Nintei Simulation*]. Tokyo: Ishiyaku Publishers, Inc..

Tsutsui, T (1999). Schematic: Better Understanding of Certification of Long-Term Care Benefits [*Zukai Yokuwakaru Yokaigo Nintei*]. Tokyo: Japanese Nursing Association Publishing Company.

Zenkoku Rojin Fukushi Mondai Kenkyukai (2001). Made them Accept Our Appeal [*Fufuku Shinsei wo Mitome Saseta*]. Yutakana Kurashi, January & February edition.

8

Sources of Financing for Long-Term Care Insurance

Before the LTCI system was enacted, only general tax revenue was used to fund social welfare-related long-term care services under the Welfare Law for the Elderly. However, LTCI is funded by premiums paid by all persons aged 40 and over, and the funds from the national, prefectural, and municipal governments (except for the 10% co-payment) were used to secure the necessary financial sources and improve and maintain the quality of care provided by LTCI. Dividing the financial sources into public funds and insurance premiums eases the burden on premiums contributed by insured individuals, maintains the supply of service, and keeps the system running smoothly.

This chapter will first illustrate how LTCI is financed by the national government, prefectural government, and municipalities to 1st and 2nd category insured persons. We will then look at how the rates of and levy premiums for 1st and 2nd category insured persons are calculated.

FINANCIAL SOURCES OF LONG-TERM CARE INSURANCE

In order to receive LTCI benefits, all beneficiaries are required to pay 10% of the cost of care services, with the remaining cost covered by the municipalities (the insurers). As of April 2000, the insurers' total revenues are obtained from contributions from 1st category insured persons (17%), 2nd category insured persons (33%), ear-marked subsidy from both prefectural (12.5%) and national governments (25%), and the municipalities' own budgets (12.5%). Of the 25% earmarked as subsidy from the national government, 20% are derived from the national treasury and 5% from the national adjustment grant. Figure 8-1 shows the breakdown of financial sources for LTCI.

Total expenditure of long-term care insurance							
Funds borne by insurers 90%						10% co-payment
Contribution from 1st category insured	Contribution from 2nd category insured	Municipalities' own general budget	Ear-marked subsidy from the prefectural governments	National government		
				Subsidy from national treasury	National adjustment grants	
17%	33%	12.5%	12.5%	20%	5%	

Note: Contribution rates are subject to review and change every 3 years. Currently, 1st category insured persons contribute 21% and 2nd category insured persons contribute 29% of the total LTCI cost. For institutional care, the prefectural governments contribute 17.5% of the total LTCI cost.

Figure 8-1 Financing of Long-Term Care Insurance

INSURED PERSONS: THE AGE OF 40 AS THE CUTOFF POINT

In the LTCI system, the municipalities are the insurers and those who pay premiums are the insured persons. All individuals aged 40 and above are required to participate in the LTCI scheme and pay premiums, even if they do not require the services. The reason for using the age of 40 as the cutoff point is that people aged 40 and above are more likely to have physical and mental conditions that require long-term care. They are also perceived as the "generations that support the expenses for elder care" for their aging parents, and thus probably have the biggest financial burden compared to other generations. For these reasons, the LTCI system perceives age 40 as the cutoff point for LTCI.

LONG-TERM CARE INSURANCE PREMIUMS

LTCI has the following characteristics: (1) even when a person becomes bedridden or requires long-term care, LTCI premiums are still collected and (2) even if one does not utilize LTCI services during his or her lifetime, the insurance premiums that have been paid into the system will not be refunded.

For both 1st and 2nd category insured persons, there are different ways of calculating the premiums charged by the municipal governments and levying methods of premiums.

Premiums of 1st Category Insured Persons

The LTCI premium collected from a 1st category insured persons is determined by each municipality government[1] in accordance with their own regulations and belongs to one of 5 premium categories depending on the insured person's income level (Table 8-1). These categories are set

Table 8-1 Calculation Formulas for Premium Rates

Categories	Eligibility	Premium rates
1st premium category	All members of the household are exempt from municipal resident taxes and are receiving public assistance and/or old-age pension.	Base amount × 0.5
2nd premium category	All members of the household are exempt from municipal resident taxes.	Base amount × 0.75
3rd premium category	The LTCI beneficiary himself/herself is exempt from municipal resident taxes.	Base amount × 1.0
4th premium category	Municipal resident taxpayer whose income is less than JPY 2.5 million.	Base amount × 1.25
5th premium category	Municipal resident taxpayer whose income is more than JPY 2.5 million.	Base amount × 1.5

according to income levels to reduce the burden on low-income earners and increase the burden on high-income earners.

As shown in Table 8-1, the premium rate for those exempted from municipal resident taxes and receiving public assistance and/or old-age pension is only 50% and the rate for those exempted from municipal resident taxes is 75% of the standard rate. The premium rates for municipal resident tax payers who fall in the 4th and 5th categories are set higher than the standard rate: 125% for those who earn less than JPY 2.5 million (4th category) and 150% for those who earn more than JPY 2.5 million. In other words, the rates for individuals who qualify for the 1st and 2nd categories are set lower than those of individuals in the other 3 premium rate categories.

Levy Methods for 1st Category Insured Persons

There are two collection methods for LTCI premiums: (1) a special levy that is deducted directly from pension payments and (2) a regular levy that requires one to pay premiums to municipalities using bank transfers (Figure 8-2). Generally, the special levy is for old-age pension recipients who receive JPY 180,000 per year (or JPY 15,000 per month) and was adopted in the Japanese social insurance system for the first time in 2000.

As per the "Special Measures for Smooth Enforcement of the LTCI Law," the national government froze the levy of LTCI premiums for half a year, from April to October 2000, and paid the premiums that 1st category insured persons were supposed to pay. From October 2000 to September 2001, 1st category insured persons were required to pay only half of the premiums and the national government paid the other half. From October 2001, the collection of the full amount of premiums was started (Table 8-2). However, those who were unable to pay the premiums due to being unemployed, bankruptcy, or a natural disaster were exempted after approval from the municipalities.

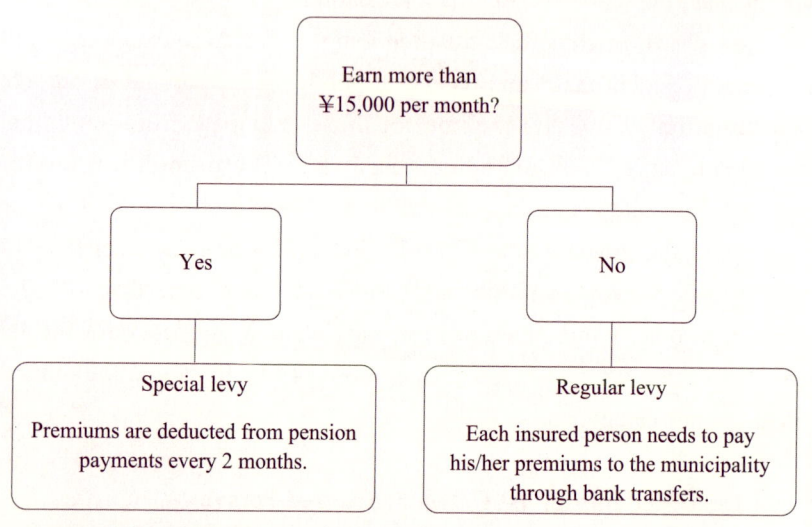

```
                    ┌─────────────────────┐
                    │   Earn more than    │
                    │  ¥15,000 per month? │
                    └──────────┬──────────┘
                ┌──────────────┴──────────────┐
          ┌─────┴─────┐                 ┌─────┴─────┐
          │    Yes    │                 │    No     │
          └─────┬─────┘                 └─────┬─────┘
                │                             │
    ┌───────────┴───────────┐     ┌───────────┴──────────────┐
    │    Special levy       │     │     Regular levy         │
    │ Premiums are deducted │     │ Each insured person needs│
    │ from pension payments │     │ to pay his/her premiums  │
    │    every 2 months.    │     │ to the municipality      │
    │                       │     │ through bank transfers.  │
    └───────────────────────┘     └──────────────────────────┘
```

Figure 8-2 Premium Levy Methods for 1st Category Insured Persons

Determining Methods of Premiums for 1st Category Insured Persons
As discussed above, the amount of insurance premium paid by 1st category insured differs by municipality. This is because the

Table 8-2 Payment Process of Premiums

From April to September 2000	From October 2000 to September 2001	After October 2001
Central government pays the full premium on behalf of beneficiaries	Insured persons pay only half of the premium	Insured persons pay the full premium
	Central government pays the remaining 50%	

difference in total municipality expenditures for LTCI is reflected in each municipality.

The following points are processes for determining the total expenditure on LTCI services:

1) First, each municipality investigates the actual status of their elderly residents and the number and availability of long-term care services to determine how many elderly residents in their municipality require what types of services in what quantities.

2) On the basis of the results, each municipality determines how much and what types of LTCI services should be provided for its eligible residents for the next 5 years.

3) Once the number and types of services are determined, each municipality determines the unit price of each service and calculates the budget required for the next 3 years[2].

This estimate of supply and demand provides a basis for determining how much would be spent on LTCI statutory benefits for eligible residents, for determining the total budget, and setting up the base amount for LTCI premiums for each municipality. If a municipality decides to provide more LTCI services, it can increase the premium amount. The adoption of this procedure creates a situation in which the municipality with a higher number of elderly residents is justified in charging a higher base amount to its residents, creating significant differences in premium rates between municipalities. Therefore, in order to prevent premiums in certain municipalities from becoming too large, national adjustment grants from the national government are provided.

Nevertheless, there still are some differences in the rates of contribution between municipalities (Table 8-3). The reasons for this are as follows:

1) Premium rates are easily influenced by the number of care services provided by the municipality. In other words, they are influenced by whether enough social resources are available for beneficiaries.

2) Premium rates depend on how much the municipality relies on home care or in-facility care services, because LTCI reimbursement, which is the payment that nursing facilities and community-based care providers receive for services rendered to LTCI recipients, for care provided in nursing facilities is considerably higher than that for home care, municipalities that depend highly on in-facility services would have to set a higher rate of contribution. Furthermore, since different reimbursement rates are set

Table 8-3 Premiums of 1st Category Insured Persons and Aging Rates by Prefecture

Prefectures that charge higher premiums	Premiums (JPY)	Aging rates (%)	Prefectures that charge lower premiums	Premiums (JPY)	Aging rates (%)
Okinawa	3,601	12.4	Nagano	2,361	19.5
Tokushima	3,332	18.6	Fukushima	2,483	17.8
Aomori	3,303	16.8	Ibaragi	2,521	14.9
Oita	3,264	18.3	Gifu	2,577	16.3
Kagawa	3,246	18.5	Tochigi	2,565	15.9

Note: As of April 2000

for each care provider based on their occupancy levels, differences in premium rates would occur.

3) Some municipalities provide their own long-term care services under their own social welfare programs using the premiums paid by their 1st category insured persons.

Because of the abovementioned reasons, differences in premium rates exist between municipalities and it is difficult to evaluate which care service is good solely based on the amount of premiums the insured persons pay.

Premiums of 2nd Category Insured Persons

Individuals aged between 40 and 64 years are 2nd category insured persons, and their rate of contribution is determined according to which medical insurance plan they enroll in and their income levels.

An overview of the premium levy method for 2nd category insured persons is shown in Figure 8-3. For those who enroll in medical care insurance offered by their employers, half of the LTCI premiums will be borne by the employers. For those who enroll in National Health Insurance, the same amount will be borne by the national government. All premiums paid by individuals aged 40-64 and medical insurers are pooled at the national level and allocated to municipalities to provide an equal percentage of the total cost of LTCI benefits.

During the first year of LTCI enactment, the premium amounts were set based on the size of their employers in addition to the type of medical insurance they enrolled in. For those who were employed by large enterprises and were enrolled in the medical insurance provided by their employers, the health insurance unions of the employers had to contribute JPY 1,965 every month. For those who were employed by small and medium-sized enterprises and were enrolled in the National Health

```
                                                    Add LTCI premiums
  Determine the      2nd category insured persons   to medical insurance
  premium rates in   (between age 40 and 64)        premiums as taxes.
  accordance with
  the income and
  base amount.       Medical insurers
                     (i.e., National Health Insurance
                     and Social Insurance)          Premiums paid by
                                                    2nd category insured
  Notify the amount                                 are pooled into the
  of contributions.                                 Social Insurance
                                                    Medical Fee
                     Social Insurance Medical Fee   Payment Fund at the
                     Payment Fund                   national level.

     Allocate 33% of premiums paid by
     medical insurers to municipalities.

                     Long-term care insurance
                     insurers
                     (municipalities)
```

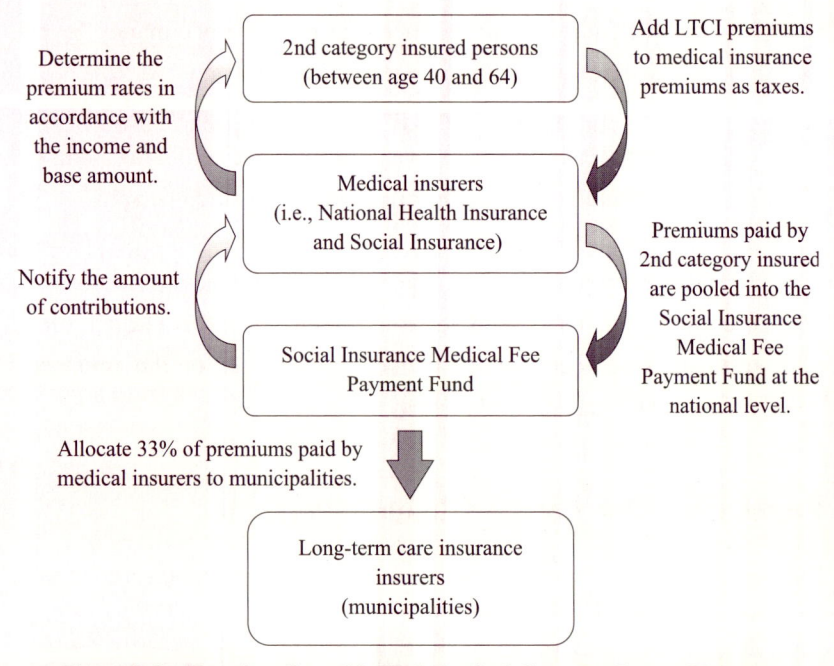

Figure 8-3   Premium Levy Methods for 2nd Category Insured Persons

Insurance, their health insurance association had to contribute JPY 1,550 every month.

Among 2nd category insured people such as those who are self-employed and enrolled in National Health Insurance, the national average premium is JPY 1,280 per month and JPY 1,410 for those enrolled in the National Health Insurance Association.

Levy Methods for 2nd Category Insured Persons

As explained above, 2nd category insured persons pay their premiums (as their taxes) to their employers, who will bear half of the premiums, which are pooled into the Social Insurance Medical Fee Payment Fund that allocates 33% of premiums to municipalities.

If the beneficiary of an insurance plan provided by the National Health Insurance Association has a dependent aged between 40 and

64, he/she has to pay an additional premium for dependent coverage even if he/she is aged 39 and below or 65 and above.

Determining Methods of Premiums for Salaried 2nd Category Insured Persons

The premium amount for 2nd category insured persons who enroll in their employers' medical insurance is determined, as a general rule, on the standardized amount of salary, which is based on monthly income and multiplied by the long-term care premium rate.

Levy and Determining Methods of Premiums for Self-Employed 2nd Category Insured Persons

Individuals who are aged 40 and above and are self-employed or unemployed must enroll in National Health Insurance or an insurance plan provided by the National Health Insurance Association, which will provide health care benefits to its beneficiaries. The Social Insurance Medical Fee Payment Fund determines the contribution amounts based on the number of enrollees and informs the insurer of this amount. The contribution amounts are set to be close to that of 1st category insured persons. The calculation formula for the premium paid by each insured person varies between insurers. For example, some insurers determine the premium amount by an income test, a means test, or the average per capita. Insurance premiums from enrollees are collected by insurers through bank transfers.

FAILURE TO PAY PREMIUMS PENALTIES

Since LTCI is a mandatory social insurance, there are some penalties set for both 1st and 2nd category insured persons who fail to pay their premiums during the grace period indicated by LTCI.

For 1st Category Insured Persons

If 1st category insured persons fail to pay their insurance premiums, there are three levels of penalty depending on the length of delay.

1) Failure to pay insurance premiums for 12 months

If 1st category insured persons fail to pay their insurance premiums for 1 year without a reasonable excuse such as facing hardship due to a natural disaster, they will have to pay for the full cost of care services and receive the reimbursement of 90% later.

2) Failure to pay insurance premiums for 18 months

If 1st category insured persons fail to pay their insurance premiums for 1.5 years without a reasonable excuse, they will be fully or partially denied of reimbursement. If they still fail to pay the premium, it will be deducted from their reimbursement checks.

3) Failure to pay insurance premiums for more than 24 months

If 1st category insured persons fail to pay their insurance premiums for more than 2 years without a reasonable excuse, their co-payments will be temporarily increased from 10% to 30% depending on the length of delay.

For 2nd Category Insured Persons

If 2nd category insured persons fail to pay their insurance premiums without a reasonable excuse, they may not be able to receive any care services when they become in need of LTCI services.

POLICY OF PREMIUM REDUCTION AND EXEMPTION

Individuals who cannot meet their premium obligations because of, for example, a natural disaster, can be given special consideration by the municipality accordingly.

For a low-income earner who is below or around the poverty line, the premium rate will be reduced to lower than that of the 1st and 2nd levels of premium rates shown in Table 8-1. Moreover, LTCI premiums will be exempted for low-income people aged between 40 and 64 who have been receiving in-kind and cash benefits from social welfare programs.

SUMMARY

Funding for LTCI comes from a variety of sources. The national government and 1st and 2nd category insured persons pay the majority, with the prefectural and municipal governments sharing part of the cost. The premium rate for 1st category insured persons is determined by each municipal government and the premiums paid by 2nd category insured persons are collected as premiums for their medical insurance. The next chapter will look into more finance-related matters such as costs of LTCI services and co-payments.

Notes

1) The average premium rate for 1st category insured persons during the fiscal years of 2000-2002 was JPY 2,911, which was increased to JPY 3,293 in 2003, JPY 4,090 in 2006, JPY 4,160 in 2009, and JPY 4,972 in 2012. See Ministry of Health, Labour and Welfare (2011) Long-Term Care Insurance to Ensure High-Quality Long-Term Care Services [Ryoshitsu na Kaigo Service no Kakuho]. In Ministry of Health, Labour and Welfare (2011) White Paper on the Labour Economy 2012 (pp.311-318). http://www.mhlw. go.jp/wp/hakusyo/kousei/11/dl/02-06.pdf (accessed September 5 2012), and Ministry of Health, Labour and Welfare (2012): The average premium rate for 1st category insured persons during 5th term [Dai 5 ki Keikaku Kikan niokeru Kaigo Hoken no Dai 1 go Hokenryo nitsuite]. http://www.mhlw.go.jp/stf/houdou/2r98520000026sdd.html (accessed September 5 2012).

2) Finance-related matters such as contribution rates and fee schedules are reviewed every 3 years.

References

Kaigo Hoken Seido Kenkyukai (2001). Premiums of Long-Term Care Insurance [*Kaigo Hoken no Hokenryo*]. Tokyo: Shakai Hoken Kenkyujo.

Kitahama, S. & Mimura, F. (2002). How Much is Premium for Long-Term Care Insurance? [*Kaigo Hokenryo no Futan wa Ikura*]. In Institute of Japan Care Work (Ed.), Introduction to Long-Term Care Insurance [*Kaigo Hoken Nyumonsho*] (pp.33-46). Tokyo: Index Press.

Nagaoka, M. (2000). No Loss on Long-Term Care Insurance e [*Son wo Shinai Kaigo Hoken*]. Tokyo: Mainichi Newspaper.

Okuno, E. (2000). Issues related to Long-Term Care Insurance and Policies of Disabled Persons [*Kaigo Hoken Seido to Shogaisha wo meguru Kadai*]. Sogo Rehabilitation, 28, 41-45.

Sakata, S. (2000). This Book Makes You Understand the System and Mechanism of Long-Term Care Insurance [*Kaigo Hoken no Shikumi to Riyoho ga Wakaru Hon*]. Tokyo: Seibido Shuppan.

Sawada, N., et.al. (1999). Better-Understanding of the Long-Term Care Insurance System [*Yokuwakaru Kaigo Hoken Seido*]. Tokyo: Ishiyaku Publishers, Inc..

Shirasawa, M. (1998). Long-Term Care Insurance and Care Management [*Kaigo Hoken to Care Management*]. The Japanese Journal of Physical Therapy, 32, 313-322.

Takai, Y. (2000). An Overview of the Long-Term Care Insurance System [*Kaigo Hoken Seido no Gaiyo*]. Sogo Rehabilitation, 28, 11-15.

Yoshikawa, K. (1998). Physiotherapy as a Care Manager [*Kaigo Shien Senmonin toshiteno Rigaku Ryoho*]. The Japanese Journal of Physical Therapy, 32, 328-335.

9

Costs of Long-Term Care Insurance-Covered Services

As previously mentioned, the LTCI system is paid for by a variety of sources, including 1st and 2nd category insured persons. Fifteen LTCI-covered care services contribute to long-term care needs, and each care service, including rental assistive devices, has its own fixed cost. It is explained in LTCI brochures, textbooks, newspapers, and service providers' websites that when LTCI-covered care services are utilized, 1st and 2nd category insured recipients are required to pay 10% of the fixed service cost as co-payment. In other words, recipients would save 90% of the expenses as a monetary benefit.

The purpose of this chapter is to discuss how to calculate the fixed costs of LTCI services, amount of co-payments (and monetary benefits), and out-of-pocket expenditures that the LTCI beneficiaries have to pay (or save).

LONG-TERM CARE INSURANCE SERVICE COSTS

A fee schedule was developed for each type of home-and community-based and institutional care service in terms of a long-term care compensation "unit"

Table 9-1 Regional Unit Pricing per Unit as of April 2000

Regions Long-term care insurance services	1st region (e.g., 23 wards of Tokyo)	2nd region (e.g., municipalities of Tokyo, Kanagawa, Aichi, Kyoto, Osaka, and Hyogo prefectures)	3nd region (e.g., municipalities of Kanagawa, Osaka, and Fukuoka prefectures)	4th region (e.g., municipalities of Hokkaido, Miyagi, Saitama, Chiba, Shizuoka, Shiga, Nara, Hiroshima, Yamaguchi, and Nagasaki prefectures)	5th region Other
Medical management Loan of assistive devices	1.0 (10)	1.0 (10)	1.0 (10)	1.0 (10)	1.0 (10)
Home health Home visit rehabilitation Day care rehabilitation Short stay program for personal care Short stay program for medical care	1.048 (10.4)	1.04 (10.4)	1.024 (10.24)	1.012 (10.12)	1.0 (10)
Home care Home bathing services Adult day services Group home for people with dementia Care services for private care facility residents	1.072 (10.72)	1.06 (10.6)	1.036 (10.36)	1.018 (10.18)	1.0 (10)

Note: Numbers in parentheses represent the unit prices in JPY. As of April 2012, there are 7 regions (see Appendix E).

Table 9-2   Calculation Formula for Determining Fixed Cost of Home Visit Rehabilitation Services

Regions	Calculation formula
23 wards of Tokyo	1.048 (unit price) × 550 units × JPY 10 = JPY 5,764
Hokkaido	1.012 (unit price) × 550 units × JPY 10 = JPY 5,566

Note: As of April 2000

(akin to a currency used to calculate the service costs), which is usually called a "point" and can be converted to the Japanese currency (yen; JPY or ¥)" after multiplying by 10.

Similar to a foreign exchange rate between two currencies, the central government of Japan determines how much 1 unit (or point) is equivalent to in JPY between different regions and named this exchange rate "unit pricing per unit." As of April 2000, the unit is set between 1.0 and 1.072, equal to JPY 10-10.72, depending upon the location (administratively, the nation is divided into 5 regions according to the average wages and salaries of employees working in the fields of long-term care; Table 9-1). For instance, as shown in Table 9-2, when an individual utilizes a home visit rehabilitation service with a per diem cost of 550 units in one of 23 wards of Tokyo, the fixed service cost is JPY 5,764, while it is JPY 5,566 in Hokkaido prefecture. Of this amount, the beneficiary is responsible for 10% of the cost (in the above example, JPY 576 for Tokyo and JPY 556 for Hokkaido; any number less than JPY 1 is rounded down) as a co-payment and the rehabilitation service provider will receive the rest of the cost as reimbursement.

FEE STRUCTURE OF LONG-TERM CARE INSURANCE SERVICES

The fee structure of LTCI services is simpler than expected. There are 4 different ways of setting up the fee schedule: (1) fixed unit price, (2) time period (hourly charge), (3) care level, and (4) combination of time period and care level (Table 9-3).

Table 9-3   Fee Structures of Long-Term Care Insurance Services

Methodologies	Types of long-term care insurance services
Fixed unit price (cost)	Home bathing services, home-visit rehabilitation, medical management, and loan of assistive devices
Time period (hourly charge)	Home care and home health
Care level	Short-stay program for personal care, short-stay program for medical care, group home for people with dementia, care services for private care facility residents, and other institutional care
Combination of time period and care level	Adult day care and day care rehabilitation

Note: As of April 2000

Fixed Unit Price Method

Four services, namely, home bathing services, home visit rehabilitation, medical management, and loan of assistive devices, are charged via fixed unit prices.

Home Bathing Services

For home bathing services, although the fixed unit price is 1250 units per service, the cost may fluctuate due to discounts (and/or extra charges) depending on the types of bathing procedures such as washing partial or full body and the number and which type of nursing staff provided bathing care (Table 9-4).

Home Visit Rehabilitation

As mentioned in the previous section, the fixed unit price for home visit rehabilitation is 550 per day.

Medical Management

Although the fixed unit price schedule for medical management varies depending on which medical/health professionals provided the

Table 9-4 Unit Price of Home Bathing Services (1250 units*)

Composition of nursing staff	Type of bath	Extra** charge and discount	Calculation formula	Unit price
1 nurse with 2 nurse's aides	Full-body bath	N/A	Regional unit price × 1250 units × JPY 10	1250 units
	Half-body bath or sponge bath	70%	Regional unit price × 1250 units × JPY 10 × 70% discount	1250 units × 70% = 875 units
3 nurse's aides	Full-body bath	95%	Regional unit price × 1250 units × JPY 10 × 95% discount	1250 units × 85% = 1188 units
	Half-body bath or sponge bath	95% and 70%	Regional unit price × 1250 units × JPY 10 × 95% discount × 70% × discount	1250 units × 95% × 70% = 832 units

* As of April 2000. See Appendix G for current fee schedule as of April 2012.
** There is an extra charge of 15% when home bathing services are provided in isolated islands and mountainous regions.

service, it is usually fixed. In addition, although there is no budget ceiling, the frequency of use is limited.

Loan of Assistive Devices

The fee schedule for loan of assistive devices is a little different from the other 3 fee schedules. LTCI indicates the devices to be covered by the insurance but does not determine its renting fees, which is set by the provider.

Time Period Method

Fee schedules for home care and home health services are determined according to the length of time the service is provided as well as the types of assistance provided. There are various fee structures and schedules, since both home care and home health care involve a variety of care activities.

Home Care (Home Help)

Home care provides a full range of care activities, which can be classified as follows: (1) nursing care, (2) homemaking activities, and (3) combination of both. The minimum length of the service is generally 30 min and the fee increases every 30 min. Homemaking is not provided for those who do not require homemaking activities for more than 30 min. If nursing care is provided in the early morning, there is an extra charge of 25%, and there is an extra charge of 50% for services provided at night. The unit price doubles if 2 home-helpers provide services together (Table 9-5). There is a discount of 5% if home-helpers who hold a 3rd class home-help certification[1] provide nursing care and a combination of nursing care and homemaking

Table 9-5   Home Care: Providing Nursing Care for Changing Diapers and Bed Sheets for 30-60 min (402 units*)

Time of day	Calculation formula
Day time	Regional unit price × 402 units × JPY 10
Night time/early morning	Regional unit price × 402 units × JPY 10 × 125% extra charge
Midnight	Regional unit price × 402 units × JPY 10 × 150% extra charge
Daytime; 2 home-helpers	Regional unit price × 402 units × JPY 10 × 2 home-helpers

* As of April 2000. See Appendix G for the current fee schedule as of April 2012.
Note: To determine the unit price for home nursing care between 60-90 min, simply change the number of units (402) to 584 and follow the formula above.

activities.

Home Health Care

Similar to home care, recipients are charged for home health care services every 30 min and are charged extra for services offered in the early morning (25%) and at night (50%). However, fee schedules differ between the type of professional used, such as licensed practical nurses and rehabilitation professionals (e.g., physical and occupational therapists). Table 9-6 shows the calculation formula for unit prices,

Table 9-6 Unit Price, Extra Charge, and Discount for Home Health Care Services for Less than 60 min (830units*)

Time of day and types of health care-related professionals	Unit prices, extra charges, and discount
Day time	830 units
Night time/early morning	830 units × 125%
Midnight	830 units × 150%
Daytime care by licensed practical nurse	830 units × 90%
Physical/occupational therapist	830 units

*As of April 2000. See Appendix G for the current fee schedule as of April 2012.

extra charges, and discount rate for home health care.

In addition, there are extra charges for emergency home health care services provided by nurses of home-visiting nursing care agencies (1370 units) and hospitals/medical clinics (840 units). Patients with home oxygen therapy, stoma, and/or catheter (condom or indwelling) are charged with extra costs (250 units) as a special management fee. In the event that terminal care is provided within 24 hours of death, an additional 1200 units is charged.

Case 1: If a person with home oxygen therapy utilizes home health care for 1 hour 4 times a month during the day, the total unit price will be as follows:

Daytime use (830 units × 4 times) + special management fee (250 units) = 3570 units

---

Care Level Method

A beneficiary's level of care will determine the per diem cost for institutional care provided at care facilities such as group homes for people with dementia, welfare facilities for the elderly, and health facilities for the elderly.

The unit price of each level for group homes for people with dementia is shown in Table 9-7, and Table 9-8 shows that for care services for private

Case 2: If a person with care-required level 1 certification is admitted to a group home for people with dementia on August 1, then the total unit price will be as follows:

Care-required level 1 (809 units × 31 days) + initial addition (30 days × 30 units)
= 25979 units

Table 9-7 Unit Prices for Group Homes by Care Level

Level of care	Unit price (per diem cost)*
Care-required level 1	809 units
Care-required level 2	825 units
Care-required level 3	841 units
Care-required level 4	857 units
Care-required level 5	874 units

* As of April 2000
Note: 30 units/day will be added for the first 30 days of admission

Table 9-8 Unit Prices for Care Services for Private Care Facility Residents by Care Level

Level of care	Unit price (per diem cost)*
Assistance-required	238 units
Care-required level 1	549 units
Care-required level 2	616 units
Care-required level 3	683 units
Care-required level 4	750 units
Care-required level 5	818 units

* As of April 2000
Note: The additional fee for functional training is 12 units/day.

care facility residents. It is important to note that an extra 30 units per day will be charged for the first 30 days of group home admission, and there is an extra charge of 12 units per day if a resident receives functional training in a private care facility.

However, the process of determining the unit price per diem for welfare facilities for the elderly, health facilities for the elderly, and designated long-term care hospitals can be complicated by differences between institutions in terms of staffing levels, work shifts, and rehabilitation staffing ratio.

Because the limited space here does not allow a detailed explanation of each institutional care facility, the following section will address the fee schedules for respite care at welfare facilities for the elderly because such institutional care is used relatively frequently.

The staffing ratio of nursing staff to short-stay resident at welfare facilities needed to provide functional training activities can be 1:3, 1:3.6, or

Table 9-9 Unit Prices for Welfare Facilities by Care Level

Level of care	Unit price (per diem cost)*
Assistance-required	914 units
Care-required level 1	942 units
Care-required level 2	987 units
Care-required level 3	1031 units
Care-required level 4	1076 units
Care-required level 5	1120 units
Functional training activity	12 units
Transportation services	184 units/one way

*As of April 2000
Note: A ratio of 1:3 means that there is 1 nursing staff for every 3 residents, but actual staffing levels may be lower than the ratio because there are PM shifts, night shifts, and work absences.

Case 3: If a person with care-required level 1 certification is admitted to a welfare facility for respite care via the facility's transportation service and the facility has 1 nursing staff for every 3 residents and is capable of providing functional training activities, the per diem cost will be as follows:

Care-required level 1 (942 units) + functional training activity (12 units) × 5 days + transportation (184 units × 2) = 5138 units

1:4.1. Using the ratio of 1:3, the per diem cost for respite care at such facilities is presented in Table 9-9.

Combination of Time Period and Care Level Method

The combination of time period and level of care determines the cost of adult day care services and day care rehabilitation. Although 2 cost determination methods are involved in the calculation formula, calculating unit prices is unexpectedly easy because both services are offered for either 2-3 hours; 3-4 hours; 4-6 hours; or 6-8 hours, and the level of care is divided into 3 categories—mild (assistance-required); moderate (care-required levels 1 and 2); and severe (care-required levels 3, 4 and 5)—and one can use all elements in a matrix method for calculation.

Other elements that should be included in the matrix method are the type and size of the provider; adult day care is usually provided by freestanding day care centers or day care centers affiliated with or within welfare

Table 9-10 Unit Prices for Day Care Rehabilitation

Time period category	Care level category	Medical facility	Small-scale medical clinic	Health facility for the elderly
2-3 hours	Mild	232	233	227
	Moderate	271	273	265
	Severe	372	375	365
3-4 hours	Mild	331	333	324
	Moderate	387	390	379
	Severe	532	535	521
4-6 hours	Mild	490	480	463
	Moderate	575	562	542
	Severe	789	772	744
6-8 hours	Mild	661	665	648
	Moderate	774	779	758
	Severe	1063	1070	1041

Note: As of April 2000

Case 4: A person with care-required level 4 certification receives rehabilitation for 4-6 hours/day, lunch, transportation, and assistance with bathing using a specialty bathtub at a health facility for the elderly 4 times/month. The total unit price per diem will be as follows:

[Severe level of care (744 units) + meal (39 units) + assistance with bathing in a specialty bathtub (60 units) + transportation (88 units)] × 4 times = 3724 units

Table 9-11 Extra Charges for Day Care Rehabilitation

Types of care/services	Extra charges*
Meals	39 units/day
Transportation	44 units/one way
Assistance with bathing (standard bathtub)	39 units
Assistance with bathing (specialty bathtub)	60 units

*As of April 2000

facilities for the elderly, and day care rehabilitation is provided by medical facilities, small-scale medical clinics, and health facilities for the elderly.

By considering all the elements, the costs for adult day care services and day care rehabilitation are calculated. Table 9-10 presents the matrix method for calculating the cost for day care rehabilitation.

In addition to the unit prices shown in Table 9-10, there are extra charges for meals, transportation, and assistance with bathing using a standard bathtub and specialty bathtub (Table 9-11).

CO-PAYMENTS AND OUT-OF-POCKET EXPENDITURES

This section explains the amount of co-payments and out-of-pocket expenditures.

Co-Payments

For home-and community-based care, as addressed in Chapter 2, there is a budget ceiling for each level of care ranging from JPY 61,500 to 358,300 per month (Table 2-3). If one is provided with home- and community-based services within the budget ceiling, then his/her co-payment is 10% of the service cost and an approximate cost can be estimated after multiplying the cost by 0.1. The reason for stating the approximate cost is that any cost less than JPY 1 is generally rounded down.

Out-of-Pocket Expenditures

When one's cost of services exceeds the budget ceiling, calculation for an approximate will be time-consuming because the calculation formula would be

$$(\text{total cost} - \text{amount of budget ceiling}) + \text{amount of budget ceiling} \times 0.1 = \text{approximate cost}$$

instead of

$$\text{amount of budget ceiling} \times 0.1 = \text{co-payment}$$

and whatever amount in excess of the budget ceiling has to be paid for out of the recipient's own pocket.

There are also some additional fees. In general, for individuals residing in any types of institutional care facilities, LTCI will cover the costs of absorbent incontinence pads, but not for other facility stock items such as soap and facial tissue. For those who utilize adult day care and day care rehabilitation centers, absorbent incontinence pads and materials of meals may not be covered by LTCI. Thus, when calculating total out-of-pocket cost, one needs to take into account the 10% co-payment, the amount that exceeds the budget ceiling (if applicable), and additional fees.

BENEFIT SUPPLY MANAGEMENT

LTCI benefit supply management is a process of monitoring and controlling the use of LTCI benefits. When home- and community-based care services are provided to a beneficiary at home, care managers are required to create a service receipt and service provider's report on a monthly basis. These measures are implemented to allow care managers to keep track of what and how many services are planned and provided within or without the budget ceiling, because the recipients have to pay 10% as co-payment and the amount that exceeds the budget ceiling, and care providers must provide services based on and must not bill services not indicated on the care plan.

Another reason is that if LTCI services are not provided according to the care plans, then care managers can use these records to determine a solution. Figures 9-1 and Figure 9-2 are samples of a service receipt and service provider's report, respectively. By creating these documents, care managers can calculate the cost of LTCI services for their clients.

SUMMARY

This chapter explored the unit prices of LTCI services, including the unit pricing per unit, calculation formula, and methods of setting up the fee schedule, co-payments, and out-of-pocket expenditures of recipients receiving LTCI services, and the importance of a benefit supply management. In determining the recipient's contribution to the cost of care, certain deductions may be made or extra charges applied under certain circumstances. In spite of high expenses, the cost of service is generously covered by LTCI, allowing beneficiaries to save money.

Service

Name of service provider	Provider number	Contents of service	Service code	No. of units	Discount: rates & no. of units	No. of services	Unit price
AAA Agency	100000000	Homemaking 2	112212	191		8	1528
AAA Agency	110000000	Homemaking 3	112311	222		4	888
AAA Agency	110000000	Home health 3	111311	584		7	4088
AAA Agency	110000000	Home care: total					[6504]
BBB Hospital	200000000	Day care rehab 1: severe level of care	161331	789		3	2367
BBB Hospital	200000000	Day care rehab 1: meal service	165100	39		3	117
BBB Hospital	200000000	Day care rehab 1: transportation	44	44		6	264
BBB Hospital	200000000	Day care rehab 1: bathing service	39	39		3	117
BBB Hospital	200000000	Day care rehabilitation: total					[2865]
CCC Agency	160000000	Home health 2	131211	830		8	6640
DDD Agency	500000000	Loan of a wheelchair	171001	600		1	600
DDD Agency	500000000	Loan of a hospital bed	171003	800		1	800
DDD Agency	500000000	Loan of a hospital bed accessories	171004	500		1	500
DDD Agency	500000000	Loan of assistive devices: total					[1900]
EEE Facility	700000000	Short stay program 1	221141	1176		3	3528
		Budget ceiling (units)			30600	Total	21437

Figure 9-1 Sample of a

Receipt

ID number: _____ Insured's name: _____

No. of units that exceeded the budget ceiling	Units within budget ceiling	Unit pricing per unit	Total amount covered by LTCI	Rate (%)	Amount of benefits	Co-payment amount	Out-of-pocket amount
	6504	10.72	69722	90	62750	6972	0
	2865	10.48	30025	90	27022	3003	0
	6640	10.48	69587	90	62628	6959	0
	1900	10	19000	90	17100	1900	0
	3528	10.48	36973	90	33275	3698	0
	21437		225307		202775	22532	0

Service Receipt

Time	Contents of service	Name of service provider	Dates of the month	1	2	3	4	5	6	7	8	9	10
			Days of the week										
7:00 8:00	Homemaking 2: early AM and night shifts	AAA Agency	Plans				1		1				
			Results				1		1				
9:00 10:30	Homemaking 3	AAA Agency	Plans	1							1		
			Results	1							1		
10:00 11:30	Home health 3	AAA Agency	Plans			1		1			1		
			Results			1		1			1		
10:00 16:00	Day care rehab 1: severe level of care	BBB Hospital	Plans							1			
			Results							1			
	Day care rehab 1: meal service	BBB Hospital	Plans							1			
			Results							1			
	Day care rehab 1: transportation	BBB Hospital	Plans							2			
			Results							1			
	Day care rehab 1: bathing service	BBB Hospital	Plans							1			
			Results							1			
14:00 15:00	Home health 2	CCC Agency	Plans				1		1				
			Results				1		1				
	Loan of a wheelchair	DDD Agency	Plans										
			Results										
	Loan of a hospital bed	DDD Agency	Plans										
			Results										
	Loan of hospital bed accessories	DDD Agency	Plans										
			Results										
	Short stay program 1	EEE Facility	Plans										
			Results										
			Plans										
			Results										
			Plans										
			Results										
			Plans										
			Results										

Figure 9-2 Sample of a

9   Costs of Long-Term Care Insurance-Covered Services   *145*

11	12	13	14	15	16	17	18	19	20	21	22	23	24	25	26	27	28	29	30	31	Total number
1		1					1		1					1		1					8
1		1					1		1					1		1					8
											1							1			4
											1							1			4
			1					1							1				1		7
			1					1							1				1		7
										1							1				3
										1							1				3
										1							1				3
										1							1				3
										2							2				6
										1							1				3
										1							1				3
										1							1				3
1			1				1			1				1			1				8
1			1				1			1				1			1				8
																					1
																					1
																					1
																					1
																					1
																					1
			1	1	1																3
			1	1	1																3

Service Provider's Report

Notes

1) Third class certification is obtained upon completion of a 50-hour training course: a minimum of 25 hours in class work, 17 hours in hands-on experience, and a further 8 hours of site visits such as home care agencies. After April 2009, LTCI will not reimburse for care services provided by those home-helpers with 3rd class certification. Incidentally, 2nd class certification can be obtained upon completion of a 130-hour training course that includes a minimum of 58 hours in class work, 42 hours of lecture on nursing skills, and 30 hours in hands-on experience in a long-term care setting such as long-term care facilities and home care agencies. Those who complete 2nd class certification training course can take a 230-hour 1st class certification training course that consists of 84 hours in class work, 62 hours of lecture on nursing skill, and 84 hours in hands-on experience.

References

All-Japan Federation of National Health Insurance Organizations (2000). Guide of Long-Term Care Insurance Reimbursements for Long-Term Care Insurance-Certified Services Providers [*Kaigo Hoken Jigyosho no tameno Kaigo Kyuhi Seikyu no Tebiki*]. Tokyo: All-Japan Federation of National Health Insurance Organizations.

Fuji Research Institute (2000). A Handbook of Long-Term Care Billing for Services Providers [*Kaigo Service Jigyosha no tameno Seikyu Jimu Handbook*]. Tokyo: Jiho Inc..

Hashimoto, S., & Senba, N. (2002). Costs of Long-Term Care Insurance [*Kaigo Service no Tanka to Shiharai wa Ikura*]. In Institute of Japan Care Work (Ed.), Introduction to Long-Term Care Insurance [*Kaigo Hoken Nyumonsho*] (pp.151-168). Tokyo: Index Press.

Kaigo Hoken Kenkyukai (2000). Reimbursement Calculation Q&A: A Guide to Billing and Reimbursement [*Kaigo Hoshu Santei Q&A: Santei kara Seikyu Madeno Tebiki*]. Tokyo: Chuohoki Publishing CO., Ltd..

Kaigo Hoken Seido Jisshi Suishin Honbu (2000). Handouts of Long-Term Care Administrative Division Meeting [*Zenkoku Kaigo Hoken Tantosha Kaigi Shiryo*]. http://www.wam.go.jp/wamappl/bb05Kaig.nsf/0/502ea675dd287e7f4925692e00836d78? OpenDocument (accessed July 1, 2012).

Kushita, Y. (2000). Benefit Management Manual for Care Managers [*Care Manager Kyufu Kanri Manual*]. Tokyo: Sairyusha.

Simizutani, S. & Inakura, N. (2007). Japan's Public Long-Term Care Insurance and the Financial Condition of Insured: Evidence from Municipality-Level Data. Government Auditing Review, 14, 27-40.

10

Care Management and Care Managers

In general, care management is defined as a multi-step process directed at coordinating existing resources to ensure appropriate care services for individuals.

Although individuals in nursing care facilities or hospitals can receive care services and support from staff members, other individuals in the community may have difficulty obtaining sufficient information regarding and finding appropriate care services. In the LTCI system, which aims to promote home- and community-based care, care management is provided as a solution to such problems faced by many community-dwelling individuals.

Creating a care plan is a part of care management that enables LTCI beneficiaries to receive a variety of complementary care services to meet their needs and desires. Based on the care plan, care providers offer care services so that beneficiaries can continue to live in the community.

This chapter begins by explaining how care services were arranged and coordinated before and after the enactment of LTCI, and moves on to highlight the role of care management and care managers in coordinating various LTCI services to ensure appropriate and continuous care; these include the type of care plan, process of care management, the process of becoming a care manager, and care managers' roles and goals.

THE CONVENTIONAL CLIENT ALLOCATION SYSTEM AND THE LONG-TERM CARE INSURANCE SYSTEM

In the conventional system, people with care needs and their families were able to receive care services only after applying at the local municipality or other relevant organizations that determine not only the necessity of providing care services, but also the types of care services and which provider to provide the services. The beneficiaries were also responsible for contacting their municipalities to reschedule the services if two or more different care providers offered different care services on the same day.

On the other hand, the current LTCI system resolved these issues by appointing care managers and establishing a care management system inspired by that in the United States, which made it more convenient for beneficiaries to receive care services. Beneficiaries now have a care manager to provide them with information regarding available care services, arrange and coordinate the delivery of services, and make referrals to service providers. Figure 10-1 shows the differences in care services coordination between the conventional client allocation system and LTCI.

CARE PLANS

A care plan is a part of care management that addresses the needs identified in the assessment and outlines the problems, type and level of care needs, types of care services provided, and roles of providers who deliver care services to beneficiaries to ensure optimal care for them. It can be created

10 Care Management and Care Managers *149*

Under the Conventional Client Allocation System

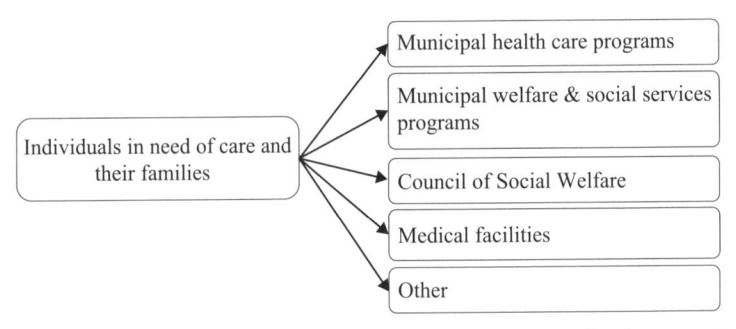

```
                                    ┌─────────────────────────────────┐
                                  ┌▶│ Municipal health care programs  │
                                  │ └─────────────────────────────────┘
                                  │ ┌─────────────────────────────────┐
                                  │ │ Municipal welfare & social      │
┌─────────────────────────────┐   ├▶│ services programs               │
│ Individuals in need of care │   │ └─────────────────────────────────┘
│        and their families   │───┤ ┌─────────────────────────────────┐
└─────────────────────────────┘   ├▶│ Council of Social Welfare       │
                                  │ └─────────────────────────────────┘
                                  │ ┌─────────────────────────────────┐
                                  ├▶│ Medical facilities              │
                                  │ └─────────────────────────────────┘
                                  │ ┌─────────────────────────────────┐
                                  └▶│ Other                           │
                                    └─────────────────────────────────┘
```

Note: Individuals search for care providers and apply for care services by contacting the municipal office and other relevant organizations, and sign the contract themselves.

Under the Long-Term Care Insurance System

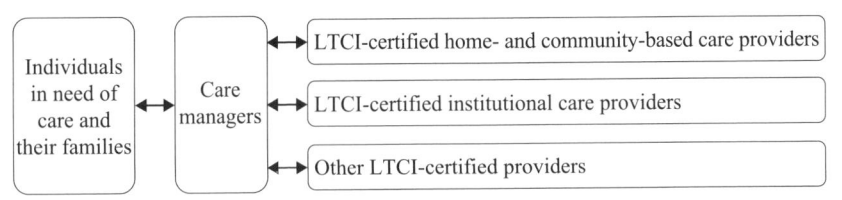

```
┌──────────────┐   ┌──────────┐   ┌─────────────────────────────────────────────────┐
│ Individuals  │   │          │◀─▶│ LTCI-certified home- and community-based        │
│ in need of   │   │   Care   │   │ care providers                                  │
│ care and     │◀─▶│ managers │   └─────────────────────────────────────────────────┘
│ their        │   │          │◀─▶│ LTCI-certified institutional care providers     │
│ families     │   │          │   └─────────────────────────────────────────────────┘
│              │   │          │◀─▶│ Other LTCI-certified providers                  │
└──────────────┘   └──────────┘   └─────────────────────────────────────────────────┘
```

Note: Care managers coordinate and arrange care services with the providers according to beneficiaries' preferences.

Figure 10-1 Difference between the Conventional Client Allocation System and Long-Term Care Insurance in Providing Care Services

by either care managers or beneficiaries themselves.

There are 2 types of care plans: (1) home-care care plans (plans for providing home- and community-based care services to individuals in the communities) and (2) in-facility care plans (plans for those who are in institutional long-term care facilities). Although both plans are called "care plans," they have different purposes.

Home-Care Care Plans

In order to meet the needs of individuals who reside in and require care at home, care plans are developed to coordinate the types and frequencies of home- and community-based care services with care providers. In other words, the care plan centers on what, when, how often, from whom to use, and how much to pay.

In-Facility Care Plans

For residents in care facilities, care plans are created to outline the nursing care/actions undertaken by the nursing staff and indicate any concerns and problems that the residents may have. As such, it is also called "nursing care plan" or "long-term care plan."

CARE PLANNING PROCESS

The process of making care plans in Japan was adopted from that of nursing homes in the United States and consists of 4 steps (Figure 10-2). These processes are similar for the creation of both home-care and in-facility care plans in Japan. The following section briefly explains the care planning process for home- and community-based care services.

Assessment

It is necessary to obtain any information related to the applicants and their families regarding LTCI benefits prior to the creation of care plans. By analyzing the obtained information, care managers can identify the needs that the beneficiaries may have.

The MHLW introduced the following 5 types of assessment tools to help care managers assess and identify beneficiaries' needs:

```
┌─────────────────────────┐
│ 1. Assessment/evaluation │◄──────┐
└───────────┬─────────────┘       │
            ▼                      │
┌──────────────────────────────────┐│
│ 2. Care providers discuss and    ││
│    develop care plans            ││
│    (Care providers' conference)  ││
└───────────┬──────────────────────┘│
            ▼                      │
┌──────────────────────────────┐   │
│ 3. Implementation of care plans│  │
└───────────┬──────────────────┘   │
            ▼                      │
┌──────────────────────────────┐   │
│ 4. Follow-up                 │───┘
│    · Monitoring              │
│    · Reassessment            │
└──────────────────────────────┘
```

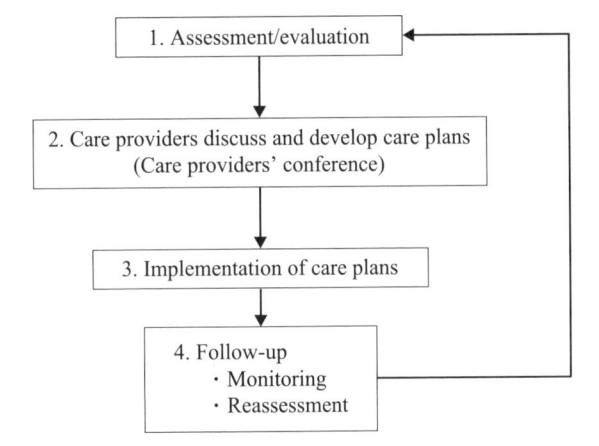

Figure 10-2 Flow Chart of the Care Planning Process

1) Minimum Data Set-Home Care
2) Three-Organization Care Plan Development Study Group Method (comprehensive assessment for providing independent support)
3) Japan Association of Certified Care Workers Method (assessment and care plan for providing independent living support while focusing on daily living assistance)
4) Japanese Association of Certified Social Workers Method (Care Management Teams Tool Kit)
5) Japan Visiting Nursing Foundation Method (Japanese Assessment & Care Plan for Long-Term Care)

Care managers are allowed to use other assessment tools that are not listed above; they are encouraged to tailor their assessment depending on the characteristics of the applicants and their caregivers and the purposes of assessment.

Care Providers Discuss and Develop Care Plans (Care Providers' Conference)

After conducting assessments, the care manager and care providers hold a meeting to discuss and plan what kind of and how often care services should be provided to an applicant by considering his/her designated care level, preferences, and physical and mental conditions. After reaching an agreement, the group creates a care plan and notifies the applicant and his/her family.

Implementation of Care Plans

When the applicant and his/her family give consent for the care plan that indicates what, when, how often, and from whom care services are provided, the creation of the care plan is complete, and the care managers will begin implementing the plan with service providers.

Follow-up: Monitoring and Reassessment

Once care services have been rendered, it is necessary to follow-up on the recipients to see whether the services are provided in accordance with the care plans, determine whether the recipients' needs are met, and check their satisfaction with the services and providers. Reassessment is conducted when there is a problem, and the care plan is revised accordingly.

CARE MANAGERS

The care manager is introduced together with the introduction of LTCI. A care manager is someone with considerable knowledge of the LTCI system and skills in arranging and coordinating care services such as LTCI- and prefectural government-certified home- and community-based care and institutional care services and coordinating team members towards the attainment of the recipient's goal. The care manager is also responsible for the assessment of the physical and mental health of recipients and the implementation of care plans for elderly and disabled persons.

Process of Becoming a Care Manager

There is a certification system for care managers. Although the qualification criteria are defined by the LTCI law, specific qualification requirements are set by municipalities (Figure 10-3). Thus, care managers are not national certification recipients; their certifications are provided by their prefectural governors after taking and completing care manager certification courses.

To be a care manager, one needs to participate in care manager certification courses and meet the following qualification criteria and requirements:

Qualification criteria are those who:
- Belong to at least one of the 21 specified professions (e.g., physicians, dentists, pharmacists, public health nurses) listed in Figure 10-3; and
- Have at least 5 years of experience in either counseling or providing direct care (10 years for direct care staff of elderly almshouses or workshop facilities for the disabled).

Qualification requirements are:
- Those who have taken and passed an enrollment exam for the care manager certification courses; and
- Those who have participated in and completed care manager certification courses provided by approved care management agencies.

Qualification criteria: Those who
1) Are physicians, dentists, pharmacists, public health nurses, midwives, registered nurses, licensed practical nurses, physical therapists, occupational therapists, certified social workers, certified care workers, orthoptists, artificial limb fitters, dental hygienists, speech therapists, practitioners of massage therapy and reflexology, acupuncturists, acupuncture and moxibustion therapists, judo therapists, nutritionists, and/or psychiatric social workers
2) Have been involved in either counseling or providing care for at least 5 years (or 10 years for some professions)

⬇

Qualification requirements: Those who
1) Have passed an examination for the care manager certification courses
2) Have participated in and completed care manager certification courses provided by approved care management agencies
3) Have received the certificate after completing care manager certification courses

⬇

Only those who meet the above criteria and requirements are certified as care managers

Figure 10-3　Care Managers' Qualification Criteria and Requirements

Individuals who meet the criteria and requirements are certified as care managers. However, they are able to perform their duties as care managers only after they are employed by a LTCI-certified home- and community-based care agency or long-term care facility. These care agencies and facilities that wish to be certified by LTCI must employ care managers in accordance with the LTCI Law. Some of them could be members of the Long-Term Care Certification Committee and conduct onsite assessments for LTCI certification and make decisions on applicants' care level.

The Role of the Care Manager

In order to successfully operate LTCI and arrange and coordinate services delivery, care managers have at least the following 3 roles:
1) Applying for LTCI benefits on behalf of the applicant as per his/her request;
2) Conducting onsite assessments at the municipality's request; and
3) Implementing care planning that involves
   - Administering assessment and identifying the beneficiary's condition, needs, and desires;
   - Matching existing resources to the beneficiary's condition, needs and desires, and preventing duplication of care services and use of inappropriate care services;
   - Coordinating the care of various disciplines and professionals;
   - Setting up a care providers conference to plan care services;
   - Obtaining informed consent from the applicant and his/her families for the care plan;
   - Conducting regular visits/calls to recipients to monitor their condition and follow up on services provided and their satisfaction; and
   - Revising the care plan when there is a change in the physical and/or mental conditions or living environment of the recipients.

Other Functions

Providing a Team Approach
Care managers are often part of multidisciplinary teams and provide a team approach for long-term care services. A team approach is a basic approach used in providing care services to individuals and their families needing assistance with health and long-term care issues. It is used for solving the multiple needs of the recipients.

Multiple disciplines and professionals with complementary backgrounds and skills (e.g., physicians, nurses, physical therapists) from multiple locations and providers working in the same team may have different understanding of the applicant/recipients based on their different professional perspectives. However, exchanging perspectives with each other enables the offer of multiple care approaches and fosters the appreciation and understanding of the roles of other disciplines and professionals, their opinions, advice, and rapport. In order to help individuals live with dignity, care managers have to bring different types of disciplines, professionals, and perspectives together.

Documentation

Care managers are responsible for documenting the care services they provide to recipients and maintaining a comprehensive record incorporating clinical, financial, and utilization data across settings in a professional manner. There are 7 types of records that they have to document and maintain: (1) face sheet, a document that contains a recipient's information such as name, gender, age, living arrangements; (2) certification of LTCI benefits and care level; (3) assessment results and care plans; (4) receipt for services rendered on a monthly basis and services provider's reports; (5) contact information of parties responsible for the recipient and service providers; (6) utilization review and monitoring records; and (7) records of the supervision that care managers receive. In case of any changes to the care plan, which can be revised whenever necessary, care managers are required to obtain informed consent from recipients the month before providing the new services.

CARE MANAGER'S BASIC GOALS

Ideally, care managers should focus on beneficiaries' independent living, normalization and dignity, and life-span development.

Independent Living

Assisting and supporting the frail elderly have two purposes, namely, helping recipients to live the best lives of their choice and assisting them to live life to the fullest by providing the appropriate care services.

Everybody has their own goals, thoughts, ideas, needs, demands, wishes, and preferences on how they want to be and live their lives. Having goals in life provides one with a motive to live and a direction in life, and/or makes life worth living. Therefore, care managers should arrange and coordinate care services and providers that help recipients to achieve the best lives possible.

Normalization and Dignity

Regardless of age and degree of disability, normalization aims to build a society where each impaired elderly individual has the right to live as normally and independently as possible, make his/her own choices, and is respected as a human being. Care managers strive to promote normalization by arranging and coordinating care services to eliminate physical and social barriers and by obtaining the full range of care services required by their clients.

Moreover, the nursing care model and practice are required to promote life with dignity even if individuals become comatose. It is therefore necessary for care managers to support their clients by providing not only the medical model of care that focus on symptom relief and illness treatment but also the nursing model of care that focuses on quality of life.

Life-Span Development

People grow, develop, and change throughout their life, and many will experience physical changes as a result of aging. However, care managers believe that aging is not a period of decline; rather, it is a period of maturity and growth. Thus, care managers provide care services with the purpose of helping their clients grow and improve.

PRACTICE OF CARE MANAGEMENT

The practice of care management is presented in the following section.

1st Stage: Application for Long-Term Care Insurance

Mr. *Taro Yamada*, a 75-year-old man who survived from a stroke 2 months ago, was hospitalized and received medical treatments and rehabilitation. Because his condition had stabilized, his attending doctor informed Taro and his wife, *Aiko*, that he was ready to be discharged soon, and suggested that he see a medical social worker. When the couple met with the medical social worker, they were encouraged to apply for LTCI benefits because Taro required assistance moving from the bed to the wheelchair. Both Taro and Aiko agreed and applied for the LTCI certification assessment.

Meanwhile, Aiko visited a community-based care agency called "Care Services" in her neighborhood to discuss alternative care services and signed a usage contract.

2nd Stage: Assessment

After several days, the care manager, *Mrs. Suzuki* of Care Services, visited Taro at the hospital, conducted an assessment, and obtained information on his current health condition, attending physician and nurses, level of care, living environment, relationship with his family, and preferences.

3rd Stage: Care Planning

Mrs. Suzuki then created the 1st draft of Taro's care plan, which indicated the types, frequency, and cost of the services and reflected Taro's needs and preferences, and explained it to both Taro and Aiko.

4th Stage: Care Providers' Conference & Care Plan Development

After Taro was classified into "care-required level 3" immediately before his discharge from the hospital, Mrs. Suzuki held a care providers' conference with the attending physician and care providers in the presence of Taro and Aiko. The care plan was discussed in detail, and the group drew up a final care plan. Figure 10-4 illustrates Taro's weekly schedule/care plan.

5th Stage: Implementation of Care Plan

The hospital bed, accessories/attachments, and wheelchair were delivered to Taro's home upon discharge, and home care, home visit rehabilitation, and day care began several days later.

	Monday	Tuesday	Wednesday	Thursday	Friday	Saturday	Sunday
4:00							
6:00							
8:00	8:00-9:00 Home care	8:00-9:00 Home care		8:00-9:00 Home care	8:00-9:00 Home care		8:00-9:00 Home care
10:00			10:00-16:00 Day care			10:00-16:00 Day care	
12:00							
14:00	14:00-15:00 Home visit rehabilitation			14:00-15:00 Home visit rehabilitation			14:00-15:00 Home visit rehabilitation
16:00							
18:00							
20:00	19:00-20:00 Home care	19:00-20:00 Home care	19:00-20:00 Home care	19:00-20:00 Home care	19:00-20:00 Home care	19:00-20:00 Home care	19:00-20:00 Home care
22:00							
24:00							
2:00							
Other services	Hospital bed, accessories/attachments, wheelchair, and purchase of assistive devices							

Note: Other than a weekly schedule, care managers also create a monthly schedule.

Figure 10-4 Sample of a Weekly Schedule and Care Plan

6th Stage: Monitoring

A week after Taro's discharge, Mrs. Suzuki visited Taro at his home to check on how he was doing and his satisfaction with the services and providers. She also checked with the providers on whether there is any concern that needs to be addressed.

7th Stage: Reassessment and Review of Care Plan

After receiving the same services for 2 months, Taro expressed his desire to increase the number of home care services so that he could bathe at home more frequently. As per his request, the care plan was revised 3 months after his discharge from hospital; the number of home care visits was increased and bathroom modification was scheduled.

SUMMARY

Care management is becoming increasingly important as the LTCI system grows. Care managers work with applicants/recipients, multidisciplinary teams, and care providers, and develop and implement care plans by considering recipients' needs, preferences, and care levels. Although some problems remain in the field of care management (e.g., some geographic areas are underserved by care providers, some applicants/beneficiaries are unable to use some services due to financial difficulties, and care providers' conferences are not always held), it continues to be the main approach to service delivery as long as LTCI exists.

References

Ishiyaku Publishers, Inc. (1998). Summary of All Curriculum for Care Managers [*Kaigo Shien Senmonin Zenka no Matome*]. Tokyo: Ishiyaku Publishers, Inc..

Kaigo Gijyutsu Zensho Henshu Iinkai (1999). Easy-to-Understand Long-Term Care [*Wakariyasui Kaigo*]. Kyoto: Minerva-Shobo.

Kunisada, M., Senba, N., Tokutomi, K., Araki, K., & Maeda, Y. (2002). Care Management and Care Managers [*Kaigo Shien Service to Kaigo Shien Senmonin*]. In Institute of Japan Care Work (Ed.), Introduction to Long-Term Care Insurance [*Kaigo Hoken Nyumonsho*] (pp.137-150). Tokyo: Index Press.

Ministry of Health and Welfare (2000). Basic Textbook for Care Managers [*Kaigo Shienin Kihon Text*]. Tokyo: Chojyu Shakai Kaihatsu Center.

Ministry of Health and Welfare, Minister's Secretariat (1999). Care Management for Disabled Persons [*Shogaisha Care Management*]. Tokyo: Chuohoki Publishing CO., Ltd..

Sawada, N., et.al. (1999). Better-Understanding of the Long-Term Care Insurance System [*Yokuwakaru Kaigo Hoken Seido*]. Tokyo: Ishiyaku Publishers, Inc..

11

Types of Professionals in the Long-Term Care Insurance System and Their Work Settings

In order to facilitate LTCI beneficiaries' access to appropriate care services and provide care services effectively and efficiently, care managers and other health and non-health professionals in hospitals, rehabilitation centers, home- and community-based care agencies and institutional care facilities must be integrated as a team. They must possess the appropriate attitude to help the elderly and their families acquire long-term care.

This chapter describes an interdisciplinary team approach, which is necessary for providing appropriate care services, and the various types of professionals involved in LTCI (Figure 11-1).

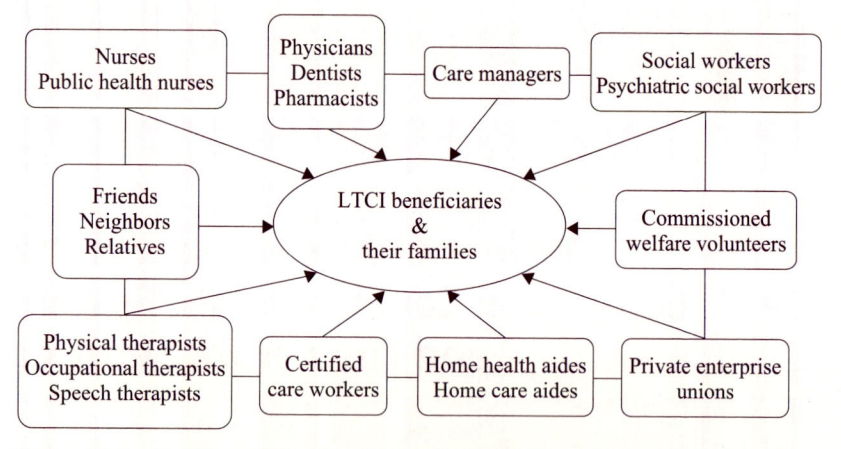

Figure 11-1 Health and Non-Health Professionals Involved in Long-Term Care

SIGNIFICANCE OF AN INTERDISCIPLINARY TEAM APPROACH

An interdisciplinary team (IDT) approach is necessary for providing quality care services. It would be easier to provide team-approach care when individuals in the IDT understand beneficiaries' situations from various professional perspectives. However, various factors such as insufficient communication within the IDT may affect their relationships within the care team and result in failure to provide appropriate care services to LTCI beneficiaries. Each professional should recognize the significance of a team approach (Table 11-1).

Table 11-1 Significance of an Interdisciplinary Team Approach

An interdisciplinary team approach was introduced when it became evident that having only one type of professionals approach and resolve problems in long-term care is insufficient. The advantages of this approach are that
· The most appropriate professional member of the IDT can solve problems efficiently and effectively.
· Each professional can perform his/her responsibilities in his/her specialized area.
· There is an increase in information about or personal understanding of long-term care.
· Team communication is improved.

WHICH PROFESSIONALS WORK IN LONG-TERM CARE SETTINGS?

Professionals who work under the LTCI system usually belong to LTCI certified home-and community-based care agencies or institutional care facilities. Each agency and facility employs various professionals such as care managers and healthcare, nursing care, rehabilitation and social services professionals. These professionals are qualified to work in long-term care settings after passing national exams to earn their credentials, graduating from vocational schools, or completing certification courses.

Care Managers

Whether the LTCI system is helpful for beneficiaries depends on the care managers. As members of IDT, care managers play a central role in arranging and coordinating care services from the beneficiaries' and team members' perspectives, assessing whether care services are provided appropriately, and managing and coordinating team activities (Figure 11-2; see Chapter 10 for more details).

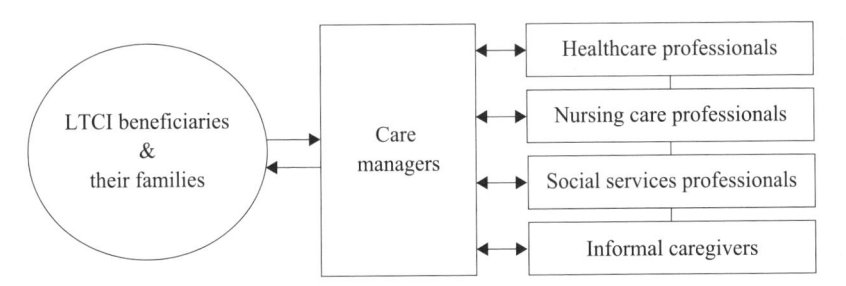

```
                                    ┌──→ Healthcare professionals
LTCI beneficiaries  ──→  Care       ├──→ Nursing care professionals
& their families         managers   ├──→ Social services professionals
                                    └──→ Informal caregivers
```

Figure 11-2 Role of Care Managers in Coordination

Healthcare Professionals

Physicians and Dentists

The Medical Practitioners Law and Dental Practitioners Law prohibit individuals who do not have medical or dental licenses from performing medical and dental care services, procedures, functions or activities, including the administration of medication and injection, monitoring vital signs, and providing electrocardiography and ultrasonography services.

Pharmacists

The role of pharmacists is to accurately prepare and distribute drugs made by manufacturers to patients in accordance with doctors' and dentists' orders, ensure that the medication treatment ordered is appropriate, and provide individualized information on dosage instructions, side effects, and interactions.

How to Become a Physician, Dentist, and Pharmacist

To become a doctor or dentist, one is required to pass a national licensure exam and receive one's license from the Minister of Health, Labour and Welfare (the Minister of HLW). Individuals who have completed 6 years of medical/dental education at a college or university in Japan, completed medical/dental education at a college or university, or have a medical/dental license in a foreign country are eligible for national exams. After passing the national licensure exam, these individuals are required to complete a residency program (2 years for physicians and 1 year for dentists).

Six years of pharmacy education at an undergraduate college is generally the minimum education requirement for the national licensure exam and for becoming a licensed pharmacist.

Nursing Care Professionals

Nurses

Nurses provide nursing care to patients and pregnant women and assist physicians when dealing with patients. Lately, the role of nurses is expanding; nurses traditionally assist patients with physical functions, but their role has expanded to include assistance with patient's psychosocial functions, if ordered by physicians. In addition, nurses closely work with nurse's aides (called "care workers" in Japan) to support elderly in long-term care facilities.

How to Become a Nurse

There are at least two types of nurses: (1) registered nurse and (2) licensed practical nurse. Each type requires different types of nursing licenses and has different education requirements.

Registered nurses: Individuals who wish to be a registered nurse must pass the national licensure exam and receive their license from the Minister of HLW. Persons who have graduated from a high school and: 1) completed 3 years of nursing education at one of the nursing schools accredited by the Minister of Education, Culture, Sports, Science and Technology (the Minister of ECSST); or 2) completed nursing courses offered at a vocational school accredited by the Minister of HLW are eligible for national exams. Recently, the number of nursing college and graduate schools is increasing.

Licensed practical nurses: Individuals who wish to be a licensed practical nurse must pass the prefectural licensure exam administered in all prefectures and obtain their license from the prefectural governor. To be eligible for the prefectural licensure exam, one needs to complete an accredited 2- or 3-year training course after graduating from junior high and/or high school.

All nurses in Japan used to be called Kango-"*FU*" (literally, "female") but after the establishment of the Public Health Nurses, Midwife and Nurses Law, this term was changed to Kango-"*SHI*" (literally, "person") to accommodate the increase in the number of male nurses.

Certified Care Workers

The "certified care worker" (CCW) is a newly established position in long-term care settings. These individuals provide assistance with ADLs and educate family caregivers if necessary. CCWs are also called "care workers," "matrons," or "care staff" in Japan. They work at home care agencies as home-helpers (discussed in the next section), or at long-term care facilities as matrons or nurse's aides.

How to Become a Certified Care Worker

Although there are several ways of becoming a CCW (Figure 11-3), they can be roughly classified into two: (1) complete more than 2 years of a training program offered at a college, university, or vocational school, and receive certification or (2) pass the national certification exam. Lately, the number of 2-year colleges and universities offering care worker curriculums has been increasing.

Those who choose to take the national certification exam instead of going through training programs must have worked as a non-certified matron, care staff, or home-helper for more than 3 years (>1,095 days of employment) and have 540 days of experience in providing direct care.

11 Types of Professionals and Their Work Settings *169*

Figure 11-3 Steps to Becoming a Certified Care Worker

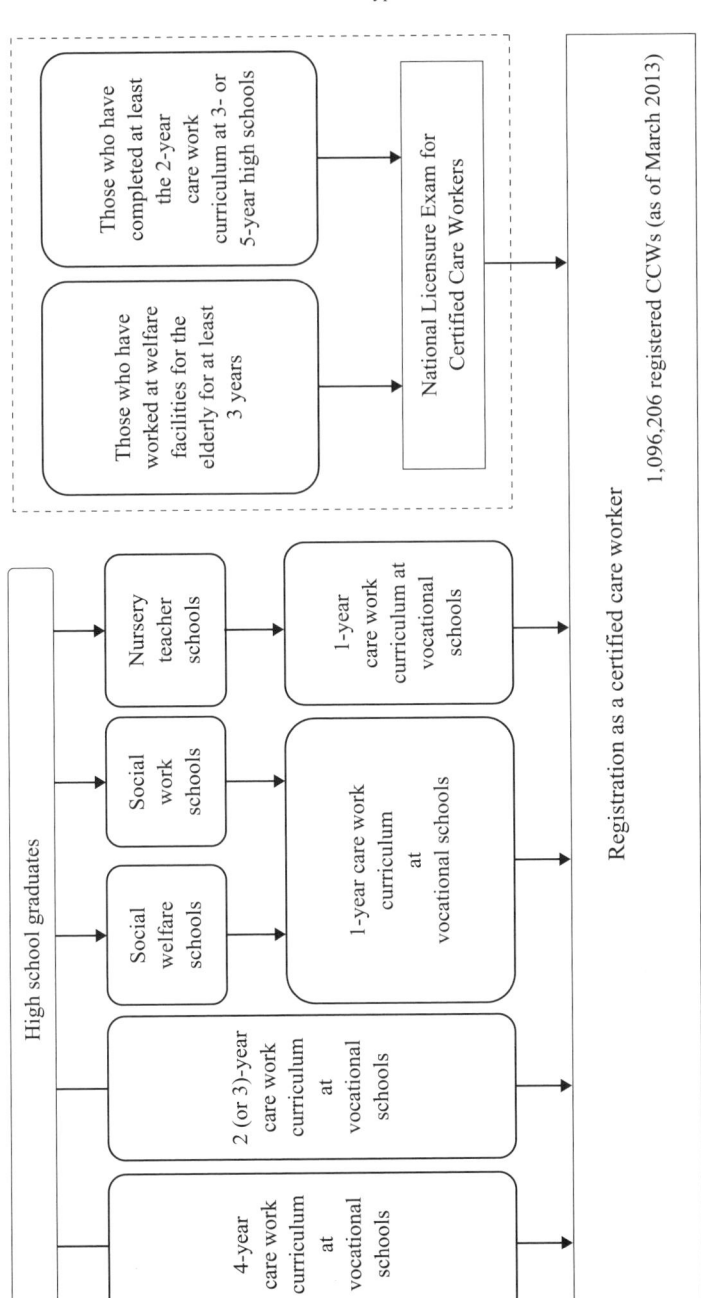

Source: Kasahara, S. (2002) Staffing and Workplaces and Center of Social Welfare Promotion and National Examination (2013) Number of Licensed Registered Social Workers, Care Workers, and Psychiatric Social Workers by Prefecture.

Home Care Aides (Home-Helpers)
Home care aides (also called "home-helpers") visit recipients' homes and provide assistance with both ADLs and IADLs. Home-helpers also educate family caregivers on the use of assistive devices such as wheelchairs and specialty beds. Spiritual support for family caregivers is also provided.

How to Become a Home Care Aide
While CCWs are nationally certified nursing staff, there is no national certification for home-helpers/care aides; prefectural governments and major cities (ordinance-designated cities) usually offer training programs for home-helpers. The length of training programs is divided into 4 levels (1st class certification course: 230 hours; 2nd class certification course: 130 hours; 3rd class certification course: 50 hours; and a continued training program for those who complete 1st class certification training course) depending on what kind of care they will be providing as a home-helper/care aide. Students who take these courses attend lectures on home care nursing and have onsite training by experienced staff to learn the basic knowledge and skills.

As of September 3, 1999, an amendment to training programs for home-helper/care aide states that CCWs who provide home-help activities are deemed to have completed the level 1 training program for home care aides.

Rehabilitation Professionals

Physical Therapists
Physical therapists are those who assist patients in reaching their maximum physical performance and level of physical function by offering physical exercises, electrical stimulation, massages, heat

therapy, hydrotherapy, ice and cold therapy, and ultrasound therapy.

Occupational Therapists
Occupational therapists are those who provide a variety of services including personal activities, productive and vocational activities, expressive and creative activities, recreational activities, and cognitive and educational activities to restore fine motor function in relation to IADLs and to maximize an individual's level of independence.

Speech Therapists
Speech therapists, also called speech language pathologists, are those who provide oral-motor and dysphagia training to restore the central function of speech, speech developmental disorder, speech delay, aphasia, motor speech disorder (cleft palate and dysarthria), and congenital and senile hearing loss.

How to Become a Physical, Occupational, and/or Speech Therapist
Similar to being a doctor or nurse, persons who want to be physical, occupational, and/or speech therapists must pass the national licensure exam and obtain their licenses from the Minister of HLW.

Persons who have graduated from a high school and completed 3 years of education for physical, occupational, and/or speech therapy at one of the rehabilitation schools accredited by the Minister of ECSST or at a vocational school accredited by the Minister of HLW are eligible for national exams.

Social Services Professionals

Certified Social Workers

Certified social workers (CSWs), or simply social workers, are those who are nationally licensed to help patients and their family caregivers with social and emotional issues. Their role is similar to that of care managers. The number of CSWs in Japan is a little under 20,000, which is lower than the number of nurses and CCWs.

Psychiatric social workers are those who are nationally licensed to assist individuals with mental disabilities to restore and/or enhance their capacity for social functioning.

Other than these types of social workers, there are also medical social workers who, in addition to providing assistance with social and emotional issues, assist and counsel patients and their families in promoting social reintegration and obtaining necessary community resources to maintain a safe and independent life after hospital discharge. There is no national license specific to medical social workers—they are usually only required to have a license for a regular social worker.

How to Become a Certified Social Worker

Becoming a CSW requires successful passage of a national licensure exam. There are 11 ways of becoming a CSW that can be grouped into at least 3 categories: (1) complete required social work courses at an undergraduate or graduate school, (2) serve as a public official in the field of social work and counseling for at least 5 years, and (3) graduate from college or university or work at a social services/welfare office for more than 4 years and complete a 1-year training program.

Long-Term Care Counselors

The MHLW started to dispatch so-called "long-term care counselors" to some municipalities from October 2000. These individuals visit the places where LTCI beneficiaries reside once or twice a week, interview them and their families (and facility staff if applicable), and ensure that beneficiaries' and their families' voices/complaints are heard. Under the LTCI system, each prefecture has established a complaints and grievances office within its Prefectural Federation of National Health Insurance Associations. However, because this system is enforced only after a problem occurs, the position of long-term care counselors was created to prevent any problems from occurring—they handle complaints on a daily basis before a problem occurs.

How to Become a Long-Term Care Counselor

Long-term care counselors must complete the courses provided by municipalities, which conduct the model programs, and act as unpaid counselors.

Commissioned Welfare Volunteers

The position of commissioned welfare volunteer was established when the Commissioned Welfare Volunteers Law was implemented in 1943.

These individuals assist residents in their assigned service areas from the residents' perspective. They refer individuals with psychosocial issues to the appropriate resources and visit elderly who are living alone and disabled persons.

As defined in the Commissioned Welfare Volunteers Law Amendments of 2000, this is not a stipend position but a voluntary one. These volunteers are appointed by the Minister of HLW based on recommendations made by each prefectural governor.

How to Become a Commissioned Welfare Volunteer

As noted earlier, the Commissioned Welfare Volunteers Law states that they are volunteers appointed by the Minister of HLW. In order to be a commissioned welfare volunteer, the person must have the right to vote in Japan. In other words, one must be a citizen of Japan. The serving term of each volunteer is 3 years and volunteers are also supposed to serve as commissioned child welfare volunteers as per the Child Welfare Law.

WHO ELSE WORKS IN LONG-TERM CARE SETTINGS?

In addition to these professionals, one should not forget that there are many volunteers and informal caregivers involved in long-term care.

Volunteers

As individuals are changing their perception of welfare problems from an individual problem to a common concern of most citizens, Japanese who had been living a passive lifestyle have begun to look for an active and diversified lifestyle. For many of them, volunteering is a way of changing their lifestyles. Volunteering is not an activity for specific individuals and groups; it is available to anyone who is interested.

Under the LTCI system, there are groups of people who offer day care services, meals-on-wheels, transportation, etc. These individuals are usually community-minded persons who are passionate about giving back to their community and want to help make a difference in an aging society.

Those who want to volunteer are recommended to consult with the Council of Social Welfare, which is a private association that aims to create favorable living environments for the disabled, elderly, and children, and which has established its branches in various locations to encourage people to participate in voluntary activities for their communities.

Informal Caregivers

There are many informal caregivers involved in long-term care and who play a pivotal role in sustaining the LTCI system. These caregivers include family members and other relatives, neighbors, and volunteers such as commissioned welfare volunteers and long-term care counselors.

NEW WORKPLACE OPPORTUNITIES CREATED BY LONG-TERM CARE INSURANCE

Professionals and disciplines who work with or under the LTCI system are usually employed by service providers participating in LTCI. These individuals have had their workplace opportunities expanded with the implementation of LTCI, which allowed private sectors to enter the field of long-term care. Many health and non-health care professionals are now working in not only the conventional medical and social welfare corporations, but also private enterprises, co-operatives (including Japan Agricultural Co-operative and Consumer Co-operative), and non-profit organizations.

This section describes these private corporations and organizations that entered the field of long-term care after the introduction of LTCI.

Private Enterprises

There were some private enterprises that provided so-called "welfare business" or "silver services" even before the introduction of LTCI. "Welfare business" and "silver services" refer to long-term care services and products for the elderly provided by private enterprises. These enterprises provided care services and assistive devices that were not covered by the social security system.

Currently, LTCI-certified enterprises provide home- and community-based care services and sell and/or loan assistive devices to LTCI beneficiaries.

The Elderly Services Providers Association, an association of private enterprises, has determined the standard level of quality services and products and established the so-called "Silver Mark System," in which a special logo was created to indicate whether the services or products met their quality standard.

Japan Agricultural Co-operative and Consumer Co-operative

Agricultural Co-operative
JAs are cooperatives where farmers pool their resources and deliver some health/medical/social benefits to its members and beneficiaries. JAs offer mutual-aids, training programs for home-helpers, and LTCI-certified services.

Consumer Co-operative
This is a cooperative that is well known for providing high quality and safe/secure food and for providing mutual aids to its members. As a LTCI-certificated care provider, its members with home-helper certification provide some home care services to the elderly.

Non-Profit Organizations

When the Non-Profit Organizations Law was founded in 1998 to encourage non-profit organizations to join the field of long-term care, non-profit organizations became eligible to provide LTCI services. Some of them provide long-term care services themselves while others offer participatory services (also called participatory home care services) where elderly and their families provide care services to people in their communities. These organizations usually assess the needs and concerns of service recipients from the recipients' perspective and try to solve problems that might be beyond the scope of the government's legitimate powers.

SUMMARY

Responsibility for the long-term care of elderly people was formerly taken care of by the family. However, it is now is taken care of by society, namely LTCI. LTCI services are provided by multidisciplinary staff, including physicians, nurses, social workers, and rehabilitation personnel, as well as non-health care professionals such as commissioned welfare volunteers. With the introduction of LTCI, there are growing workplace and volunteer opportunities in both the public and private sectors. In order to deliver the full range of services and continuum of care needed by the elderly, all professionals and disciplines must work as a team.

References

Akiyama, T. (1995). Management Theory of Social Welfare Facilities [*Shakai Fukushi Shisetsu Unei Ron*]. Tokyo: Japan National Council of Social Welfare.

Center of Social Welfare Promotion and National Examination (2013). Number of Licensed Registered Social Workers, Care Workers, and Psychiatric Social Workers by Prefecture [*Shakai Fukushi-shi, Kaigo Fukushi-shi, Seishin Hoken Fukushi-shi no Todofuken betsu Torokusha Su*]. (http://www.sssc.or.jp/touroku/pdf/pdf_t04.pdf, accessed September 13, 2013).

Kasahara, S. (2002). Staffing and Workplaces [*Kaigo Hoken ni Kankeisuru Shokushu to Shokuba*]. In Institute of Japan Care Work (Ed.), Introduction to Long-Term Care Insurance [*Kaigo Hoken Nyumonsho*] (pp.169-186). Tokyo: Index Press.

Kawamura, T. (1991). Human Resources for Healthcare and Welfare [*Iryo Fukushi no Man Power*]. Tokyo: Keisou Shobo.

Matsutani, Y., et al. (2000). Special Edition: Qualifications and Requirements for National Certification [*Tokushu: Shikaku no Yoken to Kokka-Shikaku*]. Healthcare, 42 (9), 676-681, 2000.

Okamoto, T. (1995). A Review of Social Welfare Support Techniques [*Shakai Fukushi Enjo Gijyutsu Soron*]. Tokyo: Kawashima Shoten.

Yamagata, Y., et al. (1996). Long-Term Care Work [*Kaigo no Shigoto*]. Osaka: Tokishobo.

12

Lessons from European Countries, Australia and the United States

The United Nations defines a society with more than 7% of elderly (aged 65 and over) in its population as an "aging society," a society with more than 14% of elderly citizens as an "aged society," and that with more than 21% as a "hyper-" or "super-aged society." Many developed countries have crossed the threshold into aging and aged societies. The number and proportion of elderly people have been increasing in many countries. At the same time, the number of elderly individuals who require long-term care is rising.

An increase in the elderly population raises some national issues, such as a decrease in the work force and increase in the costs of pension benefits and medical care. A common issue faced by many countries is the issue of provision of care for the elderly. Several countries have developed long-term care policies and programs to overcome the issues related to elderly care. Some of these programs and policies inspired the national government of Japan to develop its plan for LTCI.

This chapter will briefly address lessons learnt from long-term-care-related programs and policies in Denmark, Australia, the United

States of America, United Kingdom, and Germany that have influenced the framework and structure of LTCI in Japan. Table 12-1 outlines the trends in the long-term care policies and programs in the above-mentioned countries in contrast to Japan.

Table 12-1 Trends in European Countries, Australia and the United States, and Japan

	European countries, Australia and the United States	Japan
1980s	**Denmark** 1982: Reformation of the three basic principles of health, medical, and welfare services for elderly **Australia** 1985: Aged Care Reform Strategy Home and Community Care Act (the HACC Act)	1982: Health and Medical Care Services Law for the Elderly 1987: Social Workers and Care Workers Law 1989: Gold Plan
1990s	**United States of America** 1990: Implementation of the Omnibus Budget Reconciliation Act of 1987 (OBRA'87) & Nursing Home Reform Act **United Kingdom** 1993: Community Care Reforms Act **Germany** 1994: Long-Term Care Insurance Act	1990: Revision of eight laws on welfare 1993: Scheme for elderly health and welfare services 1994: New Gold Plan 1997: Long-Term Care Insurance Law 1999: Gold Plan 21
2000s		2000: Establishment of the long-term care insurance system 2005: Long-Term Care Insurance Law Amendments 2008: Medical insurance for the elderly over 75 years of age

Denmark

Denmark became an aged society when its elderly population reached 15% in 1996. A reason for Denmark becoming an aged society faster than other developed countries is that it did not suffer much damage in the two world wars. Hence, it has relatively few war-affected populations.

However, this led to more elderly people seeking health and medical care, which in turn increased the national health expenditure and placed the government under pressure to construct nursing homes for the elderly to decrease the cost for health and medical care.

Currently, Denmark provides more home- and community-based care services and is attempting to reduce the number of elderly residents in care facilities by limiting the construction of new nursing homes and converting existing nursing homes to single-occupancy rooms (Figure 12-1). This transformation from institutional care to individualized home- and community-based services was conducted to not only reduce health expenditure but also provide elderly individuals with opportunities to live

Figure 12-1 Private Room of a Home for the Aged in Denmark

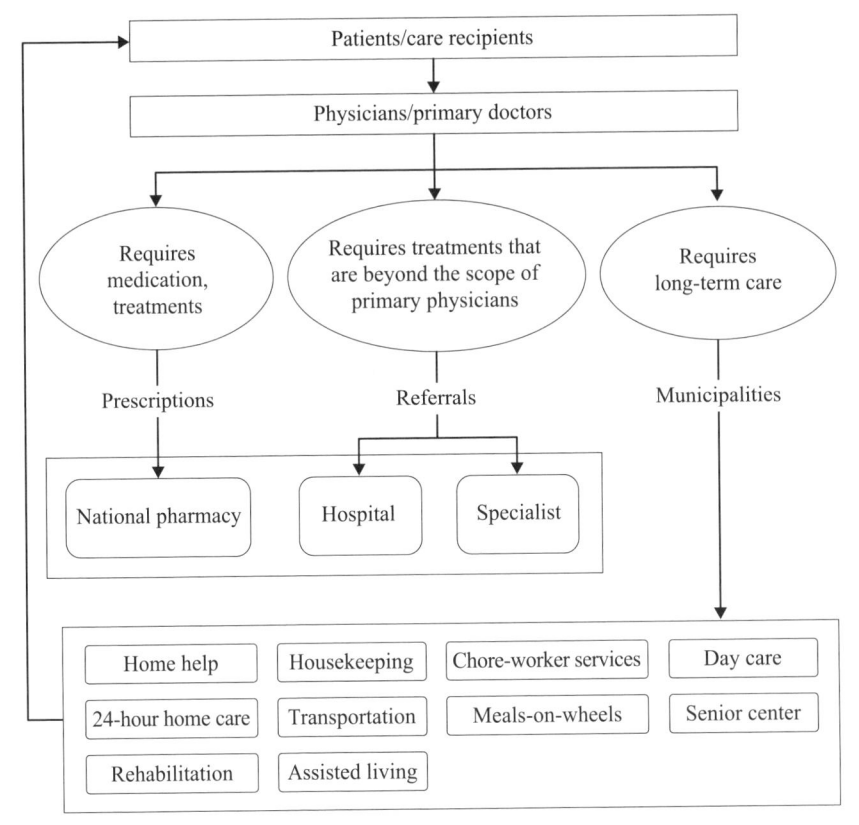

12 Lessons from European Countries, Australia and the United States 181

Figure 12-2 Medical and Long-Term Care System in Denmark

dignified lives in the community. Figure 12-2 illustrates the medical and long-term care system in Denmark.

Reformation of Three Basic Principles

The significance of the Danish system is that, in 1982, the three basic principles of health, medical, and welfare services (1. principle of consistency in human life, 2. utilization of remaining functions, and 3. respect for self-determination) for the elderly were reformed.

These three principles served as the starting point of the LTCI system of Japan. The MHW Study Group that was planning long-term care systems for elderly care reported that a self-determination system should be guaranteed for the elderly as they have a right to choose. Therefore, LTCI of Japan transformed its conventional allocation system to the free-choice system.

Australia

Similar to Denmark, Australia has also transitioned from nursing facility care to home- and community-based care by enacting the Home and Community Care Act (the HACC Act) and creating the Home and Community Care Program (HACC), a joint Australian government and state/territory government funded program for elderly people, in 1985. In the same year, aged care assessment teams (ACATs) were introduced. ACATs are groups of health professionals who provide multidisciplinary assessments with a nationwide unified standard to determine what kind of services and level of care will best meet the needs of the elderly. There are 2 levels of care: (1) high-level care that involves 24-hour care and (2) low-level care that focuses on personal care services. Based on the level of care, ACATS will provide the most suitable services to the elderly in addition to offering information and advice about their choice of care services.

ACAT assessments and approvals are necessary before those people who are no longer able to care for themselves or be cared for by family can have an Australian government subsidy for facility care or some type of home- or community-based care service (Figure 12-3). Care levels are evaluated and classified into 8 categories through the resident mix in terms of the Resident Classification Scale.

The government of Japan adopted this Australian method of classification of beneficiaries and developed its own eligibility and qualification determination system for LTCI benefits.

When elderly people in Australia choose to have home care services,

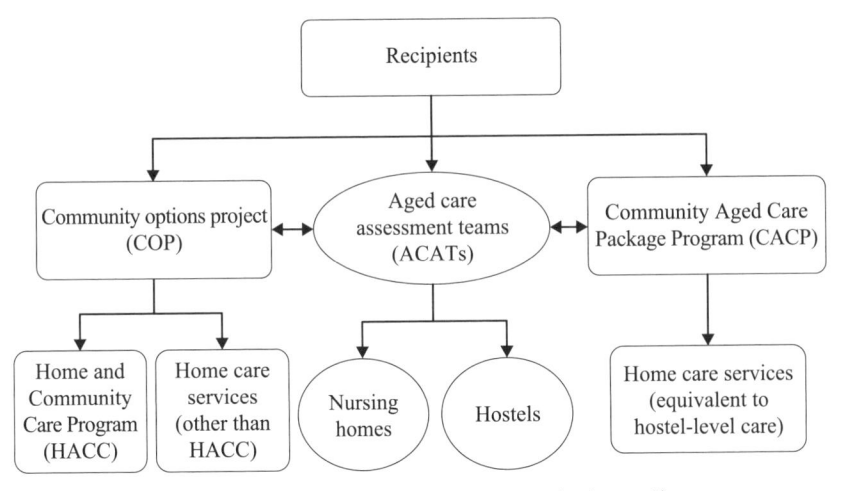

```
                    ┌─────────────┐
                    │ Recipients  │
                    └─────────────┘
                           │
    ┌──────────────────────┼──────────────────────┐
    ▼                      ▼                      ▼
┌──────────────┐   ┌──────────────┐   ┌──────────────────┐
│Community     │   │Aged care     │   │Community Aged Care│
│options project│◄─►│assessment    │◄─►│Package Program   │
│(COP)         │   │teams (ACATs) │   │(CACP)            │
└──────────────┘   └──────────────┘   └──────────────────┘
    │                │    │    │              │
    ▼                ▼    ▼    ▼              ▼
┌────────┐┌────────┐┌──────┐┌──────┐┌──────────────────┐
│Home and││Home    ││Nursing││Hostels││Home care services│
│Community││care   ││homes ││      ││(equivalent to    │
│Care Prog││services││      ││      ││hostel-level care)│
│(HACC)  ││(other  ││      ││      ││                  │
│        ││than    ││      ││      ││                  │
│        ││HACC)   ││      ││      ││                  │
└────────┘└────────┘└──────┘└──────┘└──────────────────┘
```

Figure 12-3 Long-Term Care System in Australia

the community options program (COP) analyzes the services that can be offered from multiple organizations and care providers, and at the same time, a necessary care plan is designed to provide the most suitable long-term care by considering the relevancy of the contents of long-term care. Additionally, a Community Aged Care Package (CACPs or CCPs), a package that offers a home- and community-based alternative, is also available to frail elderly people who are highly dependent on their home care service.

The United States of America

Caring for elderly people in the United States is covered by Medicare, Medicaid, private insurance, and by the elderly themselves (out-of-pocket). Medicare is a federally administered and funded social insurance program that covers people with acute conditions, who had been hospitalized for more than 3 consecutive days and are receiving rehabilitation at skilled nursing facilities (Figure 12-4) for up to 100 days of stay at a skilled nursing facility in a benefit period. Medicaid is a means-tested federal program

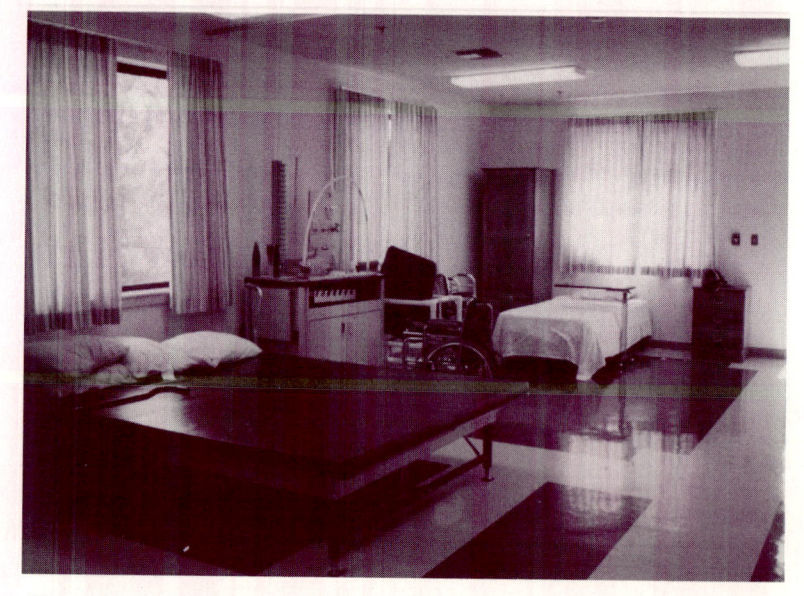

Figure 12-4   Rehabilitation Room at a Nursing Home in the United States

administered at the state level that provides health care for low-income individuals and pays for nursing home care when these individuals' incomes reach the necessary level to qualify for Medicaid benefits.

The fees for Medicare nursing homes residents are determined by assessing nursing home residents' physical, psychological, and social status with a Minimum Data Set (MDS) and by categorizing them into one of 44 patient categories called Resource Utilization Groups (RUGs). Each category has a corresponding per diem reimbursement rate, which is used to calculate the payments that nursing homes receive for services rendered to Medicare nursing home residents.

In the 1970s and 1980s, nursing homes in the United States were criticized for providing poor care to residents and the federal government was struggling to create new regulations for nursing homes to provide appropriate care. In 1987, congress passed a nursing home reform provision in the Omnibus Budget Reconciliation Act of 1987 (OBRA '87), which was enacted in 1990 to protect the rights of residents in nursing homes (which are equivalent to a mixture of welfare facilities and health facilities for the elderly in Japan).

OBRA '87 introduced the concept of care planning and mandated all Medicare- and Medicaid-certified nursing homes to develop care plans based on the MDS assessment results and Resident Assessment Protocols (RAPs). The creation of care plans and care planning involve 4 stages: assessment, planning of care, implementation, and reassessment/ evaluation.

Assessment: With the OBRA '87, which aimed to improve the quality of care in nursing homes, nursing homes assess all residents' physical, mental, and social conditions using MDS, a standardized comprehensive assessment with approximately 350 items, and RAPs upon admission, quarterly, yearly, and whenever there is a significant change in a resident's condition to determine their care problems, which will be addressed in individualized care plans.

Planning of Care: Based on the results of MDS, an interdisciplinary team consisting of nurses, nurse's aides, social services designees, activity staff, physical therapists, occupational therapists, and/or dietitians, is required to discuss the goals and desired outcomes of residents and create individualized care plans to improve any physical, mental, or social problems or needs. Nursing home residents have the right to participate in care planning and the right to refuse care/treatments/intervention actions.

Implementation: Nursing home staff members and other relevant professionals provide care/treatments/intervention actions that were developed in previous stage.

Reassessment: Reassess residents with MDS to determine whether the goals, desired outcomes, care, treatments, and intervention actions that had been provided are appropriate and adequate, and change the plan if necessary.

These procedures play an important role in improving the quality of nursing home care in the United States. It has been reported that the inappropriate use of physical and chemical restrains has decreased, as well as the number of incidents of abuse and neglect toward nursing home residents.

These procedures of care management, as mentioned in Chapter 10, were introduced in Japan for developing care plans and arranging and coordinating various care services for the frail elderly to meet their needs and maintain their dignified independent living for as long as possible.

The United Kingdom

In the United Kingdom, with the Community Care Reforms Act under the Thatcher Government, the care management system was introduced in 1993 after a series of case management trials were conducted in the 1980s and 1990s. The characteristic feature of the United Kingdom's care management system is that the organizations that are responsible for assessing and making decisions on care services are separated from the organizations that provide the services. That is, local governments are responsible for care management including assessing the needs and creating care plans for the elderly and coordinating care services while the care services are offered directly by private providers that have contracts with the local governments.

In Japan, on the other hand, care services are provided by private providers who do not have contracts with municipalities. Hence, it was difficult for the government of Japan to adopt the United Kingdom's public long-term care system. It was therefore decided that assessment for LTCI certification would be conducted by the Long-Term Care Certification Committee (part of local municipal governments) and that care management would be carried out by private parties such as home care agencies in Japan.

Germany

Almost 30 years after the world's first LTCI was established in the Netherlands in 1968, Germany introduced the LTCI system as the 5th domestic social insurance in 1994 because there was no public system that provided long-term care services. Figure 12-5 illustrates an overview of the German LTCI system.

The LTCI Act was established to provide long-term care services to all individuals who require long-term care regardless of age. It requires all individuals to pay insurance premiums. The rate of the LTCI premium was agreed to be 1.7% of an individual's gross income and pensions up to an income ceiling of 3,562.50 euros/month (as of 2006) and was raised to 1.95% in July 2008. Fifty percent of the insurance premium is borne by employers for their employees. Thus, employees bear 0.975% of their monthly income for the insurance premium.

In addition, childless people aged 23 and older must pay an

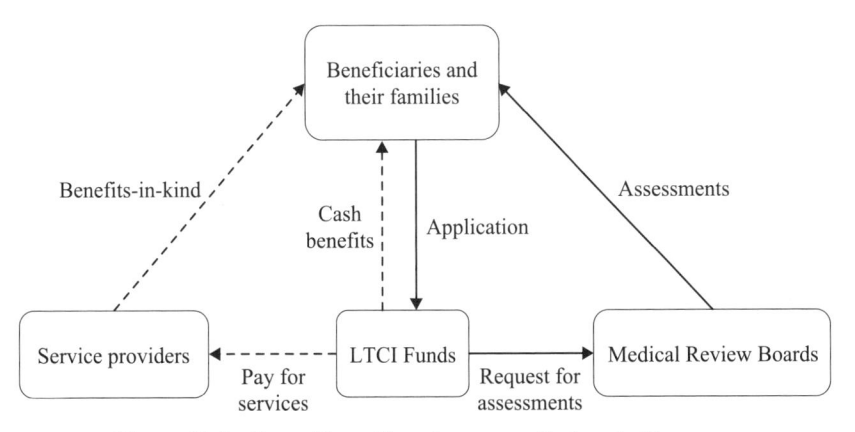

Figure 12-5 Long-Term Care Insurance System in Germany

additional contribution rate of 0.25% after 2004, i.e., the premium rate for people without children is 2.2% of their monthly incomes.

Eligibility for LTCI in Germany is "independent of the age of the dependent person" (p.54)[1]; regardless of the age or cause, once person becomes in need of long-term care for a minimum of 6 months or more, he/she is eligible for LTCI. Since the LTCI system is designed for all people regardless of age and cause in Germany, all physical and intellectual impairments and child welfare facilities are subject to LTCI. The LTCI Funds, which collect long-term care insurance premiums, are considered as health insurance funds according to German regulations.

Beneficiaries can receive LTCI benefits when they require assistance in carrying out at least two ADLs and one IADL for at least 6 months. Staff members of the Medical Review Board, (Medizinischer Dienst der Krankenversicherung), such as physicians, nurses, and nursing-related professionals, are assigned to conduct medical assessments and evaluate whether beneficiaries are entitled to LTCI benefits and classify them into one of 3 levels; "level I" is equivalent to Japan's 4th or 5th level of required care.

German LTCI benefits include home care, day care, night care, and institutional care (Figure 12-6). Once they become eligible, beneficiaries and their families are able to choose between different benefits and services and pay a flat rate for these services. Those who utilize home care services can have in-kind benefits or cash benefits, or both, up to the ceiling for each care level. The purpose for providing cash benefits is to appreciate family caregivers for taking care of their loved ones at home and to relieve some of their caregiving burden. Over 70% of beneficiaries and their families choose to receive cash benefits even though the total amount of benefits in kind is higher than the benefits in cash and a combination of the two benefits (in-kind and cash benefits).

In addition, if family caregivers provide 14 hours of care per week, LTCI will cover their social security premiums and respite care when they

Figure 12-6 Private Room of a Care Home in Germany

take a vacation to make caregiving for family members more attractive.

The LTCI system in Japan was created in reference to the LTCI system in Germany. The objective of LTCI of Japan is similar to that of Germany, which is to reduce the workload on family caregivers. The government of Japan adopted Germany's benefits eligibility determination/ assessment process as well as eligibility criteria and care levels. Like in Germany, the government of Japan included physicians as part of the LTCI system by requiring them to submit their reports on the beneficiaries' physical and mental states at the time of eligibility assessment.

SUMMARY

It is reasonable to question why policies and programs related to the elderly in some European countries, Australia and the United States of America were discussed in this book. The reason is that many of these policies and programs influenced the framework and structure of LTCI of Japan; Japan learned from Denmark to transform the conventional allocation system to the free-choice system; Australia provided Japan with an idea of how to determine eligibility for LTCI beneficiaries; the United States introduced the concept of care management; Japan got the idea of having both public and private sectors involved in the field of long-term care from the United Kingdom; and Germany, importantly, made Japan realize the need for the LTCI system. Because of the lessons learned from these policies and programs related to the elderly in the above mentioned countries, Japan was able to develop LTCI and deliver care for its elderly citizens.

References

Adachi, M. (1998). The Long-Term Care Systems in Each Country [*Kakkoku no Kaigo Hosho*]. Kyoto: Houritsu Bunka Sha.

Campbell, J. C., Ikegami, N. & Gibson, M. J. (2010). Lessons from Public Long-Term Care Insurance In Germany and Japan. Health Affairs, 29(1), 87-95.

Inazu, T., Sumii, H., & Oba, M. (2002). The Long-Term Care System in the World [*Sekai no Kaigo Hosho towa*]. In Institute of Japan Care Work (Ed.), Introduction to Long-Term Care Insurance [*Kaigo Hoken Nyumonsho*] (pp.243-262). Tokyo: Index Press.

Nakamura, Y. & Ichibangase, Y. (2000). Social Welfare in the World [*Sekai no Shakai Fukushi*]. Tokyo: Junposha.

OECD (2006). Long-term Care for Older People. OECD.

Rothgang, H. & Igl, G. (2007). Long-Term Care In Germany. The Japanese Journal of Social Security Policy, 6(1), 54-84. (http://www.ipss.go.jp/webj-ad/WebJournal.files/ SocialSecurity/2007/Spring/Rothgang%20&%20Igl%20final.pdf, accessed June 13, 2013).

Sakai, S. (1998). World's Social Welfare and Japan's Long-Term Care Insurance [*Sekai no Shakai Fukushi to Nihon no Kaigo Hoken*]. Tokyo: Akashi Shoten.

Shibata, Y. (1996). Social Security in the World [*Sekai no Shakai Hosho*]. Tokyo: Shin Nihon Shuppansha.

Stuart, M. & Weinrich, M (2001). Home- and Community-Based Long-Term Care: Lessons from Denmark. The Gerontologist, 41(4), 474-480.

Sumii, H. (2002). The Start of Long-Term Care Insurance [*Kaigo Hoken no Start*]. In Institute of Japan Care Work (Ed.), Introduction to Long-Term Care Insurance [*Kaigo Hoken Nyumonsho*] (pp.1-22). Tokyo: Index Press.

Sumii, H. (2004). Social Security from Managed Care to Long-Term Care and NPOs in the USA. Okayama: University Education Press.

Sumii, H., et al. (2008). Introduction to Long-Term Care Insurance in Japan - To Support "Kaigo" Security. International Journal of Welfare for the Aged, 19, 17-39.

13

Revisions to the Long-Term Care Insurance System

The LTCI system implemented in April 2000 has become very popular with the public, as its services are widely utilized and it has been established as a pillar of the social security system that supports senior citizens' lives. The MHLW reviews LTCI regularly: every 5 years for the LTCI system itself and every 3 years for a wide range of finance-related matters such as contribution rates and fee schedules. There were several reviews after implementation and so far, the system has undergone 3 major reviews: in 2005, in 2008, and in 2011. These reviews revealed that the LTCI system has some issues in terms of continuity, equality, and quality assurance of care. Accordingly, the national government has made some major revisions to the system, especially after the first review in 2005. The revisions include the following 5 changes:

1) Introduction of the preventative care services package;
2) Introduction of new classification criteria;
3) Levy of cost of room and board;
4) Establishment of community-focused services—small-scale multi-purpose care centers;

5) Establishment of comprehensive community support centers; and 6) Introduction of a public reporting system of care providers' quality of care.

This chapter explains the background of and attempts to provide an understanding of the revisions to the LTCI system, followed by the current status of the system.

BACKGROUND

Five years after LTCI was implemented, the MHLW (2006) found that the number of LTCI recipients had significantly increased (from 1.49 million in 2000 to 3.29 million; 121%) in 2005 (Figure 13-1), and that there was a rapid increase in total costs of the LTCI system (from JPY 3.6 trillion in 2000 to JPY 6.4 trillion in 2005; Figure 13-2). Moreover, it is well expected that by 2015, the number and proportion of people aged 65 and older in Japan will dramatically increase when baby boomers join the ranks of the elderly, and by 2025, it is expected that the number of elderly people aged 75

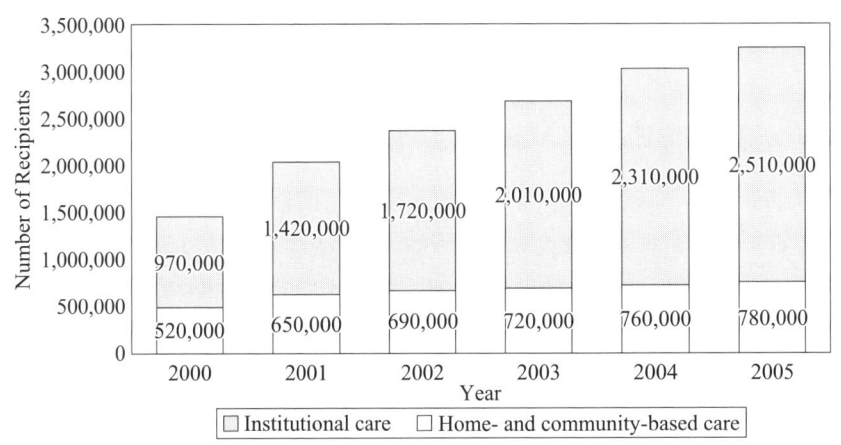

Source: Ministry of Health, Labour and Welfare (2011) White Paper on the Labour Economy 2011.

Figure 13-1 Number of Recipients: 2000-2005

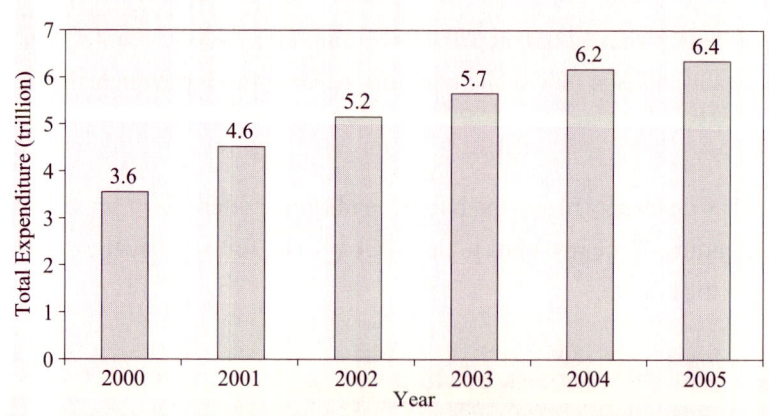

Source: Ministry of Health, Labour and Welfare (2011) White Paper on the Labour Economy 2011.

Figure 13-2   Total Expenditure: 2000-2005

or older would be 35 million. In addition, since the establishment of LTCI, it was revealed that many elderly people are socially isolated, housebound, and suffer from depression, and that more elderly people are diagnosed with dementia.

In response to these circumstances and to contain costs, the national government proposed and approved an amendment to the LTCI Law in June 2005 and implemented it in April 2006.

INTRODUCTION OF THE PREVENTATIVE CARE SERVICES PACKAGE

As stated previously in this part, the number of LTCI recipients has remarkably increased. The reasons for the rapid increase may include (1) a decline in the ability of family members to take care of their frail parents or grandparents due to a growing number of nuclear family households and of single-person households, (2) excessive marketing of the governments and long-term care industry, (3) increased awareness of government support for caregiving, (4) a decreased sense of guilt in some people because of being taken care of by society, and (5) the revision of the computer program used for the initial classification of LTCI applicants in April 2003.

The bulk of the increase was in the levels of assistance-required and 1st degree care-required; while the number of those certified as 2nd and 3rd degree care-required increased by 1.5 times, the number of those certified as assistance-required and 1st degree care-required increased by more than twofold.

Moreover, 48.9% of assistance-required recipients were reported to be at risk for inactivity (disuse syndrome), falling, fractures, and joint pain, and show reduced physical function even though they had been using care services. Hence, there is a need to review the content and types of care services appropriate for the 2 lowest eligibility levels.

During first 5 years of LTCI, the cost for home- and community-based care services increased rapidly from 32% to 46% (May 2001 to Oct 2005), while that of institutional care diminished successively from 65% to 50% (May 2001 to Oct 2005). Therefore, it was argued that the cost for home care services needs to be somehow controlled and contained.

Thus, the national government proposed and approved a new "preventative" care services package that delivers physical exercise programs, oral health services, nutritional counseling, depression prevention/support programs, dementia prevention/support programs, and social isolation prevention programs to elderly people who are at risk of being frail and receiving long-term care in the near future.

INTRODUCTION OF NEW CLASSIFICATION CRITERIA

At the same time, the classification criteria for LTCI certification were revised by adding the 2nd degree of assistance-required. In other words, as of 2005, there are 7 levels of care instead of 6, and some individuals who were classified as 1st degree care-required were reclassified as assistance-required level 2 (Figure 13-3). The preventative care services are available only for individuals certified as assistance-required levels 1 and 2 through

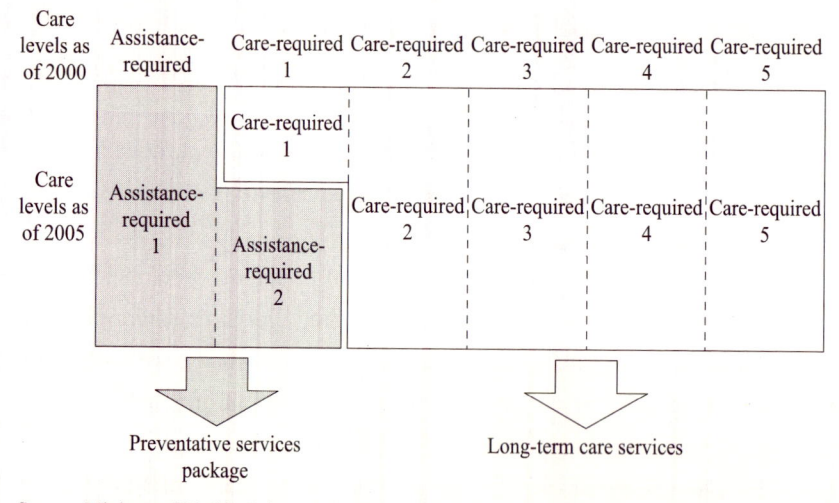

Care levels as of 2000	Assistance-required	Care-required 1	Care-required 2	Care-required 3	Care-required 4	Care-required 5
Care levels as of 2005	Assistance-required 1 / Assistance-required 2	Care-required 1	Care-required 2	Care-required 3	Care-required 4	Care-required 5

Preventative services package ⇩   Long-term care services ⇩

Source: Ministry of Health, Labour and Welfare (2006) Summary of the Long-Term Care Insurance System Revisions.

Figure 13-3   New Classification of Care Levels

Table 13-1   Budget Ceiling for Home- and Community-Based Services: 2000 and 2006

Level of care	Budget ceiling per month (JPY)	
	2000	2006
Assistance-required level 1	61,500	4,970
Assistance-required level 2	N/A	10,400
Care-required level 1	165,800	
Care-required level 2	194,800	
Care-required level 3	267,500	
Care-required level 4	306,000	
Care-required level 5	358,300	

the new classification system while long-term care services are provided in the same manner as before for people certified as care-required.

Accordingly, the budget ceilings of care levels for home- and community-based care services were revised (Table 13-1)—there was a 20% reduction for 1st degree assistance-required and 40% reduction for 2nd degree assistance-required.

LEVY OF COST OF ROOM AND BOARD

In an effort to contain costs and maintain equality between recipients who receive home- and community-based services and institutional care, starting from October 2005, the national government also proposed to levy the costs on room and board, and utilities such as water, gas, and electricity for long-term care facility residents (approximately JPY 40,000 per month on average), in addition to the cost for facility stock items and beauty shop services, since home- and community-based care recipients are responsible for taking care of their own homes and their utility bills while institutional care residents had no need to do so (Figure 13-4). The extra charge for

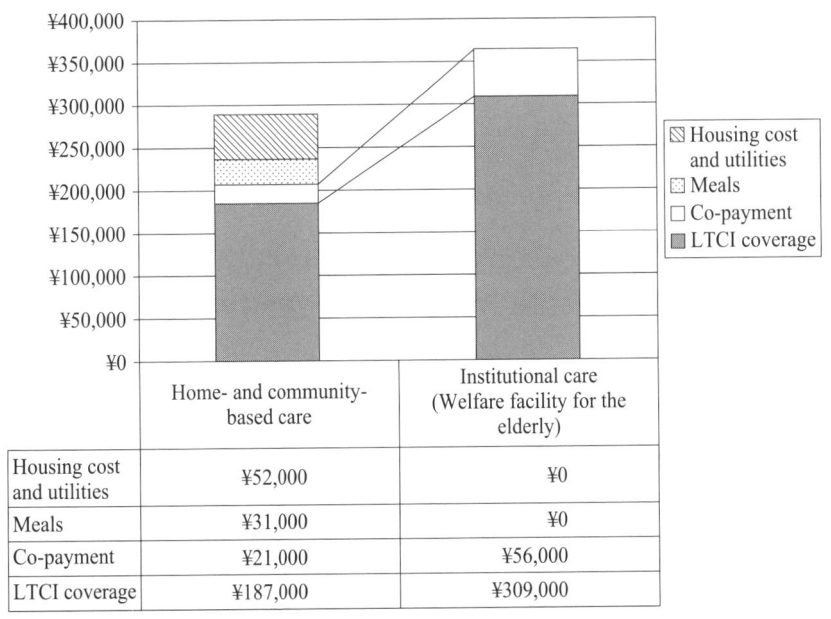

	Home- and community-based care	Institutional care (Welfare facility for the elderly)
Housing cost and utilities	¥52,000	¥0
Meals	¥31,000	¥0
Co-payment	¥21,000	¥56,000
LTCI coverage	¥187,000	¥309,000

Source: Ministry of Health, Labour and Welfare (2006) Summary of the Long-Term Care Insurance System Revisions.

Figure 13-4 Cost of Living at Home and in Institutional Settings per Month[1]

residents in single-room accommodations is higher than that in semi-private and multiple-resident rooms, and is somewhat cheaper for residents with low incomes. Recipients admitted to long-term care facilities for short-stay respite care will be charged with room and board, facility stock items, and beauty shop services.

ESTABLISHMENT OF COMMUNITY-FOCUSED SERVICES: SMALL-SCALE MULTI-PURPOSE CARE CENTERS

To improve the delivery of the continuum of care, the national government decided to provide a "small-scale multi-purpose care center" in each school district-sized area of a municipality as a community-focused service that provides an array of services to meet the needs of elderly in the community, such as meals, activities, bathing services, adult day care, home care, and institutional care for up to 25 elderly individuals who live at home. This is believed to distribute the continuum of care, enable elderly people to stay at home, and delay or avoid institutionalization, because most of the care services are conveniently provided in one location.

ESTABLISHMENT OF COMPREHENSIVE COMMUNITY SUPPORT CENTERS

Similar to the purpose of establishing small-scale multi-purpose care centers, comprehensive community support centers were established in each municipality to offer the continuum of care. These centers are responsible for coordinating various resources, such as health and medical care professionals and social welfare programs to ensure that appropriate services are provided to elderly individuals.

Each center employs care managers, public health nurses, and care workers with knowledge and skills in arranging and providing care for the elderly population within assigned areas. These individuals develop care plans for preventative care services packages (for the 1st and 2nd assistance-required levels), establish networks to link elderly people and the community, provide information and referrals, education and training to the elderly and caregivers, and protect the rights of the elderly in the community. They also apply for LTCI certification on behalf of the applicants.

INTRODUCTION OF THE PUBLIC REPORTING SYSTEM OF CARE PROVIDERS' CARE QUALITY

During the review and discussion for revisions of the LTCI system, the Elderly Care Study Group of the MHLW pointed out that ensuring and improving the quality of long-term care services is one of the most important issues in Japan. In response to that, in April 2006, the national government launched a mandatory public reporting system that contains information about LTCI-certified home- and community-based care providers and long-term care facilities in Japan, hoping that the system will encourage consumers to choose high-quality providers who will in turn improve the quality of care.

This reporting system requires all LTCI-certified care providers to submit their basic information such as contact information, ownership, staffing levels, and resident room size. It also requires assessors of prefecture-appointed public reporting centers to conduct an onsite evaluation and interview service providers to determine whether they have policies and procedure manuals for preventing abuse and neglect, pressure ulcers and wound care, complaints and grievances, and whether they have in-service training for staff on dementia and wound care. In other words, the system focuses on structure and process, not outcome.

As of April 2006, the system mandated all LTCI-certified care providers to pay administrative fees for releasing their information on the Internet. Fees vary from region to region, ranging from JPY 36,633 (Chiba prefecture) to JPY 60,000 (Shimane prefecture).

OTHER REVISIONS

There are a few more revisions made to the LTCI system. For example, being influenced by the "trinity reform," as shown in Figure 13-5, prefectural governments now have to contribute 17.5%, instead of 12.5%, and the national government contributes 20%, instead of 25%, of the total LTCI cost for institutional care. Moreover, calculation formulas for LTCI premium rates were also altered by adding a premium category and changing eligibility criteria (Table 13-2).

Other 2005 revisions include:
1) The requirement that LTCI-certified care providers renew their certification every 6 years;
2) The requirement that care managers renew their certification every 5 years by taking training courses;
3) A revision of certification assessment items—the number of

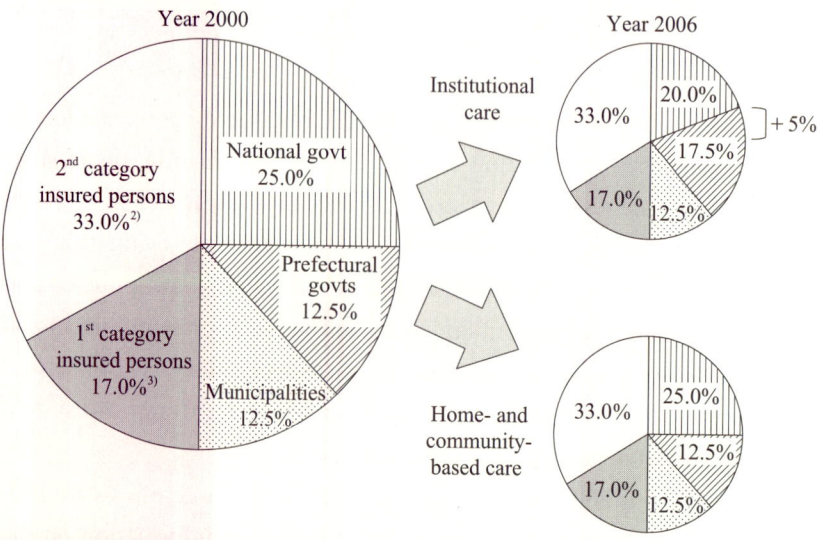

Source: Ministry of Health, Labour and Welfare (2006) Summary of the Long-Term Care Insurance System Revisions.

Figure 13-5 Contribution Rates for Long-Term Care Insurance: 2000 and 2006

Table 13-2 Calculation Formulas for Premium Rates as of 2006

Categories	Eligibility	Premium rates
1st premium category	LTCI beneficiary who receives public assistance and/or old-age pension.	Base amount×0.5
2nd premium category	All members of the household are exempt from municipal resident taxes and the LTCI beneficiary himself/herself has old-age pension of less than JPY 800,000.	Base amount×0.5
3rd premium category	All members of the household are exempt from municipal resident taxes and the LTCI beneficiary himself/herself has old-age pension of more than JPY 800,000.	Base amount×0.75
4th premium category	The LTCI beneficiary himself/herself is exempt from municipal resident taxes (some members of his/her household pay resident taxes).	Base amount×1.0
5th premium category	Municipal resident taxpayer whose income is less than JPY 1.9 million.	Base amount×1.25
6th premium category	Municipal resident taxpayer whose income is more than JPY 1.9 million.	Base amount×1.5

assessment items was decreased to 82;

4) The assessment of the possibility of attainment or maintenance of functioning by the Long-Term Care Certification Committee in addition to making the final decision on care levels;

5) The addition of terminal cancer to the list of specified age-related diseases; and

6) The restriction of LTCI-certified home care agencies and institutional care facilities in applying for LTCI certification on behalf of applicants.

2008 revisions include:

1) Authorizing the national, prefectural, and municipal governments to conduct onsite inspections of LTCI-certified care providers' headquarters to determine compliance with regulatory requirements if fraud in LTCI is suspected;

2) Authorizing the national, prefectural, and municipal governments to monitor and correct care provider's failure to comply with regulations and decide whether to cancel or renew the LTCI certification of care providers; and
3) A revision of certification assessment items—the number of assessment items was reduced to 74.

2011 revisions include:
1) The legal permission for care workers to remove sputum using the suction system;
2) Establishment of around-the-clock and on-call home health, home care, and home visit rehabilitation services;
3) Promotion of adult protective programs (e.g., adult guardianship and conservatorship) and other services (e.g., meals-on-wheels and monitoring services); and
4) Review of the public reporting system of care providers including discontinuation of onsite evaluation for provider's quality of care.

CURRENT STATUS OF THE LONG-TERM CARE INSURANCE SYSTEM

According to the MHLW (2011), the LTCI system is currently serving more than 4 million recipients, and of those, 2.94 million are receiving home- and community-based care services (Figure 13-6). In addition, more than 60% of the respondents of the study conducted by the MHLW in 2010 rated the system as good to excellent.

However, there are 67,000 LTCI-covered home- and community-based care services recipients who require a high level of care (e.g., recipients with chronic conditions, such as cerebrovascular disease) and are currently on the waiting list for welfare facilities for the elderly (420,000 elderly people in total). In addition, in spite of attempts to suppress costs incurred by LTCI,

13 Revisions to the Long-Term Care Insurance System 203

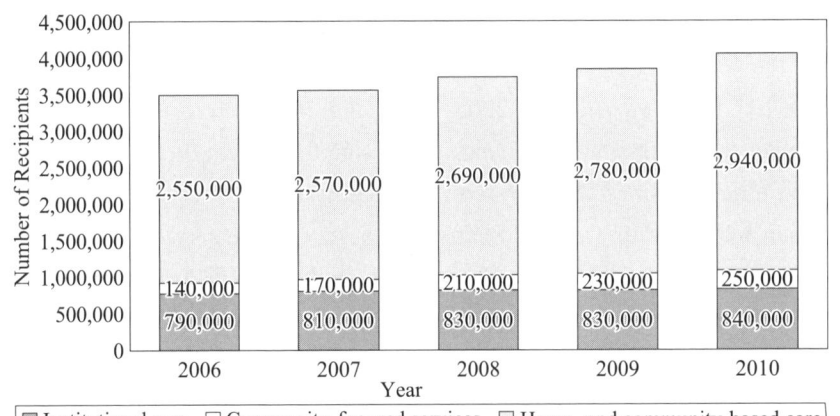

	2006	2007	2008	2009	2010
Institutional care (top)	2,550,000	2,570,000	2,690,000	2,780,000	2,940,000
Community-focused services	140,000	170,000	210,000	230,000	250,000
Home- and community-based care	790,000	810,000	830,000	830,000	840,000

■ Institutional care □ Community-focused services □ Home- and community-based care

Source: Ministry of Health, Labour and Welfare (2011) White Paper on the Labour Economy 2011.

Figure 13-6 Number of Recipients: 2006-2010

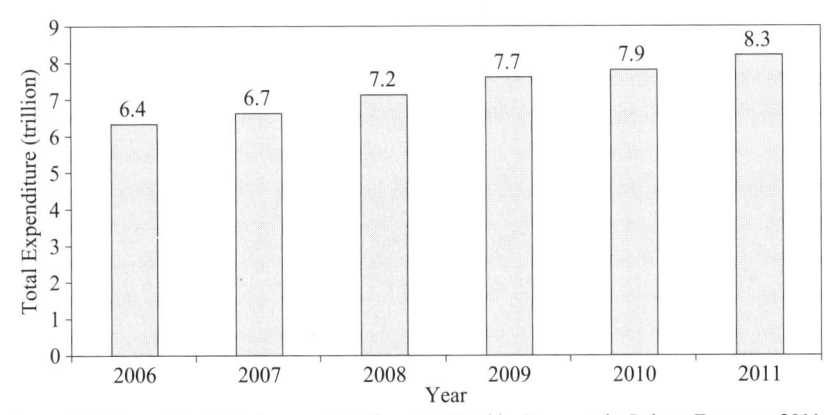

Year	2006	2007	2008	2009	2010	2011
Total Expenditure (trillion)	6.4	6.7	7.2	7.7	7.9	8.3

Source: Ministry of Health, Labour and Welfare (2011) White Paper on the Labour Economy 2011.

Figure 13-7 Total Expenditure: 2006-2011

the total expenditure has continued to increase from JPY 6.4 trillion in 2006 to JPY 8.3 trillion in 2011 (Figure 13-7), and it is expected that by the time the baby boomers become old-old (over age 75) in 2025, LTCI may require approximately JPY 19 to 24 trillion a year.

Although the system has gained popularity in the public eye, the operation of the system may require further discussion.

SUMMARY

The LTCI Law revisions of 2005, 2008, and 2011 were discussed in this chapter to illustrate the importance of revising the system. It has been more than a decade since the long-term care safety net has been developed in Japan by integrating medical care and social welfare services via LTCI. However, in spite of its popularity with the public, the LTCI system is fairly new and still in the process of developing appropriate frameworks, plans, and revising its policies and programs for frail elderly people.

Of the three major revisions, those made in 2005 led to the most significant alterations in the LTCI system (e.g., introduction of new preventative care services package and classification criteria and establishment of community-focused services). These revisions are currently in effect and have been serving as a base or starting point of LTCI. There might be many more revisions by the time the scheduled review in 2015 is conducted, which would hopefully create the ideal LTCI system.

Notes

1) Data are for those who are classified as 5th level of care required.
2) The contribution rate for 1st category insured persons during the fiscal years of 2006-2008 was 19%, was increased to 20% in 2009, and is currently 21%.
3) The contribution rate for 2nd category insured persons during the fiscal years of 2006-2008 was 31%, was decreased to 30% in 2009, and is currently 29%.

References

Ministry of Health, Labour and Welfare (2006). Summary of the Long-Term Care System Insurance Revisions [*Kaigo Hoken Seido Kaikaku no Gaiyo*]. http://www.mhlw.go.jp/topics/kaigo/topics/0603/dl/data.pdf (accessed June 28, 2013).

Ministry of Health, Labour and Welfare (2008). Announcement of Partial Amendments to the Long-Term Care Insurance Law and Welfare Law for the Elderly [*Kaigo Hokenho oyobi Rojin Fukushi Ho no Ichibu wo Kaisei suru Horitsu nitsuite*]. http://www.mhlw.go.jp/topics/kaigo/gaiyo/k2008_02.html (accessed June 29, 2013).

Ministry of Health, Labour and Welfare (2010). Budget Ceiling of Care Levels [*Kubun Shikyu Gendogaku Kijyungaku nitsuite*]. http://www.mhlw.go.jp/shingi/2010/05/dl/s0531-13d_17.pdf (accessed June 29, 2013).

Ministry of Health, Labour and Welfare (2011). Long-Term Care Insurance to Ensure High-Quality Long-Term Care Services [*Ryoshitsu na Kaigo Service no Kakuho*] in MHLW, White Paper on the Labour Economy 2011. http://www.mhlw.go.jp/wp/hakusyo/kousei/11/dl/02-06.pdf (accessed July 6, 2013).

Ministry of Health, Labour and Welfare (2013). Long-Term Care Insurance Premiums for 1st Category Insured Persons [*Kaigo Hoken no Hokenryo: Dai Ichi Hihokensha*]. http://www.mhlw.go.jp/topics/kaigo/zaisei/sikumi_03.html (accessed July 4, 2013).

Saito, Y. (2008). Present Conditions and the Subject of Long-Term Care Insurance in Japan. International Journal of Welfare for the Aged, 19, 175-190.

Sawada, Y., et al. (2009). Comparison of the Information Disclosure Systems for the Nursing Facilities in Japan and the U.S.. Japanese Society for the Study of Social Welfare, 50(1), 95-108.

Sumii, H., et al. (2010). 2005 Revision of the Long-term Care Insurance System in Japan and Its Future Prospective. International Journal of Welfare for the Aged, 22, 67-86.

Tokyo Metropolitan Government (2012). Long-Term Care Insurance. http://www.fukushihoken.metro.tokyo.jp/kourei/koho/kaigo_pamph.files/kaigohoken-english.pdf (accessed June 29, 2013).

Appendix

Appendix A. Assessment Form: Background Information

Please assess applicant when he/she is lucid. If not, please re-assess	Insurance ID No:	Insured person's No:

Assessment form: Basic Information
I. Interviewer Information

Date of assessment: / /	Location: Applicant's home / Hospital / Care facility / Other ( )
Name of interviewer:	Employer:

II. Applicant Information

| Reason for assessment: Initial / Re-application | Results of previous assessment: |
| Date of previous assessment: / / | Ineligible / Assistance-required level ( ) / Care-required level ( ) |

Name:	Sex: Male / Female	Date of birth: / / (Age:)
Address:		TEL: ( ) -
Family's name:		Relationship:
Family's address:		TEL: ( ) -

Appendix 209

III. Current Services

Home- and community-based care services (average number of use during last 90 days; numbers of purchased assistive devices at the time of assessment; and numbers of loaned assistive devices during last 180 days.)

☐ Home care (home help)	/ month	☐ Loan of assistive devices		item(s)
☐ Home bathing services	/ month	☐ Short-stay program: personal care		/ month
☐ Home health care	/ month	☐ Short-stay program: medical care		/ month
☐ Home visit rehabilitation	/ month	☐ Group home for people with dementia		/ month
☐ Medical management	/ month	☐ Care services for private care facility residents		/ month
☐ Adult day care	/ month	☐ Purchase of assistive devices		item(s)
☐ Day care rehabilitation	/ month	☐ Home modifications		Yes / No
☐ Municipality-funded special benefits [			]	
☐ Non-LTCI home- and community-based services [			]	

Institutional care services

☐ Welfare facility for the elderly	Facility's information
☐ Health facility for the elderly	Name:
☐ Designated long-term care hospital	Address:
☐ Other ( )	TEL: ( ) -

IV. Indicate Current Diagnoses, Family Situation, Living Environments, and Experience of Abuse

Appendix B. Assessment Form: General Assessment

Date of assessment: _____

Insurance ID No: _____   Insured person's No: _____

1-1 Paralysis (circle all that apply)

⇒ **Go to Assessment Form: Additional Comments 1**

| 1. None | 2. Left upper extremity | 3. Right upper extremity |
| 4. Left lower extremity | 5. Right lower extremity | 6. Other |

1-2 Limitation of joint mobility (circle all that apply)   ⇒ **1**

| 1. None   2. Shoulder   3. Elbow   4. Thigh   5. Knee   6. Foot and ankle   7. Other |

2-1 Ability to roll over (circle one that applies)   ⇒ **2**

| 1. Totally able   2. Able with assistive device   3. Totally unable |

2-2 Ability to get up and down (circle one that applies)   ⇒ **2**

| 1. Totally able   2. Able with assistive device   3. Totally unable |

Appendix 211

2-3 Ability to maintain a sitting position with feet on the ground (circle one that applies)

| 1. Totally able | 2. Able with hands | 3. Able with assistance | 4. Totally unable | ⇒ 2 |

2-4 Ability to maintain a sitting position without feet on the ground (circle one that applies)

| 1. Totally able | 2. Able with hands | 3. Able with assistance | 4. Totally unable | ⇒ 2 |

2-5 Ability to keep a standing position (circle one that applies)

| 1. Totally able without assistive device | 2. Able with assistive device | 3. Totally unable | ⇒ 2 |

2-6 Ambulation (circle one that applies)

| 1. Totally able without assistive device | 2. Able with assistive device | 3. Totally unable | ⇒ 2 |

2-7 Transfer (circle one that applies)

| 1. Independent | 2. Supervision | 3. Limited assistance | 4. Total assistance | ⇒ 2 |

3-1 Ability to stand up (circle one that applies)

| 1. Totally able | 2. Able with assistive device | 3. Totally unable | ⇒ 3 |

3-2 Ability to stand on one foot (circle one that applies)

1. Totally able without assistive device	2. Able with assistive device	3. Totally unable ⇒ 3

3-3 Ability to get in/out of bathtub (circle one that applies)

1. Independent	2. Limited assistance	3. Total assistance	4. Activity did not occur ⇒ 3

3-4 Ability to wash own body (circle one that applies)

1. Independent	2. Limited assistance	3. Total assistance	4. Activity did not occur ⇒ 3

4-1 Pressure ulcer (circle all that apply for each)

A. Presence of pressure ulcer	1. No	2. Yes
B. Presence of other skin problems	1. No	2. Yes

⇒ 4

4-2 Ability to raise hand/arm up to chest level (circle one that applies)

1. Totally able	2. Able with assistive device	3. Totally unable ⇒ 4

4-3 Ability to swallow (circle one that applies)

1. Independent	2. Supervision	4. Total assistance ⇒ 4

4-4 Ability to feel the urge to urinate and move bowels (circle one that applies for each)

A. Feel urge to urinate	1. Yes	2. Sometimes	3. No
B. Feel urge to move bowel	1. Yes	2. Sometimes	3. No

Appendix 213

4-5 Ability to clean up after urination (circle one that applies) ⇒ 4

| 1. Independent | 2. Indirect assistance | 3. Direct assistance | 4. Total assistance |

4-6 Ability to clean up after bowel movements (circle one that applies) ⇒ 4

| 1. Independent | 2. Indirect assistance | 3. Direct assistance | 4. Total assistance |

4-7 Eating (circle one that applies) ⇒ 4

| 1. Independent | 2. Supervision | 3. Limited assistance | 4. Total assistance |

5-1 Personal hygiene (circle one that applies for each) ⇒ 5

	Independent	Limited assistance	Total assistance
A. Oral hygiene (e.g., brushing teeth)	1	2	3
B. Washing face	1	2	3
C. Combing hair	1	2	3
D. Nail hygiene	1	2	3

5-2 Dressing (circle one that applies for each) ⇒ 5

	Independent	Limited assistance	Total assistance
A. Button and unbutton clothes	1	2	3
B. Put on and remove clothing	1	2	3
C. Put on and remove a pair of pants	1	2	3
D. Put on and remove a pair of socks	1	2	3

5-3 Ability to clean up own room (circle one that applies)

| 1. Independent | 2. Limited assistance | 3. Total assistance | ⇒ 5 |

5-4 Administration of medication (circle one that applies)

| 1. Independent | 2. Limited assistance | 3. Total assistance | ⇒ 5 |

5-5 Management of money (circle one that applies)

| 1. Independent | 2. Limited assistance | 3. Total assistance | ⇒ 5 |

5-6 Severe memory loss (circle one that applies)

| 1. Yes | 2. Sometimes | 3. No | ⇒ 5 |

5-7 Apathy or loss of interest in surroundings (circle one that applies)

| 1. Yes | 2. Sometimes | 3. No | ⇒ 5 |

6-1 Vision (circle one that applies) ⇒ 6

1. Adequate (no problems with daily activities)
2. Able to see visual assessment symbol from 1 meter away
3. Able to see visual assessment symbol placed right in front of face
4. Unable to see well
5. No vision

6-2 Hearing (circle one that applies) ⇛ 6

1. Adequate
2. Minimal difficulty in hearing normal speech, may miss some part of message
3. Hears loud noises
4. Unable to hear well
5. Unknown/unable to assess

6-3 Communication (circle one that applies) ⇛ 6

1. Able to express self
2. Able to communicate at times
3. Able to communicate sometimes
4. Rarely able to communicate

6-4 Responds to instructions (circle one that applies) ⇛ 6

| 1. Understood | 2. Sometimes understood | 3. Unable to understand |

6-5 Comprehension (circle one that applies for each) ⇛ 6

A. Able to understand daily routine	1. Yes	2. No
B. Able to recall his/her birthday and age	1. Yes	2. No
C. Able to recall what he/she was doing right before the assessment	1. Yes	2. No
D. Able to recall his/her own name	1. Yes	2. No
E. Able to recall current season	1. Yes	2. No
F. Able to recall current location	1. Yes	2. No

Behavior patterns (circle one that applies for each) ⇒ 7

A. Expression of unrealistic distress (e.g., being robbed)	1. Yes	2. Sometimes	3. No
B. Makes up stories	1. Yes	2. Sometimes	3. No
C. Sees and hears something that does not exist	1. Yes	2. Sometimes	3. No
D. Cries and laughs due to fluctuation of mood	1. Yes	2. Sometimes	3. No
E. Day-night reversal	1. Yes	2. Sometimes	3. No
F. Verbal and physical aggressiveness	1. Yes	2. Sometimes	3. No
G. Repetitive (repeats the same story, makes disruptive sounds)	1. Yes	2. Sometimes	3. No
H. Screaming	1. Yes	2. Sometimes	3. No
I. Resists advice or care	1. Yes	2. Sometimes	3. No
J. Moves with no rational purpose	1. Yes	2. Sometimes	3. No
K. Repetitive verbalization (e.g., "going home") and unstable mood	1. Yes	2. Sometimes	3. No
L. Unable to locate his/her own home/room	1. Yes	2. Sometimes	3. No
M. Insists on going out alone and requires supervision	1. Yes	2. Sometimes	3. No
N. Hoarding	1. Yes	2. Sometimes	3. No
O. Unable to keep watch on a stove	1. Yes	2. Sometimes	3. No
P. Destruction of objects/clothes	1. Yes	2. Sometimes	3. No
Q. Socially inappropriate behavior	1. Yes	2. Sometimes	3. No
R. Puts inedible objects in mouth	1. Yes	2. Sometimes	3. No
S. Sexual behavior that is troublesome to others	1. Yes	2. Sometimes	3. No

Appendix 217

8 **Medical care in the last 14 days** (circle all that apply) ⇛ 8

Types of medical care	1. Intravenous fluids	2. Central venous nutrition	3. Dialysis
	4. Stoma care	5. Oxygen treatment	6. Respirator
	7. Tracheostomy treatment	8. Pain management	9. Tube feeding
Special medical care	10. Vital sign monitors (e.g., blood pressure, heart rate, and oxygen levels)		
	11. Treatment of pressure ulcer		
Incontinence care	12. Catheter (condom or indwelling)		

9 **Independence level** (circle one that applies for each)

Independence level of the disabled elderly (degree of disability)	Normal	J1	J2	A1	A2	B1	B2	C1	C2
Independence level of elderly with dementia	Normal	I	II a	II b	III a	III b	IV	M	

Appendix C. Assessment Form: Additional Comments

Date of assessment: _____
Insurance ID No: _____ Insured person's No: _____

Assessment Form: Basic Information

1. Paralysis and Contracture
1-1 Paralysis and 1-2 limitation of joint mobility

( ) _____
( ) _____
( ) _____

2. Basic Movements
2-1 Rolling-over; 2-2 getting up; 2-3 sitting with feet on the ground; 2-4 sitting with feet off the ground; 2-5 standing; 2-6 ambulation; and 2-7 transfer

( ) _____
( ) _____
( ) _____

3. Complex Movements and Tasks
3-1 Standing up; 3-2 standing on one foot; 3-3 getting in/out of the bathtub; and 3-4 bathing (washing body)

( ) _____
( ) _____
( ) _____

4. Special Care
4-1 Bedsore; 4-2 ability to raise hand/arm up to chest level; 4-3 swallowing; 4-4 urination and bowel movements; 4-5 cleaning up after

urination; 4-6 cleaning up after bowel movements; and 4-7 dietary intake

( )
( )
( )

5. Personal Care
5-1 Personal hygiene; 5-2 dressing; 5-3 ability to follow instructions; 5-4 administration of medication; 5-5 cleaning own room; 5-6 management of money; 5-7 severe memory loss; and 5-8 apathy or loss of interest in surroundings

( )
( )
( )

6. Communication, Hearing, Memory, and Recall Ability
6-1 Vision; 6-2 hearing; 6-3 ability to express self; 6-4 responds to instructions; and 6-5 comprehension

( )
( )

7. Problem Behaviors
7 Behaviors

( )
( )

8. Special Medical Care
8 Special medical care

( )
( )

Please use an extra page if necessary

Appendix D. Physician's Report

Date of completion of this form: _____

Applicant	Name:		Sex	Address:
	Birth date:	(Age:)	M / F	Tel:

I hereby state that the below statement is true to the best of my knowledge and valid, and that I understand that this information is used to make a decision about the applicant's LTCI certification application.

☐ Agree ☐ Disagree

Physician's name:
Employer: Tel: (   )
Address: Fax: (   )

Date of last physical exam	.... Month Day Year
Number of times of making physician's report for the applicant	☐ Initial ☐ More than 2 times
Seen by other physicians?	☐ No ☐ Yes (if yes, check all that apply) ☐ Internal ☐ Psychiatrist ☐ Surgeon ☐ Orthopedician ☐ Neurosurgeon ☐ Dermatologist ☐ Urologist ☐ Gynecologist ☐ Optometrist ☐ Otolaryngologist ☐ Rehabilitation ☐ Dentist ☐ Other ( )

Appendix   *221*

1. Applicant's Diagnosis

Diagnosis (use the "primary diagnosis" box for diagnosis that is causing the "designated specific disease" or disability) and date of onset.
Date of onset (Month/Day/Year/Time)
Primary diagnosis _____
Secondary diagnosis _____
Tertiary diagnosis _____
Stability of symptoms ☐ Stable ☐ Unstable ☐ Unknown
Prognosis of long-term care ☐ Improve ☐ No change ☐ Deteriorate
Indicate these diseases that have a relationship to current disability status, treatment plans, and the patient's process (indicate any changes in the last 6 months and evidence for diagnosis of one of the specified diseases).

2. Medical Care (check all medical treatments rendered within the last 14 days)

Types of medical care	☐ IV management	☐ IVH	☐ Dialysis
	☐ Stoma	☐ Oxygen therapy	☐ Respirator
	☐ Tracheostomy	☐ Pain nursing	☐ Tube feeding
Special medical care	☐ Vital sign monitors (e.g., blood pressure, heart rate, and oxygen level)		
	☐ Pressure ulcer		
Incontinence care	☐ Catheter (condom or indwelling)		

3. Physical and Psychological Status

Independence level of daily living (check one that applies for each)

Independence level of disabled elderly (degree of disability) ☐ Normal ☐ J1 ☐ J2 ☐ A1 ☐ A2 ☐ B1 ☐ B2 ☐ C1 ☐ C2

Independence level of elderly with dementia: ☐ Normal ☐ I ☐ IIa ☐ IIb ☐ IIIa ☐ IIIb ☐ IV ☐ M

Comprehension and memory (check one that applies for each)

Short-term memory ☐ Adequate ☐ Inadequate

Cognitive skills for daily decision-making ☐ Independent ☐ Some difficulty ☐ Require supervision ☐ Severely impaired

Communication skill ☐ Capable ☐ Some difficulty ☐ Limited to making concrete requests ☐ Incapable

Eating ☐ Independence/eat with some difficulty ☐ Total assistance

Problem behaviors

Presence of problem behaviors ☐ No ☐ Yes (if yes, check all that apply)

☐ Delusion or auditory hallucination ☐ Delusion ☐ Day-night reversal ☐ Verbal abuse ☐ Physical abuse
☐ Resist care ☐ Wandering ☐ Mismanagement of fire ☐ Socially inappropriate behavior ☐ Pica behavior
☐ Troublesome sexual behavior ☐ Other ( )

Appendix 223

Presence of Psychiatric Symptoms & Neurological Symptoms

☐ Present (Symptoms:) ☐ Absent
(if present) → seen by a specialist? ☐ Yes (   ) ☐ No

Physical Status

Dominant arm (☐ Right ☐ Left) Weight: _____ kg Height: _____ cm

Location	Severity		
Amputation of limbs ( )	☐ Mild	☐ Moderate	☐ Severe
Paralysis ( )	☐ Mild	☐ Moderate	☐ Severe
Muscle weakness ( )	☐ Mild	☐ Moderate	☐ Severe
Pressure ulcer ( )	☐ Mild	☐ Moderate	☐ Severe
Other skin diseases ( )	☐ Mild	☐ Moderate	☐ Severe

Contracture of joints
- Shoulder ☐ Right ☐ Left
- Elbow   ☐ Right ☐ Left
- Hip   ☐ Right ☐ Left
- Knee   ☐ Right ☐ Left

☐ Dysfunction/
- Upper   ☐ Right ☐ Left
- Trunk   ☐ Right ☐ Left
involuntary movements
- Lower limb ☐ Right ☐ Left

Legend

Need for Long-Term Care

Disease/disability the patient is currently at risk of developing and its treatment plans

☐ Incontinence ☐ Fall/fracture ☐ Wandering ☐ Pressure ulcer ☐ Aspiration pneumonia ☐ Intestinal obstruction
☐ Opportunistic infection ☐ Cardiopulmonary dysfunction ☐ Pain ☐ Dehydration
☐ Other (   )
→ Treatment plan (   )

The need for medical management (underline the one that is most required for the patient)
- [ ] Doctor's home visit
- [ ] Home health
- [ ] Home visit rehabilitation
- [ ] Day care rehabilitation
- [ ] Short-stay program
- [ ] Visiting dentist
- [ ] Visiting dental hygienist
- [ ] Visiting medication management
- [ ] Visiting dietitian
- [ ] Other (   )

Points of concern from medical perspective of long-term care services (e.g., bathing services, homecare)

Blood pressure	[ ] No	[ ] Yes ( )
Swallowing	[ ] No	[ ] Yes ( )
Eating	[ ] No	[ ] Yes ( )
Transfer (e.g., between surface - to/from bed and chair)	[ ] No	[ ] Yes ( )
Other ( )		

Presence of contagious/infection diseases (if present, please explain)
- [ ] Present (   )
- [ ] Absent
- [ ] Unknown

Remarks

Please indicate any other opinions/concerns that are associated with the certification of LTCI. If you are provided with information from other specialists, please indicate the content of the information (if necessary, please attach a copy of the information you received from other specialists or patient's disability certification notice).

Appendix E. Regional Unit Pricing per Unit as of April 2012

LTCI Services \ Regions*	1st region	2nd region	3rd region	4th region	5th region	6th region	7th region
Medical management Loan of assistive devices	1.0 (10)	1.0 (10)	1.0 (10)	1.0 (10)	1.0 (10)	1.0 (10)	1.0 (10)
Home health care	1.126 (11.2)	1.105 (11)	1.084 (10.8)	1.070 (10.7)	1.042 (10.4)	1.021 (10.2)	1.0 (10)
Home visit rehabilitation Day care rehabilitation	1.099 (10.9)	1.083 (10.8)	1.066 (10.6)	1.055 (10.5)	1.033 (10.3)	1.017 (10.1)	1.0 (10)
Short stay program for personal care Short stay program for medical care	1.081 (10.8)	1.068 (10.6)	1.054 (10.5)	1.045 (10.4)	1.027 (10.2)	1.014 (10.1)	1.0 (10)
Home care Home bathing services	1.126 (11.2)	1.105 (11)	1.084 (10.8)	1.070 (10.7)	1.042 (10.4)	1.021 (10.2)	1.0 (10)
Adult day service Group home for people with dementia Care services for private care facility residents	1.081 (10.8)	1.068 (10.6)	1.054 (10.5)	1.045 (10.4)	1.027 (10.2)	1.014 (10.1)	1.0 (10)

* See Appendix F for the municipalities for each region
Note: Numbers in parentheses represent the unit prices in JPY.

Appendix F. List of Municipalities for Each Region

1st region	23 wards of Tokyo
2nd region	Tokyo (Tama, Inashiro, Nishi-Tokyo) Kanagawa (Kamakura) Osaka (Osaka)
3rd region	Tokyo (Hachioji, Tachikawa, Musashino, Fuchu, Akishima, Chofu, Machida, Kodaira, Hino, Kokubunji, Kunitachi, and Komae) Kanagawa (Yokohama and Kawasaki) Aichi (Nagoya) Osaka (Suita and Neyagawa) Hyogo (Nishinomiya, Ashiya and Takarazuka)
4th region	Saitama (Saitama) Chiba (Chiba) Tokyo (Mitaka, Koganei, Higashimurayama and Higashikurume) Kanagawa (Yokosuka) Kyoto Kyoto) Osaka (Sakai, Toyonaka, Ikeda, Takatsuki, Moriguchim Hirakata, ibaraki, Yaoa, Daito, Mino, Kadoma, Settsu, Takaishi, Higashi-Osaka, Shijonawate, Shimamoto) Hyogo (Kobe and Amagasaki) Fukuoka (Fukuoka)
5th region	Miyagi (Sendai) Saitama (Kawagoe, Kawaguchi, Tokorozawa, Sayama, Koshigaya, Warabishi, Toda, Asaka, Shiki, Wako, Niiza, Fujimi, Fujimino, and Miyoshimachi) Chiba (Ichikawa, Funabashi, Matsudo, Narashino, Kashiwa, Urayasu and Yotsukaido) Tokyo (Ome, Fussa, Kiyose Hamura, Akiruno and Hinodecho) Kanagawa (Sagamihara, Hiratsuka, Fujisawa, Chigasaki, Zushi, Atsugi, Yamato, Isehara, Ebina, Zama, Ayase, Hayama and Samukawamachi) Shizuoka (Shizuoka) Shiga (Otsu) Kyoto (Uji) Osaka (Kishiwada, Izumiotsu, Kaizuka, Izumisano, Tondabayashi, Kawachinagano, Matsubara, Izumi, Habikino, Fujiidera, Katano, Osaka-Sayama and Tadaokacho) Hyogo (Itami, Kawanishi and Sanda) Nara (Nara and Yamatokoriyama) Hiroshima (Hiroshima and Fuchucho)
6th region	Hokkaido (Sapporo) Ibaraki (Mito, Tsuchiura, Koga, Ishioka, Yuki, Ryugasaki, Shimotsuma, Joso, Toride, Ushiku, Tsukuba, Moriya, Naka, Chikusei, Bando, Inashiki, Sakuragawa, Tsukubamirai, Amimachi, Kawachimachi, Yachiyocho, Goka SakaiMachi and Tonemachi) Tochigi (Utsunomiya, Tochigi, Kanuma, Nikko, Koyama, Moka, Otawara, Sakura, Shimotsuke, Mibu and Nogi)

Appendix   227

6th region (cont.)	Gunma (Maebashi, Takasaki, Isesaki, Ohta, Shibukawa, Shinto village, Tamamura, Chiyoda, Machi and Oizumimachi) Saitama (Gyoda, Hanno, Kazo, Matsuyama, Kasukabe, Hunyu, Kounosu, Ageo, Soka, Iruma, Okegawa, Kuki, Yashio, Misato, Hasuda, Sakado, Satte, Tsurugashima, Hidaka, Yoshikawa, Moroyama, Ogose, Namekawa, ranzanmachi, Kawashima, Yoshimi, Hatoyama, Tokigawa, Miyashiro, Shiraoka, Sugito and Matsubushi) Chiba (Kisarazu, Noda, Sakura, Togane, Ichihara, Nagareyama, Yachiyo, Abiko, Kanagaya, Kimitsu, Sodegaura, Yachimata, Inzai, Shirai, Tomisato, Sanmu, Shisui, Sakae, Oamishirasato, Nagaramachi and Chonan-machi) Tokyo (Higashiyamato, Musashimurayama, Mizuhon and Hinohara village) Kanagawa (Odawara, Miura, Hadano, Ninomiyamachi, Nakai, Oi, Yamakita, Hakonemachi, Aikawa and Kiyokawa village) Ishikawa (Kanazawa) Fukui (Fukui) Yamanashi (Kofu) Nagano (Nagano, Matsumoto and Ueda) Shizuoka (Hamamatsu, Numazu, Mishima, Fujinomiya, Shimada, Fuji, Iwata, Yaizu, Kakegawa, Fujieda, Gotemba, Fukuroi, Susono, Kosai, Kannami, Shimizumachi, Nagaizumicho, Koyamacho, Kawanehoncho and Morimachi) Aichi (Toyohashi, Okazaki, Ichinomiya, Seto, Handa, Kasugai, Toyokawa, Tsushima, Hekinan, Kariya, Toyota, Anjo, Nishio, Gamagori, Inuyama, Konan, Komaki, Inazawa, Shinshiro, Tokai, Obu, Chita, Chiryu, Owariasahi, Takahama, Iwakura, Toyoake, Nisshin, Aisai, Kiyosu, Kita-Nagoya, Yatomi, Miyoshi, Ama, Nagakute, Togo, Toyoyama, Oguchi, Fuso, Kanie, Tobishim, Agui, Higashiura and Kota) Mie (Tsu, Yokkaichi, Kuwana, Suzuka, Nabari, Kameyama, Inabe, Iga, Kisosaki, Toin and Kawagoe) Shiga (Hikone, Nagahama, Kusatsu, Moriyama, Ritto, Koka, Yasu, Takashima, Maibara and Tagacho) Kyoto (Kaneoka, Joyo, Muko, Nagaokakyo, Yawata, Kyotanabe, Nantan, Kizugawa, Kumiyama, Ide, Ujitawara, Kasagi, Seika and Minamiyamashiro) Osaka (Kashiwara, Sennan, Hannan, Toyono, Kumatori, Tajiri, Misaki and Chihayaakasaka) Hyogo (Himeji, Akashi, Kakogawa, Miki, Takasago, Ono, Kasai, Kato, Inagawa Inami and Harima-cho) Nara (Tenri, Kashihara, Sakurai, Gojo, Ikoma, Kashiba, Katsuragi, Uda, Yamazoe, Heguri, Sango, Ikaruga, Ando, Kawanishi, Tawaramoto, Soni village, Asuka village, Kanmaki, Oji, Koryo, Kawai and Yoshino Wakayama (Wakayama, Hashimoto, Kinokawa, Iwade and Katsuragi) Okayama (Okayama) Hiroshima (Hatsukaichi, Kaita and Saka) Yamaguchi (Shunan) Fukuoka (Kitakyushu, Iizuka, Chikushino, Kasuga, Onojo, Dazaifu, Fukutsu, Itoshima, Nakagawa, Umi, Shime, Sue, hisayama and Kasuya) Nagasaki (Nagasakai)
7th region	Other than the above mentioned municipalities/cities

Appendix G. Fee Criterion for Long-Term Care Insurance Care Services

All 1st and 2nd category insured recipients are required to pay 10% of the service cost as co-payment.
LTCI finance-related matters such as contribution rates and fee schedules are subject to review and revision every 3 years.

Home- and Community-Based Care Services

Home Care (as of 2000 and 2012)

Length of service	Physical care (JPY) 2000	Physical care (JPY) 2012	Homemaking (JPY) 2000	Homemaking (JPY) 2012	Combination of physical care and homemaking (JPY) 2000	Combination of physical care and homemaking (JPY) 2012	Transportation (JPY) 2000	Transportation (JPY) 2012
Less than 30 min	2,100	2,540	N/A	N/A	N/A	N/A	N/A	
30 min to 1 hour	4,020	4,020	1,530	2,290	2,780	N/A	N/A	1,000/ service
1 hour to 1.5 hour	5,840	N/A	2,220	2,910	4,030	N/A	N/A	
Every 30 min thereafter	2,190	830	830	N/A	1,510	N/A	N/A	

Note: Fees may vary between providers and regions. Extra charge of 25% for care services provided between 6:00 am and 8:00 am, and 6:00 pm and 10:00 pm. Extra charge of 50% for care services provided between 10:00 pm and 6:00 am. There is another extra charge of 15% for home bathing services provided in isolated islands and mountainous regions. As of April 2012, there is a discount of 30% when home helpers with a "3rd class home help certification" provide nursing care and a combination of nursing care and homemaking activities.

Home Visit Bathing Service: 1 Nurse and 2 Care Workers Per Service

Year	Fee per service (JPY)
2000	12,500
2012	12,500

Note: Fees may vary between providers and regions. Extra charge of 15% for isolated islands and mountainous regions.

Home Health Care (as of 2000 and 2012)

Length of service	2000 Home health care agency (JPY)	2000 Medical facility (hospitals and clinics) (JPY)	2012 Home health care agency (JPY)	2012 Medical facility (hospitals and clinics) (JPY)
Less than 20 min	N/A	N/A	2,850	2,300
Less than 30 min	4,250	3,430	4,250	3,430
30 min to 1 hour	8,300	5,500	8,300	5,500
1 hour to 1.5 hours	11,980	8,450	11,980	8,450

Note: Fees may vary between providers and regions. Extra charge of 25% for care services provided between 6:00 am and 8:00 am, and 6:00 pm and 10:00 pm. Extra charge of 50% for care services provided between 10:00 pm and 6:00 am. Extra charge of 15% for isolated islands and mountainous regions. There is a discount of 10% if home health care is provided by an assistant nurse.

Home Visit Rehabilitation

Year	Fee per service (JPY)
2000	5,500
2012	3,050

Note: Fees may vary between providers and regions. Extra charge of 15% for isolated islands and mountainous regions.

Medical Management Per Service (as of 2000 and 2012)

2000 Doctors and dentists (up to 1x/mo) (JPY)	2000 Pharmacists (up to 2x/mo) (JPY)	2000 Registered dieticians (up to 2x/mo) (JPY)	2000 Other (up to 2x/mo) (JPY)	2012 Doctors and dentists (up to 2x/mo) (JPY)	2012 Pharmacists Hospital (up to 2x/mo) (JPY)	2012 Pharmacists Pharmacy store (up to 4x/mo) (JPY)	2012 Registered dieticians (up to 2x/mo) (JPY)	2012 Other (up to 2x/mo) (JPY)
9,400	5,500	5,300	5,000	5,000	5,500	5,000	5,300	3,500

Note: Fees may vary between providers and regions. Fee schedule for doctors and dentists from a hospital/office that are designated as a "comprehensive medical examination center" is JPY 5,100 in 2000 and JPY 2,900 in 2012. Recipients are required to bear the full cost of services.

Adult Day Care Service (as of 2000)
· Freestanding Adult Day Care Center

	3 to 4 hours (JPY)	4 to 6 hours (JPY)	6 to 8 hours (JPY)
Assistance-required	3,320	4,740	6,640
Care-required level 1 Care-required level 2	3,830	5,470	7,660
Care-required level 3 Care-required level 4 Care-required level 5	5,140	7,340	10,280

Note: Fees may vary between providers and regions. Additional fee of JPY 390 for meals, JPY 440 for transportation (one-way), JPY 390 for bathing, and JPY 600 for bathing with special bathtubs.

· Institutional Care Facility Affiliated Adult Day Care Center

	3 to 4 hours (JPY)	4 to 6 hours (JPY)	6 to 8 hours (JPY)
Assistance-required	2,800	4,000	5,600
Care-required level 1 Care-required level 2	3,310	4,730	6,620
Care-required level 3 Care-required level 4 Care-required level 5	4,620	6,600	9,240

Note: Fees may vary between providers and regions. Additional fee of JPY 390 for meals, JPY 440 for transportation (one-way), JPY 390 for bathing, and JPY 600 for bathing with special bathtubs.

Appendix 231

· **Freestanding Adult Day Care Center for People with Dementia**

	3 to 4 hours (JPY)	4 to 6 hours (JPY)	6 to 8 hours (JPY)
Assistance-required	4,430	6,330	8,860
Care-required level 1 Care-required level 2	5,110	7,300	10,220
Care-required level 3 Care-required level 4 Care-required level 5	6,870	9,810	13,730

Note: Fees may vary between providers and regions. Additional fee of JPY 390 for meals, JPY 440 for transportation (one-way), JPY 390 for bathing, and JPY 600 for bathing with special bathtubs.

· **Institutional Care Facility Affiliated Adult Day Care Center for People with Dementia**

	3 to 4 hours (JPY)	4 to 6 hours (JPY)	6 to 8 hours (JPY)
Assistance-required	3,730	5,330	7,460
Care-required level 1 Care-required level 2	4,410	6,300	8,820
Care-required level 3 Care-required level 4 Care-required level 5	6,160	8,800	12,320

Note: Fees may vary between providers and regions. Additional fee of JPY 390 for meals, JPY 440 for transportation (one-way), JPY 390 for bathing, and JPY 600 for bathing with special bathtubs.

Adult Day Care Service (as of 2012)
· **Assistance-Required Levels**

Year	Fee per month (JPY)
Assistance-required level 1	20,990
Assistance-required level 2	42,050

Note: Fees may vary between providers and regions, and include transportation but do not include meals and absorbent incontinence pads. Additional fess of JPY 2,250 for motor function improvement program, JPY 1,500 for oral care, JPY 1,500 for nutritional improvement program, and JPY 1,000 for group activities for improving daily skills.

· Care-Required Levels

	3 to 5 hours (JPY)	5 to 7 hours (JPY)	7 to 9 hours (JPY)
Care-required level 1	4,610	7,000	8,090
Care-required level 2	5,290	8,250	9,510
Care-required level 3	5,960	9,500	11,000
Care-required level 4	6,630	10,740	12,480
Care-required level 5	7,290	11,990	13,950

Note: Fees may vary between providers and regions and include transportation but do not include meals and absorbent incontinence pads. Additional JPY 500 for bathing, JPY 1,500 for oral care, JPY 1,500 for nutritional improvement program, and JPY 600 for care of persons with early-onset dementia.

Day Care Rehabilitation (as of 2000)

	3 to 4 hours (JPY)			4 to 6 hours (JPY)			6 to 8 hours (JPY)		
	Medical facility	Small-scale medical clinic	Health facility for the elderly	Medical facility	Small-scale medical clinic	Health facility for the elderly	Medical facility	Small-scale medical clinic	Health facility for the elderly
Assistance-required	3,310	3,300	3,240	4,900	4,800	4,630	6,610	6,650	6,480
Care-required 1 / Care-required 2	3,870	3,900	3,790	5,750	5,620	5,420	7,740	7,790	7,580
Care-required 3 / Care-required 4 / Care-required 5	5,320	5,350	5,210	7,890	7,720	7,440	10,630	10,700	10,410

Note: Fees may vary between providers and regions. Additional JPY 390 for meals, JPY 440 for one-way transportation, JPY 390 for bathing care, and JPY 600 for bathing with special bathtubs.

Day Care Rehabilitation (as of 2012)
· Assistance-Required Levels

Year	Fee per month (JPY)
Assistance-required level 1	24,120
Assistance-required level 2	48,280

Note: Fees may vary between providers and regions and include transportation but do not include meals and absorbent incontinence pads. Additional JPY 2,250 for motor function improvement program, JPY 1,500 for oral care, and JPY 1,500 for nutritional improvement program.

· Care-Required Levels

	1 to 2 hours (JPY)	2 to 3 hours (JPY)	3 to 4 hours (JPY)	4 to 6 hours (JPY)	6 to 8 hours (JPY)
Care-required 1	2,700	2,840	3,860	5,020	6,710
Care-required 2	3,000	3,400	4,630	6,100	8,210
Care-required 3	3,300	3,970	5,400	7,170	9,700
Care-required 4	3,600	4,530	6,170	8,240	11,210
Care-required 5	3,900	5,090	6,940	9,310	12,710

Note: Fees may vary between providers and regions, are subject to change based on the number of service recipients each provider has, and include transportation but do not include meals and absorbent incontinence pads. Additional JPY 500 for bathing, JPY 1,500 for oral care, JPY 1,500 for nutritional improvement program, and JPY 600 for care of persons with early-onset dementia.

Group Home for People with Dementia: Per Diem (as of 2000 and 2012)

	2000 (JPY)	2012 (JPY)
Assistance-required level 1	N/A	N/A
Assistance-required level 2	N/A	8,310
Care-required level 1	8,090	8,310
Care-required level 2	8,250	8,480
Care-required level 3	8,410	8,650
Care-required level 4	8,570	8,820
Care-required level 5	8,740	9,000

Note: Fees may vary between providers and regions.

Short-Stay Program for Personal Care (as of 2000)
· **Freestanding Facility**

	Fee per diem (JPY)		
Staffing ratio of nursing staff to short-stay residents	1:3	1:3.5	1:4.1
Assistance-required	9,480	8,720	8,280
Care-required level 1	9,760	8,970	8,510
Care-required level 2	10,210	9,370	8,890
Care-required level 3	10,650	9,770	9,260
Care-required level 4	11,100	10,170	9,640
Care-required level 5	11,540	10,570	10,010

Note: Fees may vary between providers and regions.

· **Facility Affiliated with Welfare Facilities for the Elderly**

	Fee per diem (JPY)		
Staffing ratio of nursing staff to short-stay residents	1:3	1:3.5	1:4.1
Assistance-required	9,140	8,380	7,940
Care-required level 1	9,420	8,630	8,170
Care-required level 2	9,870	9,030	8,550
Care-required level 3	10,310	9,430	8,920
Care-required level 4	10,760	9,830	9,300
Care-required level 5	11,200	10,230	9,670

Note: Fees may vary between providers and regions.

Appendix 235

Short-Stay Program for Personal Care (as of 2012)
· Freestanding Facility: Per Diem

	Private room (JPY)	Multiple-bed room (JPY)	Small-unit-based private and semi-private room (JPY)
Care-required level 1	6,550	7,370	7,550
Care-required level 2	7,260	8,080	8,260
Care-required level 3	7,960	8,780	8,960
Care-required level 4	8,670	9,490	9,670
Care-required level 5	9,370	10,190	10,270

Note: Fees may vary between providers and regions.

· Provider Affiliated Welfare Facility for the Elderly: Per Diem

	Private room (JPY)	Multiple-bed room (JPY)	Small-unit-based private and semi-private room (JPY)
Care-required level 1	6,210	7,030	7,210
Care-required level 2	6,920	7,740	7,920
Care-required level 3	7,620	8,440	8,620
Care-required level 4	8,330	9,150	9,330
Care-required level 5	9,030	9,850	9,930

Note: Fees may vary between providers and regions.

Short-Stay Program for Medical Care (as of 2000)
· Health Facility for the Elderly

	Fee per diem (JPY)	
Staffing ratio of nurse to short-stay residents	1:3	1: 3.6
Assistance-required	9,940	9,280
Care-required level 1	10,260	9,560
Care-required level 2	10,760	10,030
Care-required level 3	11,260	10,490
Care-required level 4	11,760	10,950
Care-required level 5	12,260	11,410

Note: Fees may vary between providers and regions.

· **Designated Long-Term Care Hospital**

	Fee per diem (JPY)			
Staffing ratio of nurse to short-stay residents	1:6	1:6	1:6	1:6
Staffing ratio of care worker to short-stay residents	1:3	1:4	1:5	1:6
Assistance-required	13,310	12,650	12,190	11,880
Care-required level 1	13,590	12,920	12,450	12,140
Care-required level 2	14,050	13,360	12,860	12,540
Care-required level 3	14,510	13,790	13,280	12,940
Care-required level 4	14,970	14,220	13,690	13,340
Care-required level 5	15,430	14,650	14,110	13,750

Note: Fees may vary between providers and regions.

Short-Stay Program for Medical Care (as of 2012)

	Private room (JPY)	Multiple-bed room (JPY)	Small-unit-based private and semi-private room (JPY)
Care-required level 1	7,460	8,450	8,480
Care-required level 2	7,950	8,940	8,970
Care-required level 3	8,480	9,470	9,500
Care-required level 4	9,020	10,010	10,040
Care-required level 5	9,550	10,540	10,570

Note: Fees may vary between providers and regions.

Reimbursement for Purchasing Assistive Devices

Year	Fee per year (JPY)
2000	100,000
2012	100,000

Reimbursement for Home Modifications

Year	Fee per person (JPY)
2000	200,000
2012	200,000

Institutional Long-Term Care Services

Welfare Facility for the Elderly (as of 2000)

	Fee per diem (JPY)		
Staffing ratio of nursing staff to residents	1:3	1:3.5	1:4.1
Care-required level 1	7,960	7,170	6,710
Care-required level 2	8,410	7,570	7,090
Care-required level 3	8,850	7,970	7,460
Care-required level 4	9,300	8,370	7,840
Care-required level 5	9,740	8,770	8,210

Note: Fees may vary between providers and regions.

Health Care Facility for the Elderly (as of 2000)

	Fee per diem (JPY)	
Staffing ratio of nursing staff to residents	1:3	1:3.6
Care-required level 1	8,800	8,100
Care-required level 2	9,300	8,570
Care-required level 3	9,800	9,030
Care-required level 4	10,300	9,490
Care-required level 5	10,800	9,950

Note: Fees may vary between providers and regions.

Designated Long-Term Care Hospital (as of 2000)

	Fee per diem (JPY)			
Staffing ratio of nurse to short-stay residents	1:6	1:6	1:6	1:6
Staffing ratio of care worker to short-stay residents	1:3	1:4	1:5	1:6
Care-required level 1	11,930	11,260	10,790	10,480
Care-required level 2	12,390	11,700	11,200	10,880
Care-required level 3	12,850	12,130	11,620	11,280
Care-required level 4	13,310	12,560	12,030	11,680
Care-required level 5	13,770	12,990	12,450	12,090

Note: Fees may vary between providers and regions.

Welfare Facility for the Elderly: Per Diem (as of 2012)

	Private room (JPY)	Multiple-bed room (JPY)	Small-unit-based private and semi-private room (JPY)
Care-required level 1	5,770	6,390	6,570
Care-required level 2	6,480	7,100	7,280
Care-required level 3	7,180	7,800	7,980
Care-required level 4	7,890	8,510	8,690
Care-required level 5	8,590	9,210	9,290

Note: Fees may vary between providers and regions.

Health Care Facility for the Elderly: Per Diem (as of 2012)

	Private room (JPY)	Multiple-bed room (JPY)	Small-unit-based private and semi-private room (JPY)
Care-required level 1	7,020	7,810	7,840
Care-required level 2	7,510	8,300	8,330
Care-required level 3	8,040	8,830	8,860
Care-required level 4	8,580	9,370	9,400
Care-required level 5	9,110	9,900	9,930

Note: Fees may vary between providers and regions.

Designated Long-Term Care Hospital: Per Diem (as of 2012)

	Private room (JPY)	Multiple-bed room (JPY)	Small-unit-based private and semi-private room (JPY)
Care-required level 1	6,710	7,820	7,850
Care-required level 2	7,810	8,920	8,950
Care-required level 3	10,190	11,300	11,330
Care-required level 4	11,200	12,310	12,340
Care-required level 5	12,110	13,220	13,250

Note: Fees may vary between providers and regions.

INDEX

A

ACATs. *See* aged care assessment teams
Activities of Daily Living (ADLs), 15
 in assessing physical status, 100-101, 109
additional comments by assessors. *See* application process; intake interview; qualification assessments
additional services. *See* municipal programs, additional services
address change, importance of, 89
ADLs. *See* Activities of Daily Living
adult day care services. *See* home- and community-based care services, adult day care services
aged care assessment teams (ACATs), 182
aged society, 178
aging rates, 5, 122
aging society, 178
agricultural co-operative, 176
allocation system, 4, 7, 8, 9, 13, 88, 182
 compare to long-term care insurance, 148
 and municipal governments, 4, 7
almshouses for the elderly, 70
 eligibility, 70
 staffing, 70

amyotrophic lateral sclerosis. *See* specified diseases, amyotrophic lateral sclerosis
appeal process, 92
application forms, 23, 51, 58, 83, 85, 86
application process, 83-85
 intake interview, 96-97
 qualification assessments, 83, 95-108
 See also certification process
arteriosclerosis obliterans. *See* specified diseases, arteriosclerosis obliterans
assessment forms, for long-term care insurance
 background information, 208-209 (Appendix A)
 general assessment, 210-217 (Appendix B)
assessments
 in care management, 150-151
 issues, 103-104, 109-110
 of mental status, 23, 24
 of physical status, 23, 24
 qualification assessments, 83, 95-108
assessment scales. *See* assessment tools
assessment tools, 23, 150, 151
 85-item assessment scale, 23, 97, 109
 Hasegawa Dementia Scale, 103
 See also Japan Association of Certified Care Workers Method; Japan Visiting

Nursing Foundation Method; Japanese Assessment & Care Plan for Long-Term Care; Japanese Association of Certified Social Workers Method; Minimum Data Set; Minimum Data Set-Home Care
assistance-required. *See* care levels, assistance-required
assistive devices, 20, 30, 38, 42-54
   automatic urine collection devices, 53
   available for loan, 43-51
   available for purchase, 51-54
   bathroom aids, 53-54
   bed accessories and attachments, 46
   bedside commodes, 38, 51, 52-53
   bedside rails, 46
   canes, 43, 49, 51
   code alert systems, 43, 49-50, 51
   crutches, 43, 49
   fee schedule, 44, 51, 52
   grab bars, 47, 53
   handrails, 46, 47, 51, 56
   hospital beds, 45-46, 51
   loan of, 38, 51, 133
   platforms, 47-48
   portable bathtubs, 51, 54
   positioning and adaptive cushions, 47
   power lifts, 51
   pressure ulcer prevention and treatment devices, 47
   reciprocal walkers, 48
   rental process, 51
   safety rails, 47
   sling lifts, 50
   specialty assistive devices, 38, 51
   threshold ramps, 43, 47-48, 55
   transfer lifts, 43, 50, 51
   walkers, 48
   wheelchair accessories and attachments, 45
   wheelchair ramps, 47-48
   wheelchairs, 43-44, 51, 69
Australia, 8, 182-183
   aged care assessment teams (ACATs), 182
   community aged care package (CACPs/CCPs), 183
   community options program (COP), 183
   high-level care, 182
   Home and Community Care Act (HACC Act), 182
   home and community care (HACC) program, 182
   low-level care, 182
   Resident Classification Scale, 182
automatic urine collection devices. *See* assistive devices, automatic urine collection devices
average level of care-required. *See* care levels, average level of care-required

B

base amount of time, 107
bathroom aids. *See* assistive devices, bathroom aids
bed accessories and attachments. *See* assistive devices, bed accessories and attachments
bedridden, 22, 35, 36, 37, 64, 118
bedside commodes. *See* assistive devices, bedside commodes
bedside rails. *See* assistive devices, bedside rails
beneficiaries, of long-term care insurance, 21-23, 25, 29
benefit supply management, 141
benefits, of long-term care insurance
   home- and community-based care services, 20, 29-38, 42-59
   institutional long-term care services, 20, 62-70
budget ceiling, 25, 40, 51, 89, 91, 95, 110, 140, 196-197

C

canes. *See* assistive devices, canes
care coordination, 9, 27, 147, 148, 150, 152-153, 155, 157, 165, 198
   in the United Kingdom, 186
   in the United States of America, 185-186
   See also care management
caregivers
   daughters-in-law, 3
   family members, 3, 11, 170, 172, 175
   respite with, long-term care insurance, 11-12, 31, 36
   training of, 168, 170
care homes. *See* care houses

care houses, 38, 71
  eligibility, 71
  services, 71
care level method, 135-138
  See also fee structure
care levels
  assistance-required, 19, 23-25, 29, 30-31, 37, 83, 195-196, 197
  benefits, 20-21, 29, 30-31, 37
  qualification, 23
  average level of care-required, 69
  care-required, 19, 20, 23-25, 29, 31, 62, 72, 83, 112, 195-196
  benefits, 20, 29, 31
  qualification, 23
  issues, 112
care management, 9, 19, 20, 26, 30, 147-152
  definition, 26
  example of, 158-161
  process of, 150-152
  in the United Kingdom, 186
  in the United States of America, 26, 185-186
  See also assessments; assessment tools; care managers; care plans
Care Management Teams Tool Kit, 151
care managers, 25, 26, 27, 51, 60, 66, 73, 77, 141, 147-158, 165, 200
  basic goals of, 157-158
  certification system for, 153-154
  other functions of, 155-156
  documentation, 156
  providing a team approach, 155-156
  qualification requirements and criteria, 153-154
  roles, 155-156
  See also care management
care planning, 150-152
  assessments, 150
  care providers' conference, 152, 155, 159
  follow-ups, 152
  in health facilities for the elderly, 78
  for home- and community-based care services, 150-152
  implementation of care plans, 152
  in U.S. nursing homes, 185-186
  in welfare facilities for the elderly, 78
  See also assessments; care management

care plans
  home-care care plans, 26, 149, 150
  purpose, 150
  sample of, 160
  in-facility care plans, 26, 64, 77, 149, 150
  purpose, 150
  sample of, 79-80
care providers. See providers
care providers' conference, 152, 155, 159
care-required. See care levels, care-required
care services for private care facility residents. See home- and community-based care services, care services for private care facility residents
care staff. See care workers; certified care workers; nurse's aides
care teams, 66
  goals, 66
  principles of, 66
care workers, 27, 31, 167, 168, 198, 202
  See also certified care workers; nurse's aides
cash allowance, 12
cash benefits, 127
  in Germany, 188
  See also cash allowance
CCWs. See certified care workers
Central Government Reform, 15
cerebrovascular disease. See specified diseases, cerebrovascular disease
certification process
  application process, 23-25, 83-85
  computer analyses, 95, 108
  eligibility decision, 25
  final classification, 95, 108
  initial classification, 23, 104-107
  intake interview, 96-97
  qualification assessments, 83, 95-108
certification system
  for care managers, 153
  for home-helpers, 134, 146, 170
  for Housing Environment Coordinators for the Elderly and Disabled People, 59
  for long-term care insurance, 95-108
  issues, 109-112
  See also certification process
certified care workers (CCWs), 168-169
  education, 168-169

See also care workers; nurse's aides
certified social workers, 172
  education, 172
  roles, 172
change of address. *See* address change
chronic obstructive pulmonary disease (COPD). *See* specified diseases, chronic obstructive pulmonary disease
chronic respiratory diseases, 72
chronic rheumatoid arthritis. *See* specified diseases, chronic rheumatoid arthritis
client allocation system. *See* allocation system
code alert systems. *See* assistive devices, code alert systems
combination of time period and care level method, 138-139
  See also fee structure
commissioned welfare volunteers, 173-174
  eligibility, 174
  serving term, 174
Commissioned Welfare Volunteers Law, 173
  Amendments of 2000, 173
community aged care package (CACPs/CCPs), 183
Community Care Reforms Act, 186
community options program, 183
competition between care providers, 13-14
complaints and grievances office, 173
comprehensive community support centers, 193, 198
computer analyses. *See* certification process; computer programs; initial classification
computer programs, 23, 104, 111, 112, 194
  issues, 111, 112
consumer co-operative, 176
consumption tax, 9
contracts
  with care services providers, 13, 62, 70
  with local governments, 9
co-payments, 13, 25, 64, 140
costs
  containing, 194, 197
  home- and community-based care services, 195
  institutional long-term care, 195
  long-term care insurance, 193, 203
Council of Social Welfare, 174
Council on Health and Welfare for the Elderly, 9, 26
Council on Social Security, 9
crutches. *See* assistive devices, crutches

D

daughters-in-law, as caregivers, 3
day care. *See* home- and community-based care services, day care
day care rehabilitation. *See* home- and community-based care services, day care rehabilitation
dementia prevention/support programs. *See* preventative care services package, dementia prevention/support programs
Denmark, 180-182
  home- and community-based care services, 180
  reformation of basic principles, 181-182
Dental Practitioners Law, 166
dentists, 153, 166
  education, 166
depression prevention/support programs. *See* preventative care services package, depression prevention/support programs
designated long-term care beds. *See* designated long-term care hospitals, designated long-term care beds
designated long-term care beds for elderly with dementia. *See* designated long-term care hospitals, designated long-term care beds for elderly with dementia
designated long-term care hospitals, 20, 62, 67, 69-70
  costs, 69
  designated long-term care beds, 69
  eligibility, 67
  long-term care beds for elderly with dementia, 70
  long-term medical care beds for the elderly, 69-70
  medical insurance-designated long-term health care beds, 72-73
  eligibility, 73
  medical insurance-designated recovery-

phase rehabilitation units, 73-74
  goals, 73
  patients, 73-74
  size of room, 63
  staffing, 67
  types of beds, 69-70
designated long-term medical care beds for the elderly. *See* designated long-term care hospitals, long-term medical care beds for the elderly
diabetes, 72
diabetic nephropathy. *See* specified diseases, diabetic nephropathy
diabetic neuropathy. *See* specified diseases, diabetic neuropathy
diabetic retinopathy. *See* specified diseases, diabetic retinopathy
dignity, 30, 34, 64, 74, 75, 156, 157
discharge planning, 77, 78
  in health facilities for the elderly, 78
  in welfare facilities for the elderly, 78
disease/disability prevention services, 19
disuse syndrome, 74, 195
doctors' home visits, 34
  See also home- and community-based care services, medical management
drying of futon services. *See* municipal programs, drying of futon services
dual eligibles, 55

E

ear-marked subsidy, 117
  national government, 117
  prefectural governments, 117
education
  of care managers, 153
  of certified care workers (CCWs), 168-169
  of certified social workers, 172
  of dentists, 166
  of home care aides, 170
    See also home-help certification
  of long-term care counselors, 173
  of nurses
    licensed practical nurses, 167
    registered nurses, 167
  of occupational therapists, 171
  of pharmacists, 166
  of physical therapists, 171
  of physicians, 166

  of social workers, 172
  of speech therapists, 171
85-item assessment scale, 23, 97, 109
Elderly Care Study Group, 199
Elderly Services Providers Association, 176
electric beds. *See* assistive devices, hospital beds
eligibility, for long-term care insurance, 22, 23, 39
  See also final classification; certification process
eligibility decision, for long-term care insurance, 25
  See also final classification; certification process

F

facility stock items, 35, 36, 140, 197, 198
failure to pay premiums penalties, 125-126
family members, as caregivers, 3, 11, 170, 172, 175
fee-for-services, 72
fee schedule
  for assistive devices, 44, 51, 52, 133
  for creation of care plans, 25
  for home- and community-based care services, 132-135
  for institutional long-term care services, 136-138
  for physician's reports, 91
  See also fee structure; unit prices; unit pricing per unit
fee structure
  care level method, 135-138
  combination of time period and care level method, 138-139
  fixed unit price method, 132-133
  time period method, 133-135
feminists, 12
final classification, 95, 108
  eligibility decision, 25
  by Long-Term Care Certification Committee, 23-25, 95, 108
  See also certification process
financing, long-term care insurance, 13, 116-117, 193
first category insured persons. *See* insured persons, 1st category insured persons

first class home-help certification. *See* home-help certification, 1st class certification
fixed unit price method, 132-133
See also fee structure
flat-rate payments, 72
for-profit organizations, 14
Foundation of Long-Term Care Insurance for the Elderly, 9
functional training, 36, 67, 107, 111, 112, 137
fees for, 136, 137

G

general tax revenue, 7, 9, 116
Germany, 3, 8, 187-189
  long-term care insurance, 187-189
    benefits, 188-189
    care levels, 188
    cash benefits, 188
    eligibility, 188
    and family caregivers, 188
    in-kind benefits, 188
    medical assessments, 188
    premiums, 187-188
    respite care, 188
  Long-Term Care Insurance Act, 187
  Long-Term Care Insurance Funds, 188
  Medical Review Board, 188
Gold Plan, 6
Gold Plan 21, 64
governments of Japan
  Ministry of Health and Welfare (MHW), 15
  Ministry of Health, Labour and Welfare (MHLW), 15, 22, 25, 43, 71, 72, 74, 75, 91, 97, 110, 150, 173, 192
grab bars. *See* assistive devices, grab bars
group-based approach, 74, 75
group homes for people with dementia. *See* home- and community-based care services, group homes for people with dementia

H

haircut services. *See* municipal programs, haircut services
handrails. *See* assistive devices, handrails
Hasegawa Dementia Scale, 103
Health and Medical Care Services Law for the Elderly, 6
  Amendment to, 66
health facilities for the elderly, 6, 20, 62, 66-67
  activities, 67
  care planning, 78
  costs, 69, 135
  goals, 67
  services, 67
  size of room, 63
  staffing, 63, 66
health insurance for the elderly over 75 years of age. *See* medical insurance, for the elderly over 75 years of age
home- and community-based care services, 20, 29-38
  adult day care services, 12, 30, 35
    fee schedule, 138-139
  care services for private care facility residents, 20, 30, 38, 135-136
  day care. *See* home- and community-based care services, day care rehabilitation
  day care rehabilitation, 20, 30, 36
    fee schedule, 138-139
    goals, 36
    in Denmark, 180
  group homes for people with dementia, 20, 30, 31, 37
    eligibility, 37
    fee schedule, 135-136
    goals, 37
  home bathing services, 20, 30, 32
    fee schedule, 132
  home care, 12, 20, 30, 31-32
    combination of homemaking- and physical-care-focused services, 32
    fee schedule, 134
    homemaking-focused services, 31
    physical-care-focused services, 31
  home health care, 20, 30, 33
    fee schedule, 133, 134-135
    goals, 33
  home-help, 20, 31-32, 134
    fee schedule, 134
  home modifications, 20, 25, 30, 38, 55-60
    application process for, 58
    elimination of thresholds, 55, 56-57
    financing, 55

INDEX 245

floor modification, 55, 57
installation of handrails, 55, 56
replacement of existing doors and doorknobs, 55, 57
replacement of squat toilets with Western toilets, 55, 58
home visit rehabilitation, 20, 30, 33-34
fee schedule, 132
goals, 33-34
loan of assistive devices, 20, 30, 38
fee schedule, 51, 133
medical management, 20, 30, 34-35
doctors' home visits, 34
fee schedule, 132-133
home-based medication management programs, 34, 35
visiting dental services, 34, 35
reimbursements
application process for, 58
for home modifications, 38, 58
for purchasing assistive devices, 38, 43, 51
respite care, 20, 137, 198
short-stay program for medical care, 20, 30, 37, 132
short-stay program for personal care, 20, 30, 36, 132
types of services, 20, 30-38
Home and Community Care Act (HACC Act), 182
home and community care (HACC) program, 182
home-based medication management programs, 34, 35
See also home- and community-based care services, medical management
home bathing services. See home- and community-based care services, home bathing services
home care. See home- and community-based care services, home care
home care agencies, 85, 146, 168, 201
home care aides, 31, 170
education, 170
home-care care plans. See care plans, home-care care plans
home-delivered meals. See municipal programs, meals-on-wheels
home health care. See home- and community-based care services, home health care

home-help. See home- and community-based care services, home-help
home-help certification
1st class certification, 146, 170
2nd class certification, 146, 170
3rd class certification, 134, 146, 170
home-helpers. See home care aides
home modifications. See home- and community-based care services, home modifications
home visit nursing care stations, 33
home visit rehabilitation. See home- and community-based care services, home visit rehabilitation
hospital beds. See assistive devices, hospital beds
household budget, 12
Housing Environment Coordinators for the Elderly and Disabled People, 59
hyper-aged society, 178

I

IADLs. See Instrumental Activities of Daily Living
IDT. See interdisciplinary team
in-facility care plans. See care plans, in-facility care plans
informal caregivers, 175
initial classification, 23, 104-107
computer analyses, 95, 108
See also application process; certification process; computer programs
in-kind benefits, 12, 127
in Germany, 188
Inpatient Management Fee for Exceptionally Approved Elderly Care Hospitals, 71
institutional care facilities, 4, 20, 74, 140, 163, 165, 201
activities, 64, 67
care planning, 78
care plans
in-facility care plans, 26, 149, 150
founders, 63
services, 64, 67
types of, 20, 62, 63
See also designated long-term care hospitals; health facilities for the elderly; welfare facilities for the

elderly
institutional long-term care facilities. *See* institutional care facilities; institutional long-term care services
institutional long-term care services, 20, 62-70
  providers
    designated long-term care hospitals, 67, 68-70
    health facilities for the elderly, 66-67
    welfare facilities for the elderly, 64-66
  types of services, 64, 67
  See also institutional care facilities
Instrumental Activities of Daily Living (IADLs), 15
  in assessing physical status,107, 109
insurance card, 40, 51, 85, 87
insured persons, 21-23
  benefits for, 21-22
  eligibility, 21, 118
  1st category insured persons, 21-22
  2nd category insured persons, 21-22
insurers. *See* municipal governments
intake interview, 96-97
  See also application process; qualification assessments
integration
  for care management, 163
  for continuum of care, 163
  of medical care and social welfare services, 11, 13
interdisciplinary team (IDT), 27, 164
  in U.S. nursing homes, 185
interdisciplinary team approach. *See* interdisciplinary team

J

Japan agricultural co-operative, 176
Japan Association of Certified Care Workers Method, 151
Japan Visiting Nursing Foundation Method, 151
Japanese Assessment & Care Plan for Long-Term Care, 151
Japanese Association of Certified Social Workers Method, 151

K

kaigo, 3
kango-fu. *See* nurses

kango-shi. *See* nurses

L

Law for the Welfare of Physically Disabled Persons, 23
levy, 22, 118, 119, 123, 124, 125, 192
  of cost of room and board, 197-198
  premiums,
    for 1st category insured persons, 119-120
    for salaried 2nd category insured persons, 124-125
    for 2nd category insured persons, 124-125
    for self-employed 2nd category insured persons, 125
  regular levy, 119
  special levy, 119
licensed practical nurses. *See* nurses, licensed practical nurses
life-span development, 158
loan of assistive devices. *See* home- and community-based care services, loan of assistive devices
Long-Term Care Certification Committee, 23, 25, 92, 95, 96, 108, 154, 186, 201
  roles, 23, 25, 92, 108, 201
Long-Term Care Certification Committee Review, 108
  See also final classification
long-term care counselors, 173, 175
  education, 173
long-term care insurance
  in Germany, 187-189
  identification (ID) card, 40, 51, 85, 87
  uncovered services
    almshouses for the elderly, 70
    care houses, 71
    low-cost elder homes, 70-71
Long-Term Care Insurance Bill, 11
Long-Term Care Insurance Law, 3, 4, 13, 64, 72, 90, 95, 110, 153, 154, 194
  Article 1, 13
  Article 4, 13
  Article 13, 90
  2005 revisions to, 192, 194-201
  2008 revisions to, 201-202
  2011 revisions to, 202
long-term care plans. *See* care plans, in-facility care plans

INDEX   247

Long-Term Care Security for the Elderly by Tax, 11
low-cost elder homes, 70-71
  eligibility, 71
  type A, 70
  type B, 70-71

M
market fundamentalism, 14
matron. *See* certified care workers
MDS. *See* Minimum Data Set
meals-on-wheels. *See* municipal programs, meals-on-wheels
Medicaid, 183, 184
Medical Care Act, 72
  Amendment to, 71
medical care system for the retired, 10
medical corporations, 63
medical insurance
  designated long-term health care beds, 72
  eligibility, 72-73
  designated recovery-phase rehabilitation units, 73
  goals, 73
  patients, 73-74
  for the elderly over 75 years of age, 5, 179
medical management. *See* home- and community-based care services, medical management
Medical Practitioners Law, 166
Medical Review Board, 188
Medical Services Law Reform Bill, 11
medical social workers, 158, 172
Medicare, 183, 184
MHLW. *See* governments of Japan, Ministry of Health, Labour and Welfare
MHLW ordinance. *See* Ministry of Health, Labour and Welfare ordinance
MHW. *See* governments of Japan, Ministry of Health and Welfare
MHW Study Group. *See* Ministry of Health and Welfare Study Group
Minimum Data Set (MDS), 184, 185
Minimum Data Set-Home Care, 151
Minister of ECSST. *See* Ministers of Japan, Minister of Education, Culture, Sports, Science and Technology
Minister of HLW. *See* Ministers of Japan, Minister of Health, Labour and Welfare
Ministers of Japan
  Minister of Education, Culture, Sports, Science and Technology (Minister of ECSST), 167, 171
  Minister of Health and Welfare, 9
  Minister of Health, Labour and Welfare (Minister of HLW), 38, 166, 167, 171, 173, 174
Ministry of Health and Welfare (MHW). *See* governments of Japan, Ministry of Health and Welfare
Ministry of Health and Welfare Study Group, 7, 8, 9, 181
Ministry of Health, Labour and Welfare (MHLW). *See* governments of Japan, Ministry of Health, Labour and Welfare
Ministry of Health, Labour and Welfare ordinance, 63
multidisciplinary team. *See* interdisciplinary team
multiple system atrophy. *See* specified diseases, multiple system atrophy
municipal governments, 19, 21, 39, 55, 70, 88, 90, 91, 117, 121, 122-123
  funding
    of long-term care insurance, 116, 117
    of municipal programs, 39-40
  inspections, 201
  qualification requirements for care managers, 153-154
  special benefits, 39-40
municipal ordinance, 30, 91
municipal programs
  additional services, 39
  drying of futon services, 20
  haircut services, 39
  home modification programs, 39, 57
  meals-on-wheels, 20, 39
  on-the-side services, 39
  transportation services, 20
municipal resident taxes, 119, 201
municipalities. *See* municipal governments

N
national adjustment grants. *See* national government, national adjustment grants
National Assembly, 11
national certification exams

for certified care workers, 168
national government, 6, 39, 120, 123, 192, 194, 195, 197, 198, 199, 200
  development of computer programs, 23, 104
  funding, of long-term care insurance, 116, 117, 200
  inspections, 201
national adjustment grants, 117, 122
National Health Insurance (NHI), 5, 9, 21, 123, 124, 125
National Health Insurance Association, 124
national licensure exams
  for certified social workers, 172
  for dentists, 166
  for occupational therapists, 171
  for pharmacists, 166
  for physical therapists, 171
  for physicians, 166
  for registered nurses, 167
  for speech therapists, 171
National Universal Health Insurance. *See* National Health Insurance
New Gold Plan, 6
non-profit organizations, 176
Non-Profit Organizations Law, 176
normalization, 157-158
nurse's aides, 27, 66, 67, 69, 70, 71, 168
  See also care workers; certified care workers
nurses, 167-168
  education, 167
  kango-fu, 168
  kango-shi, 168
  licensed practical nurses, 134, 167
  registered nurses, 167
  roles, 167
nursing care plans. *See* care plans, in-facility care plans
nutritional counseling. *See* preventative care services package, nutritional counseling

O

objective assessments, 96, 97-103
  group 1. paralysis and contractures, 97
  group 2. basic movements, 100
  group 3. complex movements and tasks, 100
  group 4. special care, 100-101
  group 5. personal care, 101
  group 6. communication, hearing, memory, and recall ability, 102
  group 7. problem behaviors, 102
OBRA '87. *See* Omnibus Budget Reconciliation Act of 1987
occupational therapists, 36, 44, 59, 66, 67, 134, 171, 185
  education, 171
old-age pension, 119, 201
Omnibus Budget Reconciliation Act of 1987, 184-185
One-Minute Time Study, 105, 110
  issues, 110-111
onsite assessments, 23, 95, 96, 108
  See also assessments; application process; certification process; qualification assessments
on-the-side services. *See* municipal programs, on-the-side services
oral health services. *See* preventative care services package, oral health services
ossification of posterior longitudinal ligament. *See* specified diseases, ossification of posterior longitudinal ligament
osteoarthritis. *See* specified diseases, osteoarthritis
osteoporosis with fractures. *See* specified diseases, osteoporosis with fractures
out-of-pocket expenses, 4, 140-141
  for beauty shop services, 197
  for facility stock items, 197, 198
  for U.S. nursing homes, 183

P

Parkinson's disease. *See* specified diseases, Parkinson's disease
patient allocation system. *See* allocation system
pension coverage, 14
pharmacists, 35, 67, 166
  education, 166
physical exercise programs. *See* preventative care services package, physical exercise programs
physical therapists, 36, 170-171, 185
  education, 171

INDEX 249

physicians, 27, 34, 91, 153, 166, 189
  education, 166
  physician's report, 91, 107-108, 113,
    220-224 (Appendix D)
  fees for, 91-92
platforms. *See* assistive devices, platforms
pneumonia, 74
population estimates, in 2025, 193-194
portable bathtubs. *See* assistive devices,
  portable bathtubs
positioning and adaptive cushions. *See*
  assistive devices, positioning and
  adaptive cushions
Prefectural Federation of National Health
  Insurance Associations, 173
prefectural governments
  certification for care managers, 153
  funding, of long-term care insurance,
    116, 117, 200
  inspections, 201
  licensing of licensed practical nurses,
    167
prefectural licensure exams
  for licensed practical nurses, 167
premium categories, 118-119, 200, 201
premiums, 9, 13, 21, 22, 39, 116, 118
  average of
    for 1st category insured persons, 127
    for 2nd category insured persons,
      124
  calculation formulas, 119, 201
  failure to pay premiums penalties, 125-
    126
  for 1st category insured persons, 118-120
  in Germany, 187-188, 189
  policy of reduction and exemption,
    126-127
  rates of, 92, 119, 122-123, 127, 200
  for 2nd category insured persons, 123-
    125
presenile dementia. *See* specified diseases,
  presenile dementia
pressure ulcer prevention and treatment
  devices. *See* assistive devices, pressure
  ulcer prevention and treatment devices
preventative care services package, 194-
  195, 199
  dementia prevention/support programs,
    195
  depression prevention/support programs,
    195
  nutritional counseling, 195
  oral health services, 195
  physical exercise programs, 195
  social isolation prevention programs,
    195
preventive care benefits, 39
private pay. *See* out-of-pocket expenses
progeria. *See* specified diseases, progeria
providers
  for-profit organizations, 62
  medical corporations, 63
  municipalities, 63
  national government, 63
  non-profit organizations, 62
  prefectures, 63
  public benefit corporations, 63
  school corporations, 63
  social welfare corporations, 63
psychiatric social workers, 172
public assistance programs, 17
Public Health Nurses, Midwife and Nurses
  Law, 168
public health programs, 17
public reporting system, 193, 199, 202
  fees for, 199
public sectors, 14, 62
purpose and philosophy, of long-term care
  insurance, 11-14

Q

qualification assessments, 83, 95-108
  additional comments by assessors,
    103, 218-219 (Appendix C)
  intake interview, 96-97
  issues, 109
  objective assessments, 96, 97-103
  purpose, 95
quality assurance
  by public reporting system, 193, 199
  in the United States of America, 185
quality of care, 14, 77, 116, 193, 199
quality of life (QOL), 34

R

reapplication process, 90-91
recipients, of long-term care insurance
  numbers of, 193, 203
  numbers of, home- and community-
    based care services, 193, 202

numbers of, institutional care services, 193, 202
reciprocal walkers. *See* assistive devices, reciprocal walkers
recovery-phase rehabilitation units, 73-74
reformation of basic principles, 181-182
regional unit pricing per unit, 130, 225 (Appendix E)
registered nurses. *See* nurses, registered nurses
regular levy. *See* levy
rehabilitation services
 day care rehabilitation, 20, 30, 36
 home visit rehabilitation, 20, 30, 33-34
 recovery-phase rehabilitation, 73-74
reimbursements
 for home modifications, 38, 58
 for purchasing assistive devices, 38, 43, 51
Resident Assessment Protocols (RAPs), 185
Resident Classification Scale, 182
Resource Utilization Groups (RUGs), 184
respite care, 20, 137, 198
 in Germany, 189
RUGs. *See* United States of America, Resource Utilization Groups

S

safety rails. *See* assistive devices, safety rails
second category insured persons. *See* insured persons, 2nd category insured persons
second class home-help certification. *See* home-help certification, 2nd class certification
service provider's reports, 141
 sample of, 144-145
service receipts, 141
 sample of, 142-143
short-stay program for medical care. *See* home- and community-based care services, short-stay program for medical care
short-stay program for personal care. *See* home- and community-based care services, short-stay program for personal care

Shy-Drager Syndrome. *See* specified diseases, Shy-Drager Syndrome
Silver Mark System, 176
silver services, 175
small-scale multi-purpose care centers, 198
sochi. *See* allocation system
social admission, 7, 71, 72
Social Insurance Medical Fee Payment Fund, 124, 125
social insurance model, 9
social isolation prevention programs. *See* preventive care services package, social isolation prevention programs
social security programs
 lack of long-term care coverage, 7, 19
social welfare corporations, 14, 63, 175
social welfare programs, 9, 17, 29, 39, 88, 123, 127, 198
 for physically disabled, 22-23
social workers, 172
 education, 172
Social Workers and Care Workers Law, 179
special levy. *See* levy
Special Measures for Smooth Enforcement of the Long-Term Care Insurance Law, 120
specialty assistive devices, 38, 51
specialty beds, 45, 170
specified diseases, 15, 22, 72, 73, 108
 amyotrophic lateral sclerosis (ALS), 15
 arteriosclerosis obliterans, 15
 cerebrovascular disease, 15, 22, 73, 202
 chronic obstructive pulmonary disease (COPD), 15
 chronic rheumatoid arthritis, 15
 diabetic nephropathy, 15
 diabetic neuropathy, 15
 diabetic retinopathy, 15
 multiple system atrophy, 15
 ossification of posterior longitudinal ligament (OPLL), 15
 osteoarthritis, 15
 osteoporosis with fractures, 15
 Parkinson's disease, 15, 22, 97
 presenile dementia, 15
 progeria, 15
 Shy-Drager Syndrome, 15

INDEX 251

spinal canal stenosis, 15
spinocerebellar syndrome, 15
terminal cancer, 15, 72, 201
speech language pathologists. *See* speech therapists
speech therapists, 171
  education, 171
spinal canal stenosis. *See* specified diseases, spinal canal stenosis
spinocerebellar syndrome. *See* specified diseases, spinocerebellar syndrome
staffing
  almshouses for the elderly, 70
  designated long-term care hospitals, 63, 67
  health facilities for the elderly, 63
  welfare facilities for the elderly, 63
super-aged society, 178

T

team approach, 27, 155-156, 164
teams
  aged care assessment teams (ACATs), 182
  care teams, 66
    members of, 66
    principles, 66
  interdisciplinary team (IDT), 27, 164
    in the United States of America, 185
  multidisciplinary team. *See* teams, interdisciplinary team
technology
  assistive devices, 20, 30, 38, 42-54
  computer programs, 23, 104, 111, 112, 194
Ten Thousand Citizens' Committee to Realize a Public Elder-Care System, 11
Ten-Year-Strategy to Promote Health and Welfare for the Elderly, 6, 64
terminal cancer. *See* specified diseases, terminal cancer
third class home-help certification. *See* home-help certification, 3rd class certification
Three-Organization Care Plan Development Study Group Method, 151
threshold ramps. *See* assistive devices, threshold ramps
time period method, 133-135
  See also fee schedule; fee structure

Tokyo Chamber of Commerce and Industry, 59
total expenditures
  of health/medical care, 4, 8
  of long-term care insurance, 193, 203
total fertility rates, 5
transfer lifts. *See* assistive devices, transfer lifts
transportation services, 20, 137
tree diagrams, 105-107
  issues, 112
trinity reform, 200

U

unemployment insurance, 17
unit-based care, 74, 75
unit prices, 131-139
  for adult day care services, 138
  for day care rehabilitation, 138
  for group homes for people with dementia, 136
  for health facilities for the elderly, 135, 137
  for home bathing services, 132
  for home care, 134
  for home health care, 134
  for home visit rehabilitation, 132
  for medical management, 132-133
  for welfare facilities for the elderly, 136-138
unit pricing per unit, 129-131
United Kingdom, 9, 186-187
  care management, 186
  Community Care Reforms Act, 186
United States of America, 26, 148, 150, 183-186
  care planning in nursing homes, 185-186
  interdisciplinary team, 185
  Medicaid, 183-184
  Medicare, 183, 184
  Minimum Data Set (MDS), 184, 185
  Omnibus Budget Reconciliation Act of 1987 (OBRA '87), 184-185
out-of-pocket expenses, 183
private insurance, 183
Resident Assessment Protocols (RAPs), 185
Resource Utilization Groups (RUGs), 184

skilled nursing facilities, 183

V

visiting dental services, 34, 35
  See also home- and community-based care services, medical management
visiting nurse services. *See* home health care
volunteers, 174
  See also commissioned welfare volunteers

W

walkers. *See* assistive devices, walkers
war veterans' coverage, 17
welfare business, 175
welfare facilities for the elderly, 20, 62, 64-66
  activities, 64-65
  care planning, 78
  costs, 69, 136-137
  services, 64-65
  size of room, 63
  staffing, 63
Welfare Law for the Elderly, 4, 64, 116
Welfare of Physically Disabled Persons (WPDR), 55
Welfare of Physically Disabled Persons Law (WPDR Law), 55
wheelchair accessories and attachments. *See* assistive devices, wheelchair accessories and attachments
wheelchair ramps. *See* assistive devices, wheelchair ramps
wheelchairs. *See* assistive devices, wheelchairs
women's groups, 12
workers' compensation insurance, 17
WPDR. *See* Welfare of Physically Disabled Persons

Achievements and Future Directions of
the Long-Term Care Insurance System in Japan:
Toward Social "Kaigo" Security in
the Global Longevity Society

2014 年 2 月 28 日　初版第 1 刷発行

- ■ 著　　　者 ──── 住居　広士・澤田　如
- ■ 発 行 者 ──── 佐藤　守
- ■ 発 行 所 ──── 株式会社 **大学教育出版**
  〒700-0953　岡山市南区西市 855-4
  電話（086）244-1268　FAX（086）246-0294
- ■ 印刷製本 ──── モリモト印刷 ㈱

© Hiroshi Sumii and Yuki Sawada 2014, Printed in Japan
検印省略　　落丁・乱丁本はお取り替えいたします。
本書のコピー・スキャン・デジタル化等の無断複製は著作権法上での例外を除き禁じられています。本書を代行業者等の第三者に依頼してスキャンやデジタル化することは、たとえ個人や家庭内での利用でも著作権法違反です。
ISBN978 - 4 - 86429 - 254 - 2